The War Game

CHARLES GRANT

THE WAR GAME

With a foreword by
BRIGADIER PETER YOUNG, DSO, MC, MA, FSA, FRHistS, FRGS

KEN TROTMAN
PUBLISHING

THE WAR GAME
was first published by A. & C. Black limited in 1971
This new edition published in 2007 by
Ken Trotman Publishing
P.O.Box 505
Huntingdon PE29 2XW
www.kentrotman.com

ISBN: 978-1-905074-64-8
EAN: 9781905074648

DEDICATION

To my wife and daughter, in consideration of their forbearance during numerous wargames and in appreciation of their frequent supplying of food and drink to the participants in many a hectic battle, and to my son, still—in spite of the defeats I have suffered at his hands—my favourite opponent.

Printed by Victoire Press
Bar Hill, Cambridge

THE WAR GAME
A FOREWORD BY CHARLES STEWART GRANT

The author and son ponder the campaign map in the war game room

I cannot begin to tell you how pleased I am to see "The War Game" back in print. I would like to start by thanking Richard Brown of Ken Trotman Books for making it possible. The book, first published in 1971, provided the foundation upon which my wargaming as a young boy (and the son of the late Charles Grant) was built. With its publication once again, some thirty five years later and by popular demand, it seems that its ability to inspire both old and new wargamers is enduring.

I will not describe my father's early years in war gaming, covered in the original forward by our late friend Brigadier Peter Young, but I would like to give you a brief but entirely biased view of Charles Grant the wargamer.

In about 1957, when I was 9 years old, my father invited me into a large room where set out on a green painted, extended table tennis table, were two model armies. They were of the American Civil War period. They had been individually hand cast in lead by Dad using homemade plaster moulds. The basic master was a 40 mm advancing Britain's W scale figure. My instructions were simply – this was the wargame, if I enjoyed it fine, we would do more, but if I was not interested there was no compulsion to carry on – oh, and by the way no sound effects please! By the end of the day I was the victor of the skirmish of Sawmill Village – and a committed wargamer!

In 1967 *Charge or How to Play War Games* by Brigadier Peter Young and Lieutenant Colonel James Lawford was published. At about the same time my father began a series of articles in Tradition magazine, which would ultimately form the basis for *The War Game* published in 1971. The genesis for this was the arrival in about 1960 of a range of inexpensive plastic 30mm figures, produced under the name of Spencer Smith, supported by some outstanding lead figures by Edward Suren (Willie figures) and by Tradition. This had opened up the opportunity for us to move away from the American civil war and build two large 18th century European armies.

The War Game sets out the rules with which two fictitious countries, the Grand Duchy of Lorraine (which was my country) and the Vereinigte Freie Stadte (which was my father's country) did battle. These two countries and their armies provided the basis for much of the wargaming my father and I carried out from the late 60's to the late 70's. Over ten years or so we fought several campaigns, refought a good many historical battles, numerous scenarios and individual engagements – it is the substance of this book.

In the 1970's, we moved on to the ancient period and we revelled in battles between Greeks and Persians, Roman and Goths, Egyptians and Romans and all sorts of other combinations – but we always return to "The War Game" and the mid eighteenth century.

All I have said so far is about the history and legacy and, before I conclude, I should say something about Charles Grant the person. Since Dad died in 1979 I have met so may of those that knew him, had met him and of course been influenced by him. Without exception they have described or referred to a friendly and approachable person, knowledgeable without arrogance, moderate in his criticism, fulsome in his praise and always happy to take time, whenever he was asked, to talk about the hobby to young and old. "The War Game" reflects that modest but knowledgeable and passionate approach to the hobby.

Returning to the original War Game armies and the rules, they have proved to be hardy campaigners. Both continue to do battle between the Grants. Now however, my father's army is skilfully handled by my son, Charles Murray Grant, now 21. His Grandfather would have been delighted, as indeed he would be to see "The War Game" back in print.

The original figures and houses are still in action as seen here at the refight of Mollwitz at Partizan in 2007. *Picture courtesy of Henry Hyde, Editor of Battlegames*

Fontenoy: The Allied Attack. One of the Grants' favourite battles and the subject of one of the late Charles Grant's books; this most recent refight saw Charles Stewart (formerly Charles junior) defending (unsuccessfully) against his son Charles, the third generation of wargame Grants. The allies are on the edge of Fontenoy while their massed columns supported by cavalry are pressing the French left. *Photograph Charles Stewart Grant*

Contents

Illustrations

PHOTOGRAPHS

MAPS AND DIAGRAMS

Foreword

by BRIGADIER PETER YOUNG, DSO, MC, MA, FSA, FRHistS, FRGS

Some thirty-five years have passed since my armies first found themselves locked in battle with those of Charles Grant. Hitler's war still lay in the future, and so did our own years in the Army and the Royal Air Force respectively. The art of wargaming has not stood still in the years between. The Little Wars of H. G. Wells and the more sophisticated game evolved by the late Captain J. C. Sachs, my own military mentor, have long since been overtaken by others devised by the nimble brains of Don Featherstone, Lieutenant-Colonel James Lawford and others. In the best of these the rules are firmly founded on a serious study of Military History. Without this war games are useless. But as it is they attract such eminent military historians as my old friends and colleagues of Sandhurst days, David Chandler, author of *The Campaigns of Napoleon* and Dr. Christopher Duffy, whose attractive study of Field-Marshal von Brown is quoted in these pages. That war games have a real tactical value I can attest from practical experience on active service. No wargamer I dare assert would, for example, make such an elementary error as leaving himself without a reserve. Yet, how often has one seen officers, supposedly well-instructed in tactics at some OCTU or other, who were blithely capable of doing that very thing?

Charles Grant stands in the front rank of those who have developed the war game in Britain. Many of his ideas have seen the light in the pages of *Tradition,* the journal of the International Society of Military Collectors, but that excellent and colourful magazine is not as well known as it should be, and it is, therefore, a great pleasure to see the fruit of his experience offered to a wider public.

Charles Grant is not one of those who believe that there ought to be some universal code of rules for wargamers, and here I am entirely with him. Those who have studied the rules evolved over several years by Colonel Lawford and myself (and expounded in *Charge! or How to Play War Games* by Brig. P. Young and Lt.-Col. J. P. Lawford) will see that, though they certainly owe much to those detailed in this work, they do not altogether coincide. Indeed it may be that the Grant rules are rather more complex than the Lawford/Young ones, especially in the field of morale. They differ also in a more important aspect. The latter are based on Napoleonic warfare while the Grant rules rest on a study of the wars of Frederick the Great. In fact either set will, with slight modification, serve for any period from the Thirty Years War to the American Civil War. It is true that the pikemen of the earlier period are a complication, as is the longer effective range of musketry that followed the introduction of the Minié rifle in the Crimean War. But in general the Grant rules cover the period when war as an instrument of state policy was at its height, before it got too dangerous to be either useful or attractive. One has yet to see an enjoyable evening's play based on the destruction of Nagasaki. The days of horse, foot and guns are the thing, and in that period Charles Grant, who has read so deeply in Military History, is a sure guide. His remarks on the ponderous nature of eighteenth-century cavalry, for example, are particularly pertinent in these days when the cinema and television give such a hopelessly false impression of the cavalry tactics of olden times. The author's practical inventions, such as the Canister Cone, are not the least of his contributions.

It was a particular pleasure to the present writer to find his long-forgotten victory at Mollwitz enshrined in these pages—although the author's tasteless reflections on that great and good general, the Graf von Grunt, will be taken *cum grano salo* by the discerning reader.

I wish this book every success and am confident that every wargamer, whether experienced or a beginner, will derive pleasure from its well-sustained arguments and its engaging style of presentation.

PETER YOUNG

Lovel End,
Windsor Forest.
March 1971.

Preface

This book stems from a series of articles which appeared in *Tradition*, the journal of the International Society of Military Collectors, to whose publishers, Belmont-Maitland Publishers Ltd, sincere thanks are due for permission to use them in this volume. The original articles have been largely revised and rewritten, and a number of chapters added, especially those concerning campaigning and associated matters, together with as up-to-date information as is possible relating to the supply of war game figures and material. Thanks are also due to the photographers, Kent Photos, of King Street, Dover.

I hope it is not presumptuous of me to state that the game set out herein is an eminently practical one which has been perfected over a greater number of years than I would care to say. Certainly the rules laid down could have been made more complicated but I believe that they can be used as a basis on which to build a more complex system if so desired, although for a realistic and exciting war game nothing, or so I have been assured, need be added.

Many players have contributed directly or indirectly to the rules as they are formulated; indeed, I have never played a single war game from which no profit has been derived. Consequently, it is impossible for me to thank every player individually—their numbers are truly legion. It would be improper, however, were I not to mention Brigadier Peter Young who first introduced me to formal wargaming when we were both in our very early twenties, and to whom my debt for many years' enjoyment of an absorbing hobby is naturally quite boundless. I must also thank Doctor Alasdair Bantock, whose suggestion to me regarding the pattern of shot from a round of canister resulted (after a veritable fury of research in the library of the Royal United Service Institution, in that of the Tower of London Armouries, and in the British Museum Reading Room) in the conclusions to be found in the relevant chapter.

To them both, and to all whom I have had the pleasure of facing across the war game table, I offer my heartfelt thanks.

I
Introduction

Interest in the war game is not really a recent phenomenon. Model soldiers or small figures more or less coming into this category have existed for hundreds, indeed for thousands, of years, and without delving unnecessarily into the historical and archaeological details of such figurines as those discovered in Egyptian tombs and so forth, actual model soldiers as we know them, or something approximating very much thereto, have existed for several centuries. Even earlier than this, in ancient China and India, games not unlike present-day chess were played, their theme being a warlike one and the result dependent upon the success of simulated military tactics. Originally, however, such games do not appear to have been employed by the professional soldier as an aid to the study of his calling, and there is no evidence to suggest that the great captains of ancient or even relatively modern times used any sort of war game to further their knowledge of the military art or even as a kind of relaxation. Possibly it was held to be unnecessary, the general or leader already disposing of many thousands of men and being able to manoeuvre or exercise them when and in whatever manner he pleased.

Initially the popularity of the model soldier, certainly as far as recorded history is concerned, was rather limited by the fact they seemed invariably to be composed of a precious metal such as silver, so that the cost of their manufacture, usually by artists and craftsmen, was so prohibitive as to restrict their possession to the great ones of the time and their familiars. Louis XIII and Louis XIV of France had such models and both Frederick the Great and various Czars of Russia seem to have been similarly fortunate. Happy, therefore, are we in these enlightened times when we can raise powerful armies if the fancy takes us and wage tremendous campaigns without having to forego such essentials as food and clothes.

It was really only in the nineteenth century that the war game—here I am referring to the professional variety, that played by soldiers to obtain solutions to actual problems of warfare—became widely known, thanks particularly to the General Staff of the Prussian Army, and later that of the Imperial German successor to it. Many Teutonic military theorists drew up rules for different types of war game, all within the context of their contemporary military situation. Some of the great figures of German militarism, Von Moltke and Schlieffen for example, were enthusiastic practitioners and from Germany the cult spread to Britain and to the United States. In the former the chief proselyte was Spencer Wilkinson, who founded the Manchester Tactical Society, wrote the profoundly interesting *Essays on the War Game* and later became Chichele Professor of Military History at Oxford University. In the United States, one Major W. R. Livermore wrote *The American Kriegsspiel* but both his and Spencer Wilkinson's writings had the soldier in mind and it does not seem that either had any real idea that the game could be made popular as a pastime for the ordinary civilian. In this country at any rate this aspect of the war game was left to two singularly unmilitary figures who are in fact the ancestors of the hobby side of the game as we know it today. These were Robert Louis Stevenson, whose whimsical battle narratives have been overshadowed by the writings of H. G. Wells; the latter's fascinating *Little Wars* was the original 'vade mecum' of the wargamer although by present sophisticated standards it is naive and elementary. Understandably, it took the war game a long time to reach any degree of popularity, the years between the two world wars seeing it absolutely at its nadir, although the British Model Soldier Society, formed in the thirties, had a very small wargaming section, and immediately after World War II one member, the late Captain Sachs, most devotedly kept interest alive. His game was based on very general rules covering a period of about 1900 to the end of World War II and involved a rather heterogeneous mixture of tanks, cavalry, machine guns, etc, the results of rifle fire being arbitrarily assessed as a proportion of the number of men firing, while artillery fire was provided by matches fired from the 18-pounder and 4·7″ naval gun as manufactured by William Britain and Co, the troops being mainly the leaden 54mm figures made by the same firm. The rules were in no way complex and in retrospect seem quite unrealistic, although one concession was made to strategy in that, should one player's lines of communication be cut, if only by a solitary figure, then the game was lost, despite what was happening 'up front'. On a personal note, I have many pleasant memories of games played under Captain Sachs' genial auspices with certain wargamers, then young and limber, and now most substantial citizens but still enthusiastic notwithstanding.

In the last fifteen years or so there has been a tremendous surge of interest in the war game, more or less coincidentally with an increase in the popularity of the collecting of model soldiers. This really came with the production of figures from commercial manufacturers whose excellence entitles them to be called craftsmen if not artists. It seems that, if one was to collect model soldiers, then one might as well do something with them. Once, being interviewed for a television programme on wargaming, I was asked to explain my 'motivation' for being a wargamer. This portentous word failed to frighten me—I could only say that I found military history a fascinating subject for study, thought it extremely exciting to pit my wits against those of another in the context of tactics or strategy and enjoyed the spectacle of massed ranks of resplendent soldiery in miniature. This may have answered the question, but I am really not sure. As with every hobby, one has to have the 'bug', and should it be present it will surely manifest itself, whether it be concerned with model railways, the collection of beer mats or the playing of war games. Time was, of course, when the collector of model soldiers or the wargamer would tend to hide his light under a bushel, through modesty or possibly shame. This is not so today, for with the simultaneous appearance of a substantial literature on wargaming and of a general awareness of the more scientific and historic approach to the hobby, the enthusiast is far from concealing his absorption in what was at one time considered a pretty puerile sort of pastime—by the ignorant, certainly. In these happier days, the 'What, playing with soldiers!' attitude seems to be moribund if not completely defunct, and a good thing too.

If, then, we look at our subject in the broadest possible way, we see that the war game can run the gamut from one extreme, where a couple of small boys set up rows of toy soldiers on a table or on the floor and each will strive to knock down his adversary's men with marbles, match-firing cannon or the like, to the other, which reaches its ultimate in the highly complex theoretical manoeuvres carried out by high-ranking officers of some army staff, for example the tank battles in miniature held in America, where radio-controlled tanks are used in battles on a game area covering hundreds of square feet. The terrain is elaborate and realistic, casualties and damage being recorded by photo-electric cells and worked out to the last detail by computers. It is with such fearsome and brain-chilling devices that even more complicated politico-military games are played, especially in the United States, where each branch of the armed forces has huge computer installations employing hundreds of personnel, many with the highest scientific qualifications. All such games are devoted to the simulation of current situations in politics and, as Clausewitz had it, the inevitable extension of war; from them we turn with some relief to our own war game which has less formidable features and entails a great deal more enjoyment.

Somewhere between the two extremes I mention is the war game we know, a descendant of the original German 'Kriegsspiel', with the emphasis, however, being rather more on the 'Spiel' than on the 'Krieg'. Based on contemporary or historical strategy and tactics, it is governed by rules which are designed as far as possible to reproduce the particular conditions of the warfare of one's chosen period, and it is played by one (yes indeed, solo games in which the right hand knows not what the left is up to are not uncommon) or more players, to the discomfiture of one side and the delight of the other. Even so, the loser will as often as not find as much pleasure and excitement as the winner, and this is just as it should be. One of the most thrilling games I can recall took place in the course of a campaign wherein a raiding force I had sent, possibly unwisely, into enemy territory was hunted and chivvied all over the place, to be finally cornered and taken—it was tremendous fun.

One rather unique feature of the war game is that the players may well have to create their own 'codex' of rules, or maybe to adapt a set already existing, depending upon just what their requirements are as to available time, space and ready cash. It may seem strange, the principles of war having presumably remained constant throughout the ages, that enthusiasts have sometimes the most conflicting views on all sorts of things, for example the effect of artillery fire or the speed at which cavalry moves relative to infantry, but, just as the historian uses available facts in the way best calculated to support his thesis, so—being human—the wargamer tends to take the data he prefers to back up his opinions on this or that war game rule. (Here, I may possibly be allowed to protest that my own conclusions are as impartial as possible when formulating the rules laid down in this book). Meetings of wargamers are often fraught with fierce debates over some esoteric point of weapon capability or of troop movement. There are those who regret the apparent impossibilty of ever achieving some kind of universality in war game rules—I am not one of them, believing that controversy always stimulates interest and that it is for each player to formulate his rules in accordance with the physical circumstances in which he conducts his war game. He may have unlimited time at his disposal or he may have only the occasional spell of a few hours, and obviously the tempo of the latter game must be faster than the former. Players who have only a minimum of time may opt for a modern type of game, say one set in the World War II period, where rate of movement is high and where there are as a general rule fewer pieces representing men or transport on the war game table.

This brings me to one of the features which makes the war game so intriguing, to wit the infinite diversity of periods which one can choose as a background for one's activity. From the most remote of ancient times (and there is an extremely flourishing society whose members care for nothing more recent than the early middle ages and who fight Hittite against Israelite, Greek against Persian and Roman against Carthaginian with all the attendant delights of elephants, chariots, phalanxes, slingers and so on) right up to the present day, with aircraft, helicopters and armoured vehicles, there is literally no period of warfare which cannot be successfully reproduced in war game form. Some periods are more difficult to cope with than others, of course, modern warfare being rather a complex business to transfer to the war game table for example, and, as in orthodox figure collecting, certain eras are more popular than others. No one need be surprised, then, to learn that the wars of Napoleon are refought with great regularity, as are the campaigns of the American Civil War. The Graeco-Persian conflicts and the Franco-Prussian War both have their 'aficionados' and the measured formalism of the Seven Years War is very popular.

That the study of the military uniforms of certain countries or of their military history can be allied to one's wargaming is an attraction, but even so one need not be so circumscribed. There is nothing to hinder the creation of one's own imaginary war, no limit to the fictitious powers, all extremely bellicose, which can be brought to life, and no difficulty in finding a suitable 'casus belli' over which to commence hostilities. Several such mythical situations have been created by players who favour the ancients and, without impropriety, I can reveal that my own name is really a 'nom de plume' for Fritz von Tarlenheim, the Marshal-General of the Vereinigte Freie Städte, a sort of Hanseatic League, engaged in a permanent state of war with its neighbour, the Grand Duchy of Lorraine (whose Grand Duke Aristide claims to be my son!), while sometimes allied to one side, sometimes to the other is another ruler, the Machiavellian Elector Petrus of Teutoberg-Althaufen (a resounding pseudonym for the well-known military historian, Brigadier Peter Young, DSO, MC, and a devious and cunning opponent he is!). The period of these wars is roughly the third quarter of the eighteenth century, which we take as ranging from about the Battle of Fontenoy in 1745 up to the outbreak of the American War of Independence, a fascinating era, not at all as stodgy and devoid of military interest as was thought at one time. It saw, inter alia, the beginnings of the light infantryman and the introduction by Frederick the Great of a rudimentary horse artillery. I have participated in some really tremendous battles in this war game period, with fifteen hundred and more actual miniature figures on the table, but at the same time some of the most enjoyable affrays, and this is one of the benefits of running a campaign rather than being limited to set-piece battles, have been minor skirmishes with only small numbers involved.

This indeed is a point I cannot too strongly emphasise—some of the most exciting games may be fought with only companies rather than regiments, and anyone who might be put off the plunge into the world of war games by what might appear to be heavy initial expense in purchasing some hundreds of model soldiers has no cause for alarm. With thirty or forty men on opposing sides he could get all the thrills of conducting a major battle, and in any case, it is rather more usual for the tyro to take charge of a small unit—company, squadron or the like—than for him immediately to assume command of an army. It is certainly better to begin in a small way and work upwards.

So, at the outset, we have the beginner who is eager for battle but who first has to decide on a period of history to serve as the background for his war game. For the sake of simplicity and for the very good reason that this is the game which will be discussed in these pages let us suppose that he chooses what we call the 'horse and musket' period, which can be taken as extending from about 1700 to the middle of the nineteenth century—it could at a pinch include the American Civil War although this is stretching it somewhat. Be that as it may, the general characteristics of this epoch are the use of the smooth bore musket by the bulk of the infantry, the employment of smooth bore cannon, and the rôle of heavy cavalry as a striking force, although the last diminished with increasing rapidity as the years passed, until it practically ceased with the Napoleonic Wars, certainly against infantry. Many other lesser factors are involved but prolonged discussion of them would simply succeed in obfuscating the issue. Suffice it to say that what we are about to embark upon is a game based on the Seven Years War, which is very representative of the period of time we are concerned with, and is ideal for our purpose in that it was a time of complete military professionalism, with many outstanding generals, spectacular battles and an almost entire dissociation of the military and the civil—a time when armies marched about all over the place with the populace paying little or no heed to what they were about and thus allowing the troops to get on with the job in hand without interference from such characters as guerrillas and the like. It was, in fact, a soldiers' war.

There is also the additional and by no means negligible point that throughout the period uniforms were at their most variegated and colourful and a Seven Years War battle presents a most gratifying spectacle; the Marshal-General's Putzenkammer Grenadiers in battle array are sartorially something at which to marvel. Here it may be pointed out that the rules we are compiling, although primarily designed for a mid-eighteenth century war game, can very well be adapted for earlier in the century, and during the discussion, details will in fact be given of the changes necessary to convert these—our Seven Years War rules—into their Marlburian equivalent.

II
The Basic Requirements

Now that a decision has been made on the period we are to use as a background to the war game, it remains to equip ourselves with the requisite troops and other paraphernalia required to conduct a war in miniature. This mustering of an army can be a real joy, and never more so than at the present time when shops hold a wealth of model soldiery. The difficulty indeed lies first in selecting the appropriate size and then in the choice of the products of any amount of manufacturers. The size element, indeed, does not present much of a problem, certainly if one intends to follow general practice. It would be unwise to assemble an army of some unusual scale and subsequently discover that no one else has such an army. It would be disconcerting to find oneself without an opponent. The old size of leaden soldier, the 54mm which was used in the halcyon days of Wells and Stevenson and with which many wargamers of my generation began their battles, has long been abandoned by the serious wargamer, first in favour of the 30mm type, the size indicating the height of the foot figure from base to crown, and later for the 20mm and 25mm sizes, both these being in universal use today.

It is a little odd that manufacturers appear unable to correlate their efforts and produce a standard model soldier for war games, but this is indeed so, and in fact from the workshops of the various firms specialising in model soldiers comes many a 30mm warrior who is in fact 40mm, while 20mm men will frequently be found to tower to 25mm, thus dwarfing their companions. However, experience will determine just which manufacturers produce the same size of troops, and their soldiers can then be purchased and used together with impunity. For myself, I rather regret the eclipse of the 30mm type—he had a certain substance as well as character, and careful painting of the bare casting could produce most pleasing results, sometimes equal to anything in the way of a larger showpiece. The bulk of the photographs used in this work to illustrate various tactical points and battle narratives show 30mm plastic figures. It is sad that they are no longer obtainable, especially as they were so startlingly inexpensive that a few shillings would enable one to recruit a brigade or a regiment. They were immensely durable, some of the long service units the reader will see having served in countless battles and having withstood with equanimity the resulting scooping up by the handful for depositing in their boxes after a battle, with hardly a wound to show upon their painted coats.

So be it, the passing of the 30mm leaves us with the 20mm and 25mm sizes, and it will be with these in mind that we shall, in the proper place, give some indication as to how to obtain the troops to build up an army. For the purpose of these rules, however, the height of the soldier is not of paramount importance, the figure's base being in fact the feature which counts. The number of men occupying some particular length of ground must be constant, the ground scale being, as shall be demonstrated, the important factor.

A brigade of war game infantry, Löwenstein-Oels Grenadiers preceding Ostergotland Infantry, the Brigadier-General and his aide-de-camp riding between the two.

We are now almost ready to proceed, but first we must have a battlefield. The novice on his debut as a wargamer, deploying only small forces, will not require a very great area. For the happy individual with a spare room he can devote exclusively to his hobby there is no problem, since his table can be as large as he likes and a permanent fixture as well, but for the less fortunate it must be fairly small and convenient enough to be set up quickly and speedily removed after operations without complete disruption of domestic arrangements and the possible incurring of wifely or maternal wrath. Something like 6 feet by 4 feet would do, just—it could be a sheet of hardboard reinforced by wooden battens. If necessary, and if the appropriate skill were to hand, it could be made in two sections, hinged in the middle, for ease of stowage. My own table, which has seen much service, measures 9 feet by 7 feet and was originally a table-tennis table, to which extensive surgery added the additional area. I would not recommend anything wider than 7 feet because the problem of moving troops in the centre becomes, in default of ape-like arms, something of a problem.

Finally, we have ranged our troops on the new war game table, not necessarily vast forces at the outset, when maybe a hundred infantry, twenty or thirty cavalry and a couple of cannon will be enough for us to command. (Later, though, our forces will increase dramatically). With even such a small force as this, split into two factions, we could have a vigorous little engagement in full swing in a few minutes, but at the moment the little figures stand motionless, awaiting the guiding hand of the player to put them through their paces. To do this, and to move them as he wishes, he must obey certain rules, and it is these as they reflect the tactics of the middle eighteenth century that we are about to discuss.

III
Infantry, both Line and Light

If we except the elephants employed by the ancients and later by Indian elephant batteries, oxen used as transport animals and I suppose the occasional camel, the battlefield before the advent of the internal-combustion engine was uncomplicated by the presence of anything other than man and horse. Accordingly, rules for the movement of our troops can be based on the various speeds which may be attained by these two creatures, and our immediate aim must be to seek a convenient relationship which can be used in our operations on the war game table. To do this is quite simple. One merely takes a time interval—call it *x*—which can be seconds, minutes, or in the case of a strategical game with maps, even hours, and determines the distances covered by man or horse travelling at different speeds (march or run, trot or gallop) in that time. The relationship between the distances will be constant, irrespective of what time value one attributes to *x*, so let us set about establishing such a suitable scale of movements for our troops, arrayed and waiting upon our orders on the table.

First of all, as it is our fond hope to recreate as accurately as possible a reproduction of the atmosphere and the conditions of warfare in the middle of the eighteenth century or thereabouts, our movements, if we are to be historically correct, must be governed by the tactics of the time in question. To give an extreme example, we should be somewhat taken aback if we saw a Macedonian phalanx moving about the place with the speed of a Zulu impi, and we must therefore ensure that our Seven Years War infantry battalion manoeuvres on the war game table with the same somewhat measured and stately tread as did its original on the fields of Minden and Leuthen. In parenthesis, I hope that the mention of 'stately manoeuvring' will not be found to be too offputting. Certainly, eighteenth-century warfare can admittedly be held to be a fairly formal sort of business but let no one think that it could not be a very fluid and rapidly-moving affair; Rossbach is a fine example of how swiftly the scene could change, while the casualties in many of Frederick the Great's other battles serve most readily to show how desperately the issue could be debated.

To continue, I seem to have heard or read somewhere that the marching speed of eighteenth-century infantry was designed to make the step coincide with the heart beat, but this may be completely apocryphal. At 28″ to the pace (this seems to be a fair average) this would give a marching speed of about 60 yards to the minute, which indeed is not too far removed from what was laid down by regulation. This to some may appear to be surprisingly slow, but it must not be overlooked that this pace is carried out by long lines of infantry, dressing rigidly and kept meticulously in line by a host of officers and NCO's, the hall mark of the age of linear tactics indeed. The idea of course was to maintain the troops tightly closed up, more or less shoulder to shoulder, so that when the moment came to loose off a volley, the maximum effect could be achieved. Apart from this, it goes without saying that the obvious policy was to present 'a bristling and unbroken front of bayonets to charging squadrons of mounted swordsmen' (as Glover describes it in his *Peninsular Preparation*, published by Cambridge University Press in 1963) if enemy cavalry happened to be in the offing. It can clearly be seen that the emphasis on dressing was the reason for the deliberate pace—the longer the line the more difficult it is to keep its strict alignment, as any PBI will agree. This rate, then, 60 yards to the minute, we shall take as a basis for the various moves our infantry will make, and so we must transfer it to the war game table. What better than that we adopt a distance of 6″ to represent it. This will act as a kind of common denominator for the remainder of our moves. Not that there is any particular reason to specify a move of 6″, nor indeed is there anything against it, but it has always been popular with wargamers, and there does not appear to be any immediate need to anticipate a change to the metric system (despite the fact that in the service of the Vereinigte Freie Städte the troops are paid —when the Paymaster remembers—in 'thalers'!)

Of course infantry are not always going to move about in line and indeed the normal change of position on the battlefield will be carried out in column, and this at once brings a new speed into the picture. Without having to pay so much attention to dressing, the column (in threes in the Prussian Army, to give an example) is going to move about rather more quickly than would be the case were the men in line. We shall say then that the speed of a column can be laid down as $7\frac{1}{2}$″, this distance being covered in our time interval of x minutes.

In the case of both the 6″ and the $7\frac{1}{2}$″ move we considered infantry simply getting from Point A to Point B without taking any other action. We must now deal with the line of infantry wishing to combine an advance with the delivery of musketry. Clearly the distance of the advance, in x minutes of course, will have to be reduced to correspond with the time required to fire the desired number of volleys. This was an important part of Seven Years War tactics, and Frederick likened his battalions to 'moving batteries' which advanced steadily, firing by platoons, so that a practically continuous volley rolled from one end of the battalion to the other and back again. This, strictly speaking, is not the case, the flank platoons firing first, and the fire going thus from the outside to the centre of the battalion, but the effect was pretty much the same. This process required the ultimate in drill and discipline and the study of an eighteenth-century Prussian Drill Manual is an eye-opener if one wishes to consider with what precision the Prussian foot could manoeuvre. This 'advance and fire' technique was so organised that each platoon fired about every 16 seconds—a rate of fire which could not be emulated by other Continental armies of the time, and indeed it does not seem likely that even the Prussians could keep this up for long before fatigue began to slow it down. Be that as it may, we can reduce quite substantially the line advance of 6″ and it seems reasonable to allow in the same move an advance of 4″ coupled with a discharge of musketry (and about the latter more later).

This steady advance, together with successive volleys, was the paramount factor in the process of shattering the opposition and it was continued until the attacking infantry was in a position to come to grips with the enemy, in other words when missile fire was 'off' and the troops went in with the bayonet to finish the job. It is generally held nowadays that the actual physical clash did not take place as frequently as one might believe from one's reading, and it appears that more often than not what happened was that the defenders, pretty shaken already if the musketry of their opponents had been at all effective, did not await the onset but went, standing not upon the order of their going. At a later date, the success of heavy Napoleonic columns of infantry against European infantry in line was due not really to what they actually did when they charged, but rather to what it was thought they would do, and this resulted in the issue's seldom coming to the actual crunch. In any event, whether or not the opposition awaited their arrival, the attackers would shift into top gear and charge. Again, this is a relative word: the troops were, after all, burdened with a variety of ponderous equipment and uniform, carried musket and bayonet, plus ammunition, heavy bandoleers and the like, and the resulting gallop would break no records, I feel sure. However, their speed would be sufficient for us to allocate a longer move in our comparative scale, so we say that infantry may have a 'charge' move of 9″, provided that this brings them into actual contact with an enemy. The charge naturally carries an additional bonus in the way of impetus, that is the effect a running man would have if he cannoned into a stationary one, but of this more later. The charge is something which naturally can be carried out only at infrequent intervals and its effects and results will be discussed when we consider fighting 'at push of pike'.

Thus far we have been dealing with infantry of the line, who made up by far the greater proportion of the foot soldiery of eighteenth-century armies, but it now behoves us to consider one of the special features of the particular time. This was the arrival about the middle of the century of the light infantryman, whose original function at a time when transport columns were quite enormous was to protect them on the road, but who quickly took over additional duties as a skirmisher and as a species of scout. The armies of France and Austria contained many light infantry units, the Balkan territories of the latter nation providing numbers of highly colourful and, to tell the truth, phenomenally cut-throat troops such as Pandours and Croats, who formed an excellent light infantry and who, despite a certain unreliability in action, were eminently suitable for the 'petite guerre' of outposts, raids and ambushes. The French, too, raised many 'free corps', the Arquebussiers de Grassin, who fought with distinction at Fontenoy, the Chasseurs raised by Fischer, a one-time valet who became a notable partisan, and the Fusiliers de la Morlière being only three of the number. Frederick the Great also created some light battalions, his 'jäger', but he did not appear to be over-keen on them, possibly fearing that the independence of action which was a sine qua non of the light infantryman would encourage those who, having little or no desire to remain longer than was necessary in the Prussian service, would take an early opportunity to dissociate themselves from its ferocious discipline.

It must not be thought that these light infantrymen, even the Prussian jäger, approached even remotely the high standards of efficiency of, say, the British riflemen of the Peninsular War, and could not be truly described as 'waspish soldiery [who] lie on the ground or cover themselves behind any object offering itself and bring down their mark with unerring certainty' (thus Glover in *Peninsular Preparation*, Cambridge University Press). They were armed more or less as were the infantry of the line but, being recruited in the main from peoples whose natural habitat was the forest and the mountain, were usually more skilled in the use of firearms and could consequently be reckoned to have a reasonable chance of hitting any individual target at which they aimed. The advantage of having people who could lurk about behind trees and in ground hollows, and who could harass marching columns or even pick off officers without having to march about in serried ranks is apparent. So, our light infantryman need not remain in line or in column, but can move around quite smartly, as quickly as line infantry in column, and thus his move at all times is 7½″; as we shall see he can also move and fire in the same operation. As it is hoped to show, he is very useful but by no means omnipotent on the battlefield.

We can compile a table of infantry moves thus:

Line Infantry	in line	moves 6″ or moves 4″ and fires
	in column	moves 7½″
	charging	moves 9″
Light Infantry	at all times	moves 7½″

IV
Cavalry

Although the proportions of horse to foot varied between armies, the great bulk of the mounted troops of our period was heavy cavalry, composed of dragoons, cuirassiers and others of the same ilk. Dragoons had of course been originally a separate arm whose function it was to fight as well on foot as on horse, but they were never completely successful in this dual rôle, and by the time of which we speak they had become to all intents and purposes almost identical with the regiments of horse. So we shall consider cavalry under the simplified heads of heavy and light, in that order.

The function of the former was to provide a massive striking force which could be kept in reserve until the psychological moment when it could be unleashed against a weakened enemy or into some gap in the opposing line and then, riding in close order, the troopers would crash through enemy foot or overthrow cavalry who faced the onslaught. The numbers in our war game armies must be fairly high, certainly a quarter of the total, possibly a third. Indeed, at a time only a few years before our period, the army of Peter the Great of Russia consisted of no less than three-fifths mounted troops, although this figure may have included Cossacks and other light horse.

Consequently, as we shall shortly have to deploy such considerable numbers of heavy cavalry on the war game table, the rules governing their movements must conform accurately with their historical capabilities, and initially we must get as true a picture as possible of what mid-eighteenth century cavalry could do on the battlefield, before translating this into war game terms.

First of all, we must disabuse ourselves of the common idea of people dashing about on fiery steeds, something like a heavy field at Aintree or the Derby runners coming round Tattenham Corner. Television and the cinema have much to answer for in creating a completely erroneous image of the speed and manoeuvrability of mounted men. Indeed, if we are to accept what we see so frequently (Heaven forbid!) we must assume that the most conservative gait for any horse is a fast gallop, a speed which it can apparently maintain for hour after hour. This is of course patently ridiculous, even in modern times, and still more so during the eighteenth century.

A typical cavalry regiment on the move. The Rijkswacht te Paard in the service of the Vereinigte Freie Städte, with the Colonel and standard in the lead and subaltern officers bringing up the rear.

The horses we have to consider are far removed from being candidates for the Classics or even for the present-day hunting field; they and their riders can be well described as big men on big horses. As for the riders, the *Clothing Regulations for the Army* of 1729 stated: 'Men not under Five Foot Ten Inches, in stockings, is sufficient size for Horse and Dragoons', this at a time when five feet ten inches was considered adequate for the Foot Guards themselves. As regards the horses, the Duke of Cumberland's *Standing Orders for the Corps of Dragoons, 1755* said: 'HRH does not approve of the large-footed, hairy legg'd Cart Horses that are too commonly bought for the Dragoons.'

I have no wish to drag the reader through a lengthy and possibly dull treatise on cavalry but it seems proper to give sufficient documentation to substantiate the conclusions we reach concerning the powers and limitations of cavalry, and to feel reasonably sure we are acting in accordance with historical precedent.

If I may then make one or two references, I shall begin with Lieutenant-Colonel G. T. Dennison (*A History of Cavalry*), who writes of the Prussian mounted arm as Frederick the Great found it on coming to the throne:

> The cavalry was composed of large men mounted upon powerful horses. . . . The force was of the heaviest type and incapable of rapid movement.

Evidently our mounted troops were by no means as mobile as we may have been led to believe, but let us proceed.

In the relevant article in *Chambers's Encyclopædia* (New Caxton Library Service) the cavalry of the period is described thus:

> .... men who wore iron skull caps (under their hats) and breastplates, and were armed with a long straight sword, a pair of pistols and a short carbine. Dragoons were not armoured; they were armed with firelock muskets, broadsword, bayonet and pistols and were equipped with enormous 'cartouche' boxes; the weight on the horse must have been immense.

Finally, James Lunt, in his biography of Lieutenant-Colonel James Luard (*Scarlet Lancer*, published by Rupert Hart-Davis in 1964) writes:

> .... dragoons were invariably bigger men than the rest of the cavalry and carried heavier equipment; consequently it became necessary to provide them with something approaching carthorses if they were able to get across country.

Before us now is something quite different from what might have been our original conception. Briefly, it amounts to a man of above average size on a mount which was more often than not a 'Black Horse', a breed closely related to the earlier 'Great Horse' and which, although not approaching the later mediaeval 'destrier', was something appreciably slower and heavier than the modern riding horse.

Arab horses, it is true, had been imported as far back as the reign of Charles II, and it was earlier in the eighteenth century that the three Arab stallions, the Godolphin Barb, the Darley Arabian, and the Byerly Turk, ancestors, I believe, of most of our present racehorses, had been brought to England; but it was not until about 1800 (my authority is Major G. T. Tylden in *Horses and Saddlery*) that the 'hunter' type of remount was being acquired for service in the British Army. Possibly officers had better bred animals than had the rank and file, but in any case they would each have two or three. I think it reasonable to assume that the regimental troop horse of the eighteenth century was not tremendously dissimilar to the Drum Horse of the Household Cavalry of today.

Returning to the troops themselves, they were, as has been indicated, bigger men than the average (this fact is repeatedly stressed in contemporary accounts), and taking into consideration the weight of their uniforms, arms, equipment and horse furniture, we get a picture of something pretty ponderous indeed, not to say slow, in their manner of getting around. Indeed, as late as the last decade of the nineteenth century, the average heavy cavalry horse in European armies carried between 21 and 23 stone, which contrasts with the 18 stone laid down just after World War I in the British Army and the 16 stone of the 1934 Regulations.

Bearing all the above in mind, we must now set about deciding upon the cavalry move. Certain speeds are prescribed for cavalry in Field Service Regulations and tactical manuals, and for mounted troops the first of these is:

Cavalry at the walk—120 yards per minute.

Various authorities do vary this by a yard or two either way but this figure will suffice for our purpose. This is what one might call a parade ground speed, such as might be carried out by a column of horse on a road, and since we are proposing to deal with bodies of horse moving over possibly rough and uneven ground where any evolution is a complicated operation requiring time and an exact discipline, we have to reduce it by as much as a quarter (it might even be a third, but a quarter will be enough). We are left with a speed of 90 yards per minute, which when reduced to war game terms, as was done for infantry, gives a move of 9″. This might seem to merit a little discussion, as it is but 1½″ longer than the infantry in column move (7½″). The point, though, is that the cavalryman at the walk does not get along all that much more quickly than a man on foot. London readers can easily verify this by walking alongside the Household Cavalry party on its way to mount guard at the Horse Guards—they will be surprised how long they can keep up with the troopers without unduly stretching themselves.

Here I must digress just a little concerning a decision which the wargamer must make on the nature of his cavalry moves. Obviously, cavalry are not going to 'walk-march' wherever they go on the battlefield. Times there will be when they will be required to proceed hastily from one point to another and will have to increase their speed accordingly. Ideally, I suppose, each move, whether it be walk, trot or gallop should have its corresponding war game equivalent, but this is impracticable without a great deal of book-keeping. Cavalry, particularly the heavy type we are considering, do not dash about all over the place but must halt from time to time to have a breather. We should therefore have to ascertain the proper ratio of walk to trot and work something out on the basis of how much trot was permissible to how much walk—so many moves of one to so many of the other. Some fairly elaborate sort of record would have to be maintained to obviate unfairness and to prevent unlikely tactics. This might well daunt the wargamer, especially the beginner.

The solution is to establish a mean and we can do this by combining the walk and trot into an average of what was actually carried out. So may I again quote an authority who, although he writes of World War I, may be acceptable?

The late Captain Cyril Falls (*Armageddon 1918*, published by Weidenfeld and Nicholson in 1964) describes a journey a cavalry unit made in the Mesopotamian campaign:

> . . . marching at a speed which best combined haste and the preservation of horseflesh; trotting twenty minutes, walking twenty and halting five.

This seems to convey the impression of something in the nature of a forced march, not lightly to be undertaken, but I think it will do, with limitations, for what we might call a 'battlefield' move by our heavy cavalry. The trot (*vide* our Field Service Regulations previously referred to) is 235 yards per minute. Reducing this by a quarter to allow for movement on rough ground, we arrive at the figure of 176 yards per minute. Making our calculations on the basis of the details specified by Falls we have a table move of very nearly 12″. This is the point at which the wargamer is faced with an alternative—does he wish to use the 9″ move which can be carried on throughout a lengthy engagement, or the 12″ one which requires intervals for rest? Now, a further point is that the 9″ move represents a speed of 3 miles per hour which, in a ten-hour day, would carry cavalry a distance of 30 miles. May I again quote Falls?

> The Germans were proud that one of their [cavalry] divisions had, in the invasion of Belgium and France in 1914, covered 30 miles in a day, but it is not claimed that they did this two days running.

Evidently 30 miles in a day can be considered quite an achievement for cavalry, a fact borne out by General Hawley, who said, in 1728, in a paper on a proposed regiment of light dragoons: 'This regiment will march 30 miles a day, when a regiment of modern dragoons can march but ten'.

So even our 9″ move for eighteenth-century heavy cavalry might be subject to some qualification. However, my suggestion is that we adopt 9″ as a 'standard' move for heavy cavalry; it can be maintained throughout an entire battle, and it can be used when fighting a campaign. Then let us enact that, for every move during which the cavalry remain at rest or 'stand fast', it may subsequently have one move of 12″. A six-move sequence might be:

1 moves 9″
2 stands fast
3 stands fast
4 moves 9″
5 moves 12″
6 moves 12″

It can be seen that the 12″ move need not follow directly after the 'rest' and that, as is apparent, the longer the 'rest' the more 12″ moves can be made. Thus, by husbanding one's cavalry, a sufficient reserve of 12″ moves may be available to carry it rapidly to some spot where its presence is required—a forced march, in effect. This system necessitates only minimal book-keeping, a simple record of each occasion when one's cavalry stands fast instead of moving, or one may simply place a counter in some receptacle to indicate a move of rest, removing it when a 12″ move is made.

Wargamers may operate this system or, if they would rather not bother with any sort of record, opt for either the 9″ or the 12″ move. It is entirely dependent upon their personal taste and on how far their desire for realism takes them.

Now we come to the *raison d'être* of the heavy cavalry—the charge, a dramatic and frequently devastating affair, when the squadrons drove home upon the enemy in an attempt to overthrow him by weight and impetus. I crave the reader's indulgence for possible pedantry if I produce one or two further references to authenticate our findings.

First, I need hardly point out that to achieve the maximum effect the charge had to be carried out as one man, the troopers riding knee to knee and bursting upon the foe like a single clap of thunder. Consequently the operation had to be geared to the speed of the slowest, not the fastest horse present.

Now for the references:

Dennison (*History of Cavalry*) refers to Frederick the Great, who ordered that his cavalry 'will move off at a fast trot, and charge at the gallop, being careful to be always well closed together.'

Leonard Cooper (*British Regular Cavalry 1644–1914*, published by Chapman and Hall in 1965) says: 'in fact, all through history, far more charges have been delivered at a canter than at a gallop.'

The point is that the heavy cavalry charge had to be a very controlled movement, not a hell-for-leather 'ventre-à-terre' sort of thing with each man for himself in the manner the French described as 'en fourrageurs'.

I have in my possession some notes by Major Martin, who served in the British Regular Cavalry during and after World War I. He writes as follows:

> ... usually the charge would be sounded approx. 150–200 yards from the objective. The final gallop (charge) would take about 15–20 seconds.

Research suggests that 200 yards would be rather an excessive gallop for the much heavier horse we have in mind, the idea being to reach the objective not at the last gasp but some time before, so it seems logical to assume that in our case the charge would be sounded somewhat closer to the enemy, say 120 yards. As before, reducing by a quarter the stated speed for the gallop (about 350 yards per minute) we have a resulting rate of 260 yards per minute, in round figures. Again calculating in round figures for the sake of simplicity, 120 yards will be covered in about half a minute. As we have worked in terms of a minute throughout, half a minute remains for the approach to charging point, which would be covered at our already established 12″ per move (combined walk and trot to represent the gradual acceleration). This adds 6″ to the 12″ of the actual charge and makes the resulting 'charge move' one of 18″.

The charge move may be made, naturally enough, only when it contacts an enemy, and there is a further proviso concerning which I again quote from Major Martin's notes:

> When once committed to a charge to the front, the attempt to change direction to a flank charge would be a tactical error. Control and cohesion would be lost entirely.

So, to the rule giving cavalry a charge move of 18″ must be added the rider—

no pun intended—that it must be made in a straight line (ie no charging round corners!). As we shall consider later, charge moves cannot be made very frequently; there must be only a limited number in each battle, but the point will be discussed when we consider hand-to-hand fighting (or the mêlée).

As was observed in our introductory remarks, the Seven Years War era was productive of many experiments in the military art, one being the introduction of light cavalry. In Great Britain the first complete regiments of Light Dragoons, five in number, were raised in 1759, two more being added in the following year. They were mounted on 'well turned, nimble road horses', but a cursory examination of their equipment and arms leaves little doubt that they were not a great deal lighter than the existing categories of horse and could not really be placed in the same category as the 'light' cavalry which existed in fairly large numbers in most Continental armies. In fact it would be better not to cloud the issue at the moment with the British variety and to consider only the European type, of which we have numerous examples, most of them pretty outlandishly armed and garbed. South-eastern Europe provided Bosniaks and Pandours, Poland furnished Lancers and Russia had the Cossacks. The French raised a considerable amount of light cavalry, mostly organised as hussars or 'free corps', and Marshal Saxe had his own regiment of lancers. All were used in their classic rôle for reconnaissance and screening duties, and because of their lightness were not expected to withstand the onslaught of heavy cavalry. However, by the same token they were able to sustain a rapid march for longer, and we can expect them to get about the battlefield without the periods of rest required by the heavies. Thus, in our war game, we accord them a standard move of 12″, which they can carry out during an entire game without rest moves, but since the speed of their charge during the short period it occupied would not appreciably exceed that of heavy cavalry, it remains at 18″. The question as to the comparative effect of the two charges, by light and by heavy cavalry, is for later consideration.

Thus, finally to summarise the cavalry rules:

Heavy cavalry	standard move	9″
	'battle' move	12″(one may be made for every previous rest move)
	charge move	18″
Light cavalry	standard move	12″
	charge move	18″

V
Muskety

Before considering the rules governing musketry in our mid-eighteenth century war game, it will be as well to know a little about the actual weapon involved. It was in brief a smoothbore, flintlock musket, and variations of the type were used in all armies from the early 1700's up to and including Napoleonic times, the best known being probably the British 'Brown Bess' and the French Charleville type. They fired a solid ball of between ·69 and ·76 inch calibre, weighing about an ounce, and all were wildly inaccurate at anything much above point-blank range. The actual ball could be lethal up to three hundred yards or more, but even the most expert of marksmen could not be sure of hitting a man-sized target at any range in excess of a hundred yards. This gross inaccuracy governed infantry tactics and determined at once that individual firing was quite out of the question. The aim of infantry was, in short, to march up to the enemy and to discharge the maximum amount of musketry into his densely-packed ranks, on the simple premise that, by firing as many muskets as could be brought to bear as often as possible in the available time into the opposing mass (ie without necessarily firing at any specific individual), some of the shots were bound to be effective. Obviously, the more shots fired in the enemy's general direction, the more would be likely to hit some member of his force. Consequently, the main considerations were speed of fire and the perfection of the drill movements necessary for achieving this.

The eighteenth-century musketeer is frequently thought of as having to go through a long series of movements preparatory to firing, a process taking apparently several minutes. This is only partly correct. Loading did require a number of movements but these could be carried through very quickly and, at the start of an engagement at any rate, well trained infantry could be expected to fire up to a rate of four rounds per minute. This of course tapered off quickly as the men tired and as their muskets became fouled, but it should nevertheless be taken that a fair average rate of fire at this time would be something like three rounds a minute. Even allowing for the high proportion of misfires to which the flintlock was prone and for the mischances of battle when men became excited or frightened or both in the heat of action and forgot to prime their weapons properly or left the ramrod in the barrel when loading, a quite immense volume of fire could be delivered by an infantry battalion in a very short time. A classic example of the devastation caused by such fire is the volley fired by the British infantry at Fontenoy, which practically destroyed the Gardes Françaises as a fighting unit. The late Major-General J. F. C. Fuller (*Decisive Battles of the Western World,* Vol. II, page 419) refers to the first Prussian volley at Crefeld in 1750 when it was said that 75% of the enemy was laid low. Sir John Fortescue (*History of the British Army*) writes of 'the most perfect volley ever fired on the battlefield', which broke Montcalm's infantry on the Heights of Abraham. All this should show that, particularly at close range, musketry was far from being without its terrors and we must ensure that our war game rules give it its proper value for different ranges.

Bearing in mind all the foregoing, we must convert actual musket ranges to the war game scale and then calculate what casualties are likely to be inflicted at those ranges.

It seems that we can accept the effective maximum range of the flintlock against formed troops (that is when fire is directed at large bodies, companies at the very least) to have been in the neighbourhood of 200 yards. But at this distance the chance of inflicting any substantial loss was so remote that rarely, indeed if ever, was fire opened at over 150 yards' range, and that distance itself would be considered in practice as the absolute limit. However, let us be generous and say that extreme practicable range was 180 yards, while appreciating that at this distance musketry was virtually innocuous. Obviously, as range decreased, fire became progressively more lethal, so that at some point we have to decide—and this has to be a completely arbitrary thing depending on the wargamer—when 'extreme' range becomes 'medium' range, and when that in turn changes to 'close' range, when the effect of musketry is at its maximum. Assuming, then, that we have three distinct ranges, extreme, medium and close, we have to specify what they are and there seems no better system than to divide the 180 yards we have already decided upon as a maximum into three equal parts, giving us the resulting ranges as follows: extreme, 120 to 180 yards; medium, 60 to 120 yards; close, zero up to 60 yards.

Our next step is to tie these distances up with the war game scale we are going to use. When establishing the relative distances for various infantry and cavalry moves, we used as a basis for calculation the table scale of 1″ equalling 10 yards. Thus, as the infantry in line move is 6″, which in effect is 60 yards, this can be taken as a yardstick for musketry range, and the first we consider, close range, is obviously from zero up to 6″, the second, medium range being from 6″ to 12″ and extreme range being similarly 12″ to 18″, with the 18″ being the equivalent of the 180 yards of the maximum feasible range.

Next we have to estimate effect and this involves the consideration of probability. If we picture one battalion firing at another, the effect of its fire will range between a maximum and a minimum: between every shot hitting its target, and conversely, every one missing. Usually, of course, there will be an average result depending upon a multitude of factors, including the experience of the troops firing, their physical and mental conditions and so on, and all these things coupled with what we might call luck will determine the result of the volleys fired. At this point we produce our dice, which will be in considerable demand as we progress in the war game (they are, by the way, the simple numerical type marked 1 to 6). I once heard a television interviewer suggest to a wargamer that the use of dice would seem to reduce the war game to the level of Ludo or Snakes and Ladders! This of course was arrant nonsense. War is far from being an exact science; Gneisenau, the Prussian general and military theoretist, wrote that 'War is always and everywhere a stage of contingency and good fortune plays its part'. All kinds of unexpected events can influence strategy and tactics: the death of a commander, a sudden panic by green or battle-weary troops, the misunderstanding of an order; this is what makes war an art rather than a science and is the imponderable we represent by the use of dice. In this instance we use dice in the assessing of musketry. By so doing we obtain, within the appropriate limits, the maximum or minimum possible effect. The frequent use of dice will ensure that an average result will usually emerge, but dice being what they are, the unexpected will from time to time occur, as it did and does in every form of human activity. A volley may wipe out an entire enemy formation or, at the other extreme, may fail to register a single hit, to the extreme and understandable chagrin of the wargamer involved.

Here, then, are the mechanics of calculating the effect of musketry when two players, *A* and *B*, each have an infantry unit lined up and firing at the other. The number of men in each unit will depend upon the personal whim of the 'general' who owns it, but at this point, though meriting future discussion, the question of numbers is not immediately relevant. To use one dice throw to indicate the effect of a whole regiment's volley would nullify our principle of the average, so to avoid this we employ a larger number of dice throws to make certain that the results will operate around what we think would be a reasonable average. Thus we divide the men in the firing unit, and in the target unit for that matter, into groups of six. This again is an arbitrary figure and it could be eight, or even ten, but six has several advantages, not the least being the fact that it coincides with the number of faces on the dice.

First of all the two players concerned, *A* and *B*, throw dice to see which fires the volley which takes place in each war game move, if the players wish to fire, needless to say. This, depending on the amount of time the move represents, may be the equivalent of a single actual volley, but as more often than not the move represents a minute and sometimes longer, it will correspond to several volleys. The 'firing first' procedure merely accounts for one side firing more quickly than the other. If the same number is thrown by both *A* and *B* the firing is equal and simultaneous.

Suppose, then, for the sake of example that *A* has thrown the higher number and his men fire first. Let us take one of the firing groups of six men. Again *A* throws a die, and the result represents the casualties he has inflicted upon the target group, also of six, at which the fire was directed. Deductions are made from the number which has been thrown, to bring it down and more in keeping with a realistic average, and to graduate the effectiveness of the firing at distant, medium and close range. Thus, should the range be between 12″ and 18″ (extreme), 4 is deducted from the number thrown; if between 6″ and 12″ (medium)—3 is deducted, and if zero to 6″ is the range, then only 2 is deducted, to represent the increasingly greater efficacy of the volley as the range closes. Thus, for instance, if 5 had been thrown, deductions of 4, 3 and 2 would indicate that 1, 2 and 3 casualties had been inflicted on the target group at the appropriate ranges. To determine the individual casualties, the men in the target group are numbered 1 to 6, and dice thrown to decide which of them actually fell. If we say that 3 casualties were inflicted, three dice are thrown by *A*, the firing player. Suppose they come up as 1, 3 and 3 again, then numbers 1 and 3 in the target group are hit, the latter, poor fellow, being twice a casualty, and he and no 1 are removed from the table. Thus *B* has lost two men from his group which as an isolated unit could not then return the fire, being insufficient in number to produce an effective volley. On the other hand it can be united with other groups if, as usually happens, more than one is involved in the firefight.

All this sounds fearfully complex. Let us take a simple example and work through it with the aid of diagrams.

Here, then, are two parties of line infantry, *A* and *B*, eighteen strong each (that is, three groups of six men each), ready to engage in a musketry duel with each other at a range of between 60 and 120 yards.

A			*B*	
1	2		1	2
3	4	I	3	4
5	6		*5	6*
1	2		1	2
3	4	II	3	4
5	6		5	6
1	2		1	2*
3	4	III	3	4
5	6		5	6

(Asterisks denote casualties)

1 Players *A* and *B* throw dice to decide the order of firing. *A* wins.
2 *A* throws three dice to obtain the casualties inflicted by his three firing groups on *B*, and he gets 5, 3 and 4.
3 The range is 6″ to 12″, so 3 is deducted from each throw. Result: 2, 0 and 1.
4 *A* throws 2 dice for group I and gets 5 and 6, and one die for group III,

getting 2.

5 Nos 5 and 6 are removed from group I and no 2 from group III. With these losses, side *B* is renumbered as below.

A		*B*
1 2		1 2
3 4	I	3 4
5 6		
1 2		5 6
3 4	II	1 2
5 6		3 4
*1 2		5
3 4*	III	6 1
5 6		2 3

1 With his men renumbered thus, *B* has two firing groups (remainders are ignored) and so throws only two dice, getting 5 and 6 (good volleys!).

2 Deductions for medium range as before leave 2 and 3.

3 Concentrating on groups I and III of *A*, *B* throws two and three dice respectively for these two groups, getting first 5 and 6, then 1, 1 and 4.

4 In target group III, no 1 was hit twice, therefore *A* loses four casualties, two each from groups I and III.

The result of this little firefight is that *A* suffered four casualties and *B*, despite the disadvantage of firing second, three only.

Once the rules are grasped this process takes only a matter of seconds, much less time than it requires to describe it, but that is the way with war games; actions move much more rapidly than words.

The above concerns a firefight taking place in open country, of course, and obviously changes will have to be made when one side is under cover. This means, by the way, something pretty substantial, field fortifications, stone walls, houses and so on. It is clear that fire directed at troops under cover must be less effective than if they were in the open. So we reduce the effectiveness of a group firing at such a protected target in this way:

The deductions of 4, 3 and 2 made from the dice throws for extreme, medium and close range are increased by 1 when the target group is under cover, making them 5, 4 and 3. We see immediately that long-range firing at infantry behind a wall, for instance, is not of much use. The player has to throw a 6 to secure a hit, while the fire from behind the wall is limited as before, only by 4, 3 and 2.

There is one other circumstance which must be mentioned, and that is the first volley. The first discharge of musketry in a battle was always more deadly than succeeding ones, because:

> ... men loaded best when cool and collected, unhurried by the fear that they were entitled to feel in presence of their foe, [and so] the first volley of an engagement was the most deadly. (R. Glover: *Peninsular Preparation*, Cambridge University Press).

Loading carried out carefully in camp under supervision, with the men not forgetting to prime their muskets or not leaving the ramrod in the barrel, was much more efficient and less likely to cause misfires. Our war game first volley is rendered similarly more destructive by regulating that, for the initial volley of an infantry unit in a battle, only 3, 2 and 1 are deducted from the dice throws for distant, medium and close range respectively. If a player's nerve holds out and he can get to close range of an enemy without firing, a truly devastating point-blank volley can be delivered.

To conclude, let us give:

A Summary of the Firing Procedure

1. Players throw dice to determine the order of firing; with equal throws the volley is simultaneous.
2. The winning player throws one die for each firing group of six men.
3. Deductions for range, cover, etc., are made as follows:

Range in inches	Deductions: Ordinary volley, In open	Ordinary volley, Under cover	First volley, In open	First volley, Under cover
0–6	2	3	1	2
6–12	3	4	2	3
12–18	4	5	3	4

4. Each target group is numbered 1 to 6, and dice are thrown to indicate which men in the group have been hit. Nb a man may be hit more than once.
5. If firing has not been simultaneous, the troops in the infantry already fired at are renumbered (less casualties) into 6-man groups and the process repeated in their favour.

A Note concerning Light Infantry

In setting out the capabilities of light infantry of the mid-eighteenth century it must always be remembered that they are not (and this has been already mentioned) the British riflemen of the Peninsular War. Generally speaking, they were armed with

A battalion of light infantry (the Arquebussiers de Grassin) in open order. Note the prescribed 3″ distance between the men.

the same musket as their fellows of the line regiments but, being recruited from a class more used to firearms and of a more independent character, they could be expected to act individually and by reason of their skill with even the ordinary musket be very effective in the skirmishing rôle. In this context, then, we shall consider them.

First, moving in column or in line, light infantry obey the same rules as infantry of the line: $7\frac{1}{2}''$ in column and 6″ in line. Operating as light infantry, however, in extended order, they may move and fire at the same time, the move always being $7\frac{1}{2}''$. To act as light infantry, however, allowance must be made for their being in very open order, and so they must be 3″ apart when it is understood that they are taking advantage of terrain features, bushes, ground hollows and the like, which will make them considerably more difficult to hit than the same number of infantrymen forming a solid line.

As to their firing, two courses are open to them. The first is an important one. In contrast to line infantry, they may fire (within certain range limitations) at selected individuals in a group; they can pick off officers, for instance. The alternative is to fire into the brown in much the same way as line infantry, which is naturally easier than the former, and is less likely to cause a significant loss of morale in the target unit. Much will depend upon the circumstances as to what the light infantrymen—or their commander—will select as a target.

Here, then, are the various ranges and killing requirements for light infantry:

Firing at organised bodies of troops in the open—('into the brown')

Range 0″ to 9″	5 or 6 required to kill
Range 9″ to 18″	6 kills

Firing at specially selected individuals (picking off officers, gunners serving a gun etc.)

Range 0″ to 9″	6 required to kill
Range 9″ to 18″	cannot be done at this range, except that mounted officers of an infantry unit, or generals in the open, may be picked off, a 6 again being needed

Firing at line infantry under cover (in houses, behind walls or earthworks etc.)

Range 0″ to 9″	6 kills (there is no picking off in this case)
Range 9″ to 18″	no effect at this range

Light infantry firing at light infantry (the latter being in extended order)

In the open 0″ to 9″	5 or 6 kills
9″ to 18″	6 kills

(When one side is under cover: there is no effect at the greater range, 6 is required to kill at 0″ to 9″).

Having dealt with light infantry dealing out destruction to the line, one can only reverse the process to give line infantry the opportunity to reply, thus:

Line infantry against light infantry in the open

Range 0″ to 6″	4, 5, 6 kills
Range 6″ to 12″	5, 6 kills
Range 12″ to 18″	6 kills

Line infantry against light infantry under cover

Range 0″ to 6″	5, 6 kills
Range 6″ to 12″	6 kills
Range 12″ to 18″	no effect

In both cases, the line infantry fires in the normal groups of six, and it should be noted how, as the range closes, the fire of the line men increases significantly in effect. Light infantry tactics were therefore to keep firing at long range for, as soon as the line infantry came into close range, the sheer weight of their volleys largely nullified the greater accuracy and the concealment ability of the light infantryman.

VI
The Mêlée

Such medical evidence as is available in the shape of hospital statistics, surgeons' reports etc suggests that even during as remote a period as that with which we are concerned, the occasions when bayonets or swords were actually crossed in anger were by no means as frequent as might be imagined. Certainly in the open field, with long lines of musketeers blazing away at each other at close range, one side or the other tended to give way when the fire and casualties became unbearable, and consequently it was not really often that the opposing lines really came to 'push of pike and dint of butt'. A sustained fire from eighteenth-century infantry could be extremely devastating, as I have previously indicated, and a firefight of only a few minutes was usually sufficient for all but the most steady and disciplined men to recoil and run, or at least to retreat with considerable celerity. However, it did from time to time occur that infantry were engaged in close combat, particularly when they were obliged to take part in street fighting, to assault field entrenchments or to engage in the desperate business of storming the breach in the walls of some fortified place. Accordingly, it being necessary to have the correct rules for such a contingency, we shall first of all concern ourselves with the clash of infantry in the open, and discuss how we can cope with hand-to-hand fighting, or in one word, mêlée.

At the outset, there is the question of the way in which two opposing bodies of infantry approach each other, preparatory to engaging in close combat and it is at once obvious that the man who is under way and advancing determinedly is at a considerable advantage vis-à-vis the one who may have chosen to remain stationary and await the crunch. If it should happen that the former succeeds in reaching his enemy without the latter's having been able to put a ball into him, he may well bowl over his adversary by sheer impetus. Despite the well-tried linear tactics of the day, more than one military writer of the eighteenth century advocated the headlong attack in column, designed to break into the enemy ranks by weight and pace. These columns would have a comparatively narrow front, as it was quite impossible to maintain dressing in a charge with ranks of more than twenty to thirty men. Marshal Saxe wrote in favour of the column and so did several French theorists, as befits representatives of the nation whose forte has always been considered to be the dashing attack. Certainly, if a determined column *did* survive the advance through sustained musket fire—and the 'if' is a very considerable one—much damage could be done and the enemy line sorely pressed.

One example of how the column could almost dislocate a line can be found at the Battle of Culloden in 1746, although this instance does present some unique features. Here a column, or to be exact a great wedge of Highlanders, surged across the battlefield and with tremendous violence struck the Hanoverian line, despite having been scourged by a hail of musketry and grapeshot. The point of impact was Barrel's Regiment of Foot which suffered very heavy casualties, almost a third of its effectives, in a matter of a few minutes. The presence of a steady second line, however, and lack of support caused the Highlanders to be driven back, but although they were almost without discipline the impetuosity of their attack did for a short while create a breach in the line of Government troops. Nevertheless, this type of attack was rare in the warfare of the era and in spite of its august Continental supporters, the column did not enjoy great favour as an attack formation. It was employed occasionally, it is true, and here we shall use it as a device for bringing two bodies of infantry into hand-to-hand conflict.

Before proceeding further, we have to determine how we are to indicate the winner when two of our miniature warriors, musketeers, fusiliers or grenadiers, are matched upon the war game table. This may be done in two ways. First a formula of sorts may be employed, combining the factor of numerical strength with the imponderable of luck. Allowance may also be made for the type of troops engaged, to give greater value to élite formations as opposed to, say, militia. With this in mind, one can simply count the number of one's figures actually in contact with the enemy and multiply this number by that obtained by throwing one die. When both players have done this, the winner is naturally the one with the higher total. The actual losses may be calculated upon an agreed mathematical proportion of casualties to troops engaged or by a system of additional dice throws. This is satisfactory only up to a point. It does ensure that the numerically stronger side does not inevitably win, but the employment of a single dice throw might produce a freak result which several throws would obviate. The alternative system is to take each individual combat, that is when one soldier is in contact with another, and decide the result by a dice throw. For the player with a desire for speed or who has less time (as when the dining table does duty as a field of battle), the first method is probably preferable, but if the saving of time is not the dominant motive and a desire for realism is present then the second is more accurate, more realistic and a great deal more exciting. It is quite extraordinary how one can become identified with a tiny leaden or plastic figure. On one occasion, when a certain sabreur of mine cut down a favoured captain belonging to my then 'enemy', a man of considerable maturity and vast military experience, he was so put out by this mishap that the remainder of the battle was conducted to a barely muted obligato of curses in a variety of languages.

Assuming, then, that our two combatants are more or less armed in the same fashion and that particularly in the circumstances we are considering, a crowd of fighting, jostling soldiery, the victory of one or the other will have a strong element of luck about it, we decide each individual fight by a straight dice throw. A number of dice throws, particularly if the mêlée is a considerable one, removes any tendency towards an unreal result, although the numerically lesser side can still emerge the winner, despite the logical advantage being with the big battalion. Quite simply then, when our troops have been placed in their mêlée positions, the players dice for each combat, the higher throw as always being the winner. Now it may occur, and indeed most certainly will, that one man may be attacked by two opponents at the same time, usually when one side is markedly stronger than the other. Naturally, two have an advantage over one, but here again I must stress the nature of what we are considering. The individuals in a crowd of fighting and struggling men, furiously hacking and stabbing away at one another, are not in the most advantageous position for co-ordinating their efforts. They are piled into a mass with every man endeavouring to render his immediate adversary hors-de-combat, and at the same time trying to protect himself from other assailants. This greatly limits the effectiveness of two men in a two-to-one fight, and it is almost impossible for a third man to intervene, to

Approaching the crunch! A column (Royal La Marine Infantry) attacking a line (Löwenstein-Oels Grenadiers). The next move should bring the attackers into contact.

make it a three-to-one engagement; he will simply get in the way of the other two. He will indeed have enough to do to look after himself and has little chance of avoiding attack by other unfriendly persons. Certainly in vacuo, as it were, in the middle of a field or in a boxing ring, three men *can* operate successfully against one, but not in the midst of such a hurly-burly as I have been describing. It seems reasonable to assume then that two will be the maximum number able to join forces, and even their efforts will be somewhat limited, so, when we have two men engaged with one, the player with the two men still throws but one die, but to his resulting throw, he adds fifty per cent of what he has thrown.

> Thus with *A* versus *B* in a straight throw by both players, the higher wins.
>
> But with *A* against *B1* and *B2*, the former throws straight, the latter increases a single throw by fifty per cent of itself.
>
> Eg, if the throw for *A* is 3 and for *B1* and *B2* is also 3, the total for the *B* side is 4½ and he must win. However, should *A* throw 3, and *B1* and *B2* have only 1, making a miserable 1½, then the single man wins the fight, and bully for him!

Now we can set about bringing the infantry together for the hot encounter.

In the first instance let us take the example of a line of infantry being approached by an enemy column of foot, and let us follow the latter's progress as it advances towards the line, which is remaining stationary and firing. The numbers involved are not important just now. The mechanics of the operation are shown below, which follows the column *X* as it moves towards the line *Y*.

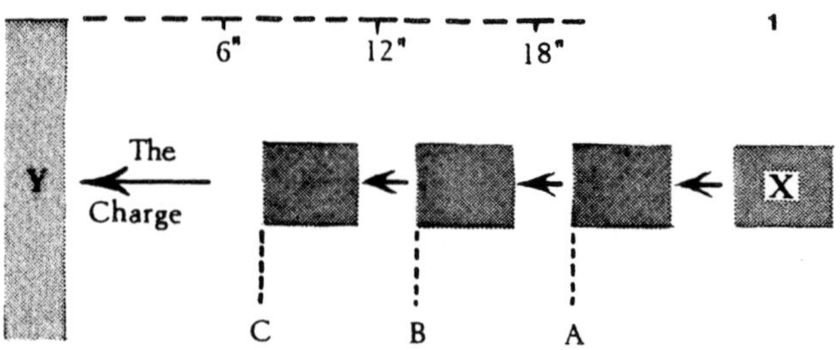

1 On the first game move with which we are concerned, the infantry column *X* has arrived at point *A*, just outside extreme musketry range (18″) from the line *Y*.

2 On the next move, *X* advances 7½″ (the infantry in column move) to position *B*, at which point it receives a volley from *Y* (at long range, 12″ to 18″) and the casualties, if any, are removed.

3 On the third move, *X* continues its forward progress by another 7½″ move to *C*, where it receives a second volley from *Y* (at medium range this time) and again losses are removed.

4 At *C* the attackers are some 7″ from their objective which they can reach on the next move by charging (the 9″ infantry charge move). During the charge, however, depending upon the rapidity of fire by *Y*, they might have to receive yet another volley, and this question is resolved by a simple dice throw by the players. If *X* wins, his column charges without having to endure another discharge of musketry. If he loses, his men have to take another volley, this time at close range (zero to 6″), before contacting the waiting line.

Having thus taken the proceedings, in diagram 1, up to position *C*, let us go on to diagram 2, which shows the details of the opposing forces at the moment when contact is about to be made.

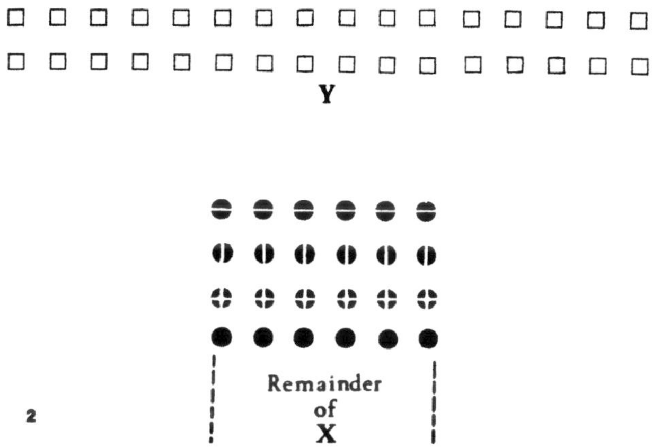

2

In diagram 2, only the first four ranks of the column are dealt with individually, as ordinarily it would be unlikely that any single soldier farther away from the enemy line would be able to contact the objective, certainly on the initial charge move.

The column has then arrived at *C*, and the players have thrown dice to see whether or not it takes a volley during the charge; *X*, shall we say, has won, and his column is ready to charge home without having to suffer further losses from musketry. (It will be noted that the attackers have suffered two volleys in making their approach, and may have to take a third before finally closing). So, with the troops poised to strike as in diagram 2, the actual contact is made in diagram 3 (overleaf).

The men in the front rank of the column are moved directly forward to make contact, each with one of the enemy, while two men from each flank of the second rank are moved forward and outward to meet the enemy on either side of the original front rank, while the centre men close up behind the front rank already at grips with the enemy. Similarly, *one* man from each flank of ranks three and four is moved outward and forward, the centre men closing up to their front, and behind them the remainder of the column comes up to the full extent of its 9″ move. The operation, which seems most complicated but is not really so, results in the situation as it is

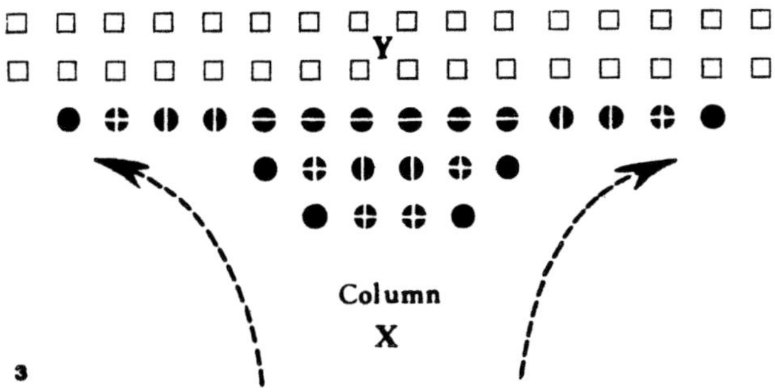

3

shown in diagram 3. In each individual case the move must not exceed 9″, and if the charge originates from a point just within the 9″ mark, it may be that fewer men will be able to contact, and the initial spread will be less. In retrospect, the general effect of this action resembles what happens if one presses the end of a pat of butter slowly against a flat surface.

This constitutes the 'contact' move and with the individual men placed as in the diagram, the combats will be decided by the dice throw. These will probably all be straight throws, one against one, as the recipients of the charge will have been in as close order as possible to prevent any two-to-one fights. There is one important difference, however, in the actual fighting. Moving at speed, the charging troops have a considerable advantage, their impetus, and each man has, therefore, on this contact move a bonus of 1, which is added to his dice throw. This quite simply represents the benefit he obtains from his speed as opposed to his opponent's having stood fast. In every individual combat, then, the attacking player adds one to his dice throw, so that should the players throw equally, say 5 each, then the attacker, who has the bonus of 1, has in effect a throw of 6 and consequently wins. This concerns only the fighting on the actual contact move, and after the charge neither player has any such bonus.

The next stage sees the contest degenerating into a general mêlée, with the attackers attempting to break through the line which is striving to hold them up. Let us suppose that, when casualties have been removed at the end of the contact-move fighting, the situation is as shown in diagram 4. Note that without specifying the actual dice throws, the attackers have lost only two men.

The combatants now rush together to continue the fight, and as it is not possible

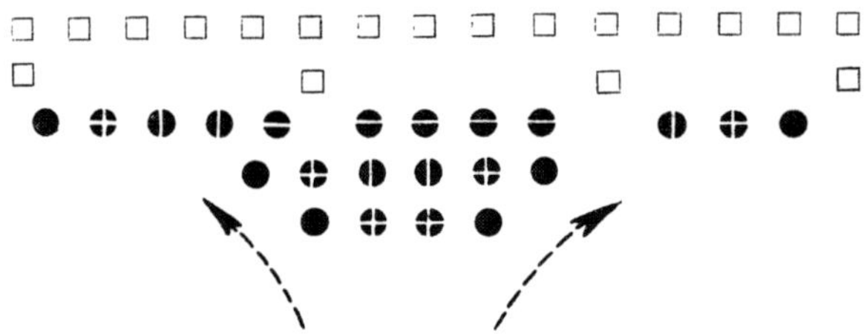

for the players to move all their troops simultaneously, nor would it be fair or realistic for one to move all his before the other, we take a convenient number, say 4, and decide whether *X* or *Y* moves first by the usual dice throw. The winner then places four of his men into contact with the enemy troops. The second player moves four of his into contact, the first another four and so on until all possible men have been moved or contacted. Once a man has been contacted, he cannot be moved himself until the combat of which he is part has been decided, and not more than two men may contact one. The move is now the standard 6″ infantry move, the charge being over. When all moves have been made, a section of the fight might be something like diagram 5.

5

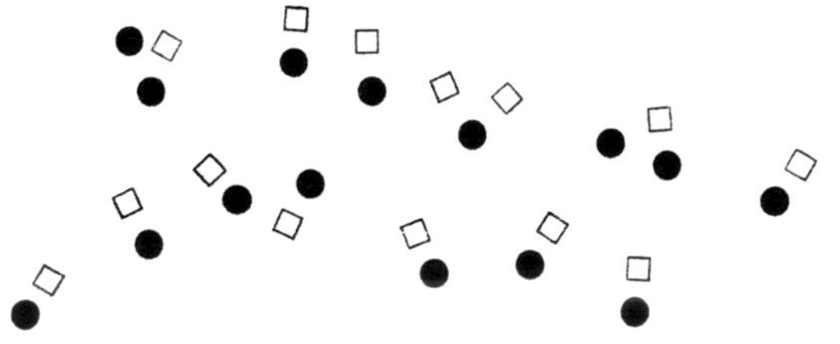

Diagram 5 shows the mêlée to be quite general, although the troops would probably be closer together than as shown, and the majority of fights are on a man-to-man basis, although some are indeed of the two-to-one variety. As with the previous moves the fighting is determined by dice throw, and the casualties are removed.

We have now had two combat moves, the initial one resulting from the charge, and one move of general fighting. What follows should really be determined by what time has been decided should represent one war game move. Certainly a fight like this would not be prolonged; casualties, fatigue and morale would in a few minutes cause one side to break and run, nor would it be without precedent for both to do so. We can but lay down a rule based on general experience of wargaming and say that after the two combat moves described the mêlée will end with one or both sides retiring, a question to be dealt with in the next chapter.

VII
More about the Mêlée

In Chapter VI we considered what took place when one stationary body of infantry in line was charged by a second infantry force in column, and we discussed the process by which this event was reproduced on the war game table. In such an engagement one side will usually have achieved a decisive advantage over the other, whether it be a moral or a material one, and will consequently have had the better of the encounter. In such a case the loser will have been obliged to pull back his forces, leaving the field and the victory to the enemy, a procedure which satisfactorily resolves the issue. I hope the reader will bear with me if I postpone the discussion of this for the moment, as it actively concerns the use of 'morale' rules, and allow me to concentrate for the time being on the problem of a situation in which no decisive advantage to either side has resulted from the fight.

In considering the attack by the column on the line of infantry, we tacitly assumed it to be part of a larger action and that it took place in open ground, there being no question of gaining some topographical or tactical feature such as a ridge, village, or entrenchment—anything, in other words, in the nature of a position. So at the end of the two moves which we had decided were to constitute the mêlée, it would be likely that the mental and physical exhaustion of both sides would cause them to fall back some distance to recover and to regroup. Thus we have a rule which lays it down that:

> Units involved in a mêlée which has been drawn will fall back two normal moves (6″ per move in the case of infantry) and will 'rest' for a further two moves before being allowed to take further part in offensive action. They may defend themselves if attacked.

For this period of what we might call 'exhaustion', such men would be at a very considerable disadvantage and obviously, if attacked during this time by fresh enemy forces, would undoubtedly find it harder to put up as effective a fight as they did in the mêlée in which they had just been embroiled. It is quite apparent that a second attack, launched immediately after a mêlée by a follow-up unit would be a deadly blow to troops who had already given of their best against another enemy unit. This question is covered by enacting that:

> If a unit is attacked by fresh troops during the four moves of 'exhaustion' (two retreat and two 'rest'), the attackers add 2 to each individual combat throw if the move is immediately following the fighting moves of the 'exhausted' side, and 1 to each throw if the 'exhausted' side has had a clear move without fighting. If fighting is continued for another move, the additions are increased to 3 and 2 respectively.

In other words, if side *A*, which has had two moves of fighting, is attacked by *B* on the third move (the first exhaustion move), side *B* adds 2 to each throw, and if the combat continues for another move, *B* adds 3 to every individual throw.

If *A* is attacked not on the first but on the second exhaustion move (thus having one move without combat), *B* adds only 1 to the throws he makes, and 2 should there be another fighting move.

Two moves of combat for the fresh attackers are all they are allowed, of course, but in any case, by this time the first unit will almost certainly be in a fairly precarious position and will very likely have sustained crippling losses. It should also be pointed out that should the follow-up unit actually charge those who are retreating, then each man will also have his charge bonus of 1 to add to the throws, thus making the advantage a really devastating one without doubt.

These two moves of retreat and two of rest (the retreat may be continued for all four moves if the player thinks it to his advantage to pull the regiment right back out of danger) apply to all sorts of units involved in hand-to-hand fighting, whether they be horse or foot.

Although all the above resulted, as we know, from an occasion when a column of infantry charged a stationary line of the same arm, we explained that this was simply a means to start the discussion, adding the proviso that, despite the writings of the eighteenth-century theorists, the column was not too highly regarded by the practitioners of linear tactics. More often than not it was a case of line approaching line, firing for some time and then, if there were no recoil by one side or the other, the lines would close and put the issue to the chances of a hand-to-hand struggle. This situation can be dealt with simply on the war games table, in this way. When two lines are within the ordinary 6″ move of each other, the 'generals' may decide that they are getting nowhere with the firefight which has been going on and that it is time to come to 'push of pike'. Dice are thrown and the winner of the throw moves four of his men into contact with the enemy, who moves four of his similarly; the first continues with four men, and this goes on until all possible troops are in contact. Individual fights are then decided in the usual manner. Supposing, however, that one player decides to move to close quarters while the other still holds back, then the latter may have the opportunity of firing a volley as his enemy comes up to contact. As before, a dice throw decides this point: if the second player wins, his men fire a volley and casualties are removed before the advancing troops are moved up. In this case, of course, the troops who fired are not moved to contact in fours as above but stand and await contact. The decision whether to take the chance of firing and not moving to meet the enemy is naturally up to the 'general' in question.

The word 'advancing' is, by the way, specifically used in the case of the line advance as it is not a charge. The men are moving up steadily in line as opposed to those coming on at speed on a much narrower front, and the advance as opposed to the charge provides no impetus bonus. When line meets line the individual fights are on the straight throw basis, or on the two-to-one system if the advancing player can manoeuvre his men accordingly.

We have dealt initially with two bodies of infantry fighting in the open, but for a variety of tactical reasons and usually for the very good one that it is numerically inferior, one of the opposing forces will in very many cases take advantage of some natural or artificial protection such as walls or field entrenchments. We must emphasise that the latter are not simply dug-out trenches or fox-holes, but something pretty substantial, raised above ground level and properly positioned and prepared by engineers. Malplaquet, Poltava and Fontenoy can be quoted as examples of the important rôle played by field works in eighteenth-century battles. To assault infantry manning such entrenchments or redoubts or protected by stone walls was something to be considered most carefully by an attacking general before he committed

Attacking troops behind a wall. It can be seen that certain of the assaulting troops have succeeded in crossing. It would be at this stage that a decision would have to be reached by the procedure described as to whether the attacking force carried the position or not.

his men to such an attack, as it would be a frightfully expensive business. The appalling losses suffered by the Black Watch in their unsuccessful attempt to storm Fort Ticonderoga in 1758 illustrates how costly such an operation could be, but the occasion did arise when the effort had to be made.

In the war game the situation is dealt with thus: we can illustrate the procedure by the example of a column of infantry attempting to storm a stone wall defended by enemy musketeers. Let us assume that *A*, in a similar manner to that already described, has brought his men to a point within 9″ of his objective, and that they will be able to charge home on the following move. This situation is shown in diagram 1, with *B* in defence of the wall.

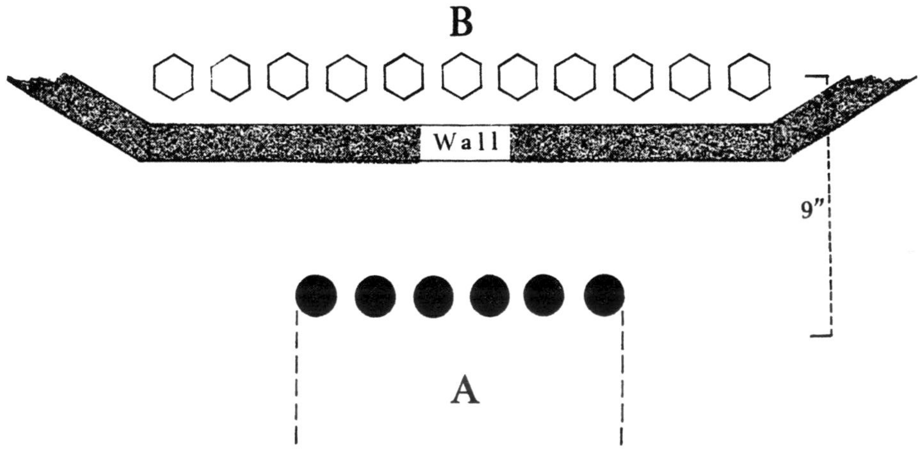

At this point *A*, whose troops have taken the appropriate number of volleys in moving up, decides to charge, and he and *B* decide, by the usual dice throw, whether or not another volley is to be received by the attackers as they rush up to the wall. If *A* wins the throw, his men reach the wall without further damage; if he loses, *B* fires another volley and casualties are removed before *A* moves up his men, which he does as in diagram 2.

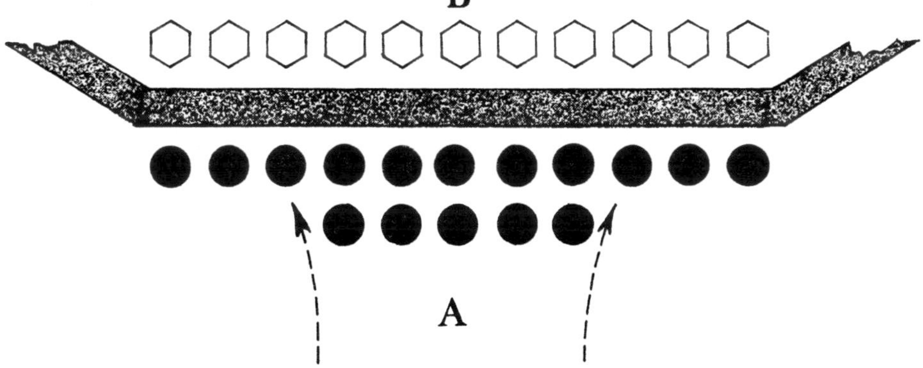

In diagram 2, fighting is going on across the wall, with *A* attempting to force his way over and *B* striving to keep him back. Observe here that although *A* made a 9″ charge move, his men will not get an impetus bonus since even a running man can make little impression on a wall and indeed, in this case, the defenders have the advantage, protected as they are. *B* adds 1 to every combat dice throw he makes for his men fighting with the protection of the wall, but otherwise the process is identical with previous combats. An example: *B* throws a 3 for one of his men, for whose attacker *A* throws 4. With the defender's 1 for protection, this means a drawn fight which will have to be continued on the next move. If two attackers engage one defender, though, and *A* throws 3 for them, giving a throw of $4\frac{1}{2}$ with the 50% addition, a throw of 4 for the defender would suffice, together with the defensive 1, to win the combat; in fact it would result in the removal of one of the attackers as a casualty. In the normal case of two private soldiers this would be the right hand man—not that there is any prejudice against him, it's simply a rule of thumb. If one of the two should happen to be an officer, however, dice throws would have to be made to determine whether he or the humbler private would fall, as a cunning player (and we of course deprecate such gamesmanship) would see to it that his officer is always the left-hand man in such circumstances.

Once the combats 'over the wall' have been settled, the position might be something like that shown in diagram 3.

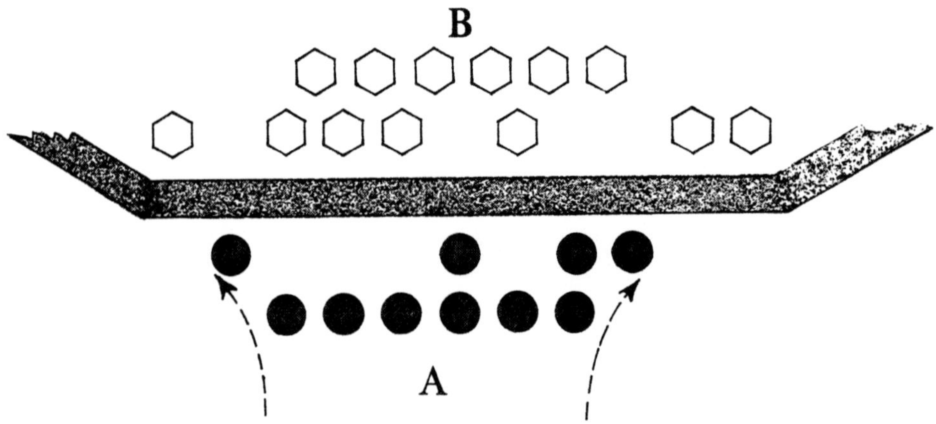

3

It will be seen that certain gaps have appeared in the line of defenders and that *A* has a second line of troops ready to move in to exploit any defensive weakness, although *B* also has some men in reserve. What would happen, in actual fact, is that those of the assaulting force who have accounted for their immediate antagonists will get over the wall as soon as they can, closely followed by their second line, while *B* will rush his men in to fill the gaps and 'pinch out' any incursion into his position. On the war game table the players throw dice to decide which shall first move four men, as in any other mêlée. If *A* wins, and let us imagine he does, he will obviously try to get as many of his men as possible over the wall. In the diagram four can do so, and *A* throws dice (one for each man) to see whether in fact they can do it. A throw of 2 to 6 shows he can, but a throw of 1 indicates he is too idle, too fat or too tired to make the crossing, and must wait for the next move to try again, that is in the unlikely event of his not being assailed by another defender. Supposing, then, that *A*'s four men are in good shape and get over the wall, then *B* has to move four of his. He will have two problems in mind, the first being how to deal with those already across, the second how to plug the gaps in his line. How he copes will be up to him, but in any case he moves four men as he thinks fit, *A* replies with another four, and so on until all troops possible are in contact, with the situation as shown in diagram 4.

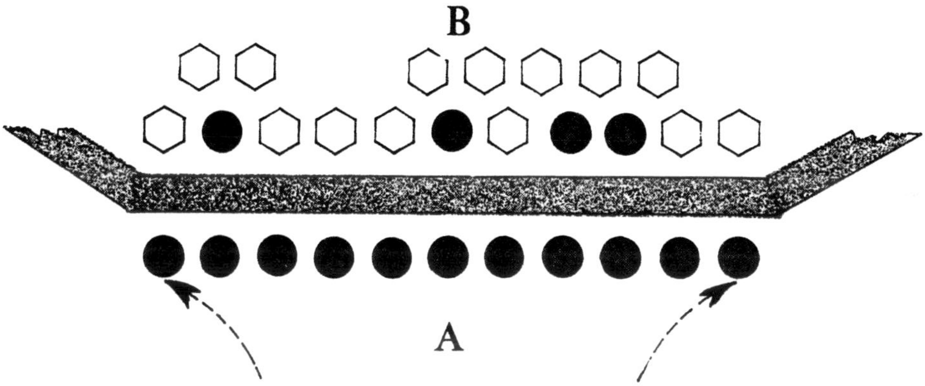

The counter-attack is in progress, most of the men who got over the wall being engaged by two defenders, although *B* is still under pressure all along the line. Once again dice throws decide the combats, with *B* still having the defence bonus for those of his men who still have the protection of the wall, although naturally he enjoys no such benefit for those engaging the enemy within; these are of course on equal terms.

At the end of this move a decision must be made in respect to what happens to the whole action. This is not the same as a fight in open country, after which both sides may fall back to rest and re-form. This has been a struggle with a definite objective, an operation to seize a certain position, and the result, if but a temporary one, has to be decided otherwise. In this case, what would chiefly influence the result, all other things being equal, would be the extent of the foothold that *A* had secured beyond the wall, ie the number of surviving troops he has in this situation; those must be given greater importance in the method used to obtain the result of the fight. We go about it in this way: the number of men each side has in contact is counted and multiplied by the imponderable factor, ie the dice throw. Every man *A* has succeeded in getting across the wall counts 2, all others as 1 only, and the player whose total is greater holds the position, the other being obliged to retreat. An example to demonstrate the system:

A has 20 men involved: 5 over the wall count 2 each = 10; 15 counting 1 each, giving a total of 25. He throws a 4, thus giving himself a final comparison total of 100.

B has 15 men involved, counting 1 each; a dice throw is 5; his total is then only 75.

With 100 as against 75 *A* has won the position.

All this is presupposing that both sides are of good morale and have not suffered so heavily that they would be obliged to abandon the fight.

Only a few words are necessary to describe the last type of mêlée with which we need concern ourselves, that involving cavalry against infantry. The former advances in the normal way, and will receive a volley when it arrives within musket range of its objective. Musket range (18″) is of course the charge move, so on the next move the players dice to see whether the cavalry receives another volley as it is charging or whether it is moving too fast for this to happen. If the infantry player wins the throw, his men fire and the cavalry casualties are removed before contact is made. Should he lose the throw, then there is no second volley. He has a choice, however. He may, should he so wish, abstain from firing the first volley and can then choose to deliver a volley at either medium or close range, depending upon whether he throws a low or a high dice against his opponent. What it means is that he can get one volley against the charging cavalry, the dice deciding whether his men are sufficiently well drilled to wait these extra few seconds before firing. Once in contact (and allowing for the breakthrough process described elsewhere) the ordinary cavalryman versus infantryman combat is decided by dice throw, wherein the player with the mounted man *doubles* his dice throw against a straight one for the foot soldier. In the general mêlée two infantrymen, not more, can combine against one cavalryman. Should the latter win, the right hand infantryman is the casualty.

VIII
Artillery: the Roundshot

Having now dealt in a general sort of way with firepower, movement and mêlée in so far as they relate to infantry and, to a limited extent, cavalry, it is time to carry on with a consideration of the third arm, the artillery, and to establish rules for cannon fire in the war game.

As always, a little background is necessary first, to make sure we have the correct facts and to prevent our giving too much or too little effect to the field pieces we are to use in our war game battles. The article on artillery in the *Encyclopædia Britannica* refers to the eighteenth century, with which we are of course concerned, as 'a period of marked ordnance activity on the part of all major European armies', and certainly many reforms and innovations were found in this period, particularly from the middle of the century onwards. The old, very slap-happy system or rather lack of system whereby every army had guns of all sorts and sizes and every variety of calibre came to an end and an era in which standardisation and uniformity were watchwords took its place. Taking France as an example, Valière and Gribeauval were two pioneers who had great influence on their country's artillery, and among the changes largely attributable to them was the reduction of the numerous calibres of French field pieces to only three, corresponding to 4–, 8–, and 12–pounders. This may seem an elementary sort of thing to us but it was quite revolutionary in its day. Prussia and Austria were also active in their efforts to improve their ordnance, and in the former country Frederick the Great was instrumental in introducing the first horse artillery to be seen in war. The field howitzer was also developed and the horse teams drawing the guns were organised in pairs instead of being employed in single file. The personnel serving the guns became more professional; in this country the two companies which provided the basis for the future Royal Artillery were raised in 1716, and four years later in France the Regiment Royal de L'Artillerie was created from the already existing battalions of Royal-Artillerie and Royal-Bombardiers. Thus, by the time with which we are concerned, most European armies had a fairly sophisticated and well-organised corps of artillery, some more efficient than others, but all made up of the same ingredients of field gun and howitzer. Within our self-imposed terms of reference which are limited by our aim to provide initially a not over-complicated framework of rules for an eighteenth-century war game, it is not proposed to deal other than basically with either; I must also point out that, in the matter of artillery's effectiveness, range and mobility, there are certainly as many divergent opinions among wargamers as are to be found concerning any other facet of the game. Consequently, criteria I may consider logical and valid may not be acceptable to another wargamer, and bearing this in mind my hope is to found my obiter dicta on historical fact, if I can.

Proceeding, then, we can for our purposes divide field artillery in two types, the field gun and the howitzer, and of course it goes without saying that both were smooth bore. The first is the long-barrelled weapon for long range work firing roundshot—solid iron spheres which progressed in a series of bounds after they had first pitched, each ricochet becoming weaker and weaker until the ball simply rolled along the ground until it came to rest, although even a rolling ball could take off a man's foot, as was proved by more than one ill-advised soldier who tried to stop one in this way. By our period there was no question of loose powder being stuffed down the barrel to form the propellant charge. In fact the technique had become considerably more advanced quite earlier, charge and ball being attached and sewn together in a kind of canvas bag, a primitive type of large cartridge. Field gun trajectory was relatively flat, in contrast to that of the howitzer which threw its projectile (a shell fused to explode, it was hoped, on impact) much higher into the air, so being able to direct plunging fire on targets not in direct vision. The difference is best shown in the diagram.

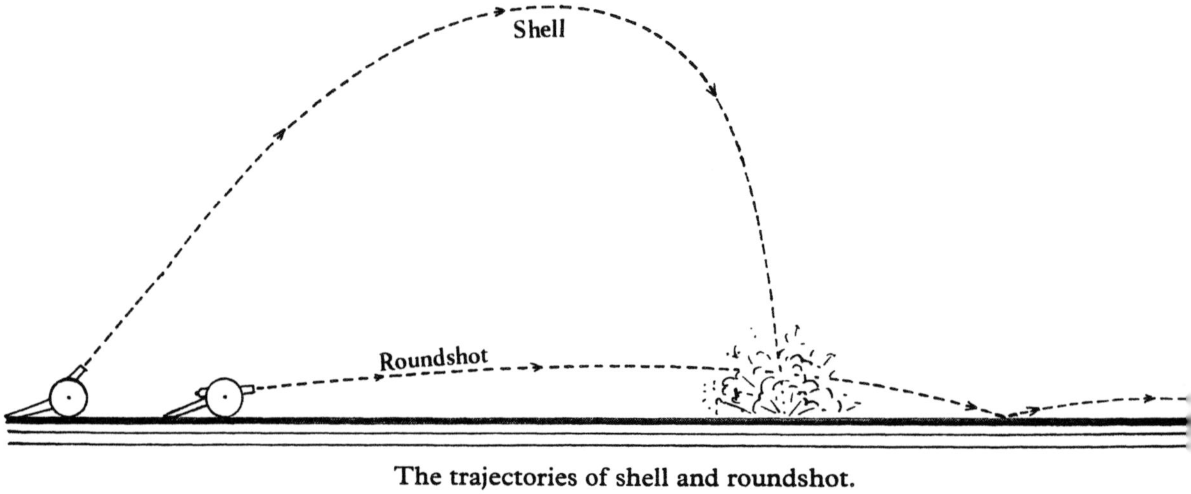

The trajectories of shell and roundshot.

Now, without going too deeply into ballistics we must establish one or two facts concerning the powers of our cannon, and first let us examine the field gun firing roundshot, the best methods for its use and most important, its effective range. It seems that, when roundshot was fired, the intention was that it should ricochet, the effect being similar to that produced when one skids a flat stone across the surface of a pond in a series of bounds. The roundshot, in fact, was aimed to pitch in front of the enemy, whence it was intended that it should plough its way through the opposing ranks in decreasing 'hops'; in theory, each ricochet would be half the length of the previous one, but I daresay that the state of the ground, whether it was rocky or muddy, would have some considerable effect on that. With the vagaries of eighteenth-century powder it was presumably easier to do this than to attempt to hit a small target and under- or overshoot.

Before laying down a range for our field gun, we have to decide on which calibre of piece we are going to employ, especially as at this point we do not want to make our gunnery rules too complicated by using cannon of different capabilities. During our period, guns of 4-, 6-, and 8-pounder calibre were extensively used by all European armies, the second being extremely popular on the Continent, and it seems a good idea to accept it as an average (note that the 12-pounder was not found in great numbers until the time of Napoleon, who was very partial to what he termed his 'plus belles filles'). The wargamer who wishes may, of course, have guns of varying sizes but I think it best to discuss one only here.

In his *Essai General de Tactique* of 1775 Guibert, the French military writer, gave the roundshot ranges of the 8- and 4-pounder as being 800 yards and 500 yards respectively. These are what are called 'effective' ranges, or if I may use the term, what might be considered 'practical' ranges. Now very obviously, if a gun is given maximum charge and elevation, it will send its projectile to the greatest possible distance, but this is not much good if, when it strikes, the distance is such that it is not possible to see the result. Furthermore, the greater the distance travelled by the ball, the greater becomes any initial error in its aim and the more subject it is to atmospheric conditions. This is the consideration which must govern our gunfire. How far can the piece be aimed, and by corollary, at what distance can its effect be seen by the gunner to enable him to make necessary corrections? There is no point in making a rule concerning a possible maximum range for a gun without reference to its use and performance in practice. In any case, without unlimited ammunition, gunners are not going to waste shot on targets which are too distant to warrant an effort being made to hit them, or which by reason of their range cannot be identified as friend or foe.

In the days of which we are speaking, not all that many perspective glasses were available, and the first limiting factor to gunnery was visibility, this being far more of a restriction than many people realise, wargamers particularly giving the human eye far more power than it really possesses. If one cares to carry out a few tests on a clear day over measured distances the results will be found to be more than surprising. At anything over five or six hundred yards there is an appreciable loss of colour and anything in the way of groups of people appear simply as black blobs. No wonder then that one finds so many errors of identification in warfare, friendly troops firing into each other and so on. In his *Journal of the Waterloo Campaign*, published by Peter Davies in 1969, Captain Mercer, whose narrative is very well known and tremendously readable, describes such an incident thus:

> There we saw two dense columns of infantry pushing forwards at a quick pace towards us...Everyone, both of the 14th and ourselves, pronounced them French, yet still we delayed opening fire on them. Shouting, yelling and singing, on they came, right for us; and being now not above 800 or 1000 yards distant, it seemed folly allowing them to come nearer. The commanding officer of the 14th, to end our doubts, rode forward, but was returned, assuring us that they were French. The order was already given to fire, when luckily, Colonel Gould recognized them as Belgians.

This seems to suggest quite plainly that at a thousand yards or less identification becomes virtually impossible, although mounted troops can be distinguished from infantry, but only by reason of size. Without going more deeply into the matter it is safe to say that on a dullish sort of day visibility would be even more restricted. At 1500 yards large groups could be picked out only if they were on the skyline or against a very light background, and against ploughed fields, for example, would be practically invisible.

Furthermore, in the circumstances we are considering, ie during a battle, there would be an added consideration in the shape of the dense clouds of smoke produced by the frequent discharge of thousands of muskets and scores of cannon. So immense and ubiquitous were those great banks of smoke that it seems a man was lucky if he could see what was going on only a short distance from him. Captain Mercer, if I may quote him again, has this to say with reference to the subject:

> ...I saw through the smoke the leading squadrons of the advancing column coming on at a brisk trot, and already not more than one hundred yards distant, if so much, for I don't think we could have seen so far.

Anyhow, all this seems enough time devoted to background and theory so we shall now get on with the business of determining our field gun's effective range, that is the distance beyond which, for any of the reasons given above, the gunners could not or would not fire.

It is possible of course to have a scale of ranges depending upon natural visibility, or how long the battle had been in progress, thus allowing for the amount of smoke about, but these are refinements best left to the individual taste of the wargamer, if he desires to go so far with realism.

We shall therefore take 600 yards as being the effective roundshot range of our field gun, which thus corresponds roughly with the 6-pounder. I am aware that this distance may seem to some wargamers to be too short but I deem it better to err, if at all, on this side rather than on the other, and another reference may support my contention. John Naylor in his book *Waterloo* (Batsford, 1960) discusses the artillery used, which of course was in no way different from that of the preceding half-century, and writes:

> The extreme range of the twelve-pounder, the largest gun commonly used in battle, was about 3,600 yards, but the extreme effective range was 1,200 to 1,700 yards. It was only at little more than half this distance, however, that firing usually began.

It seems that if a 12-pounder opened fire at 600 to 850 yards, a cannon of half the calibre would not do so at more than the lesser figure given.

Using our previously established table scale of 10 yards to 1 inch, we arrive at a maximum table range of 60″ or 5 feet. At this distance our roundshot is going to be used with the ricochet technique and we shall have to work out the lengths of the said ricochets, at the same time allowing for the fact that due to erratic behaviour of the gun, lack of uniformity in powder quality or minute variations in the size of the ball, the ball might do one of three things when fired. It might hit the point at which it was aimed, or it might either overshoot or undershoot, and each subsequent bound would be dependent upon the first bounce. So we produce our first device which is shown in the diagram below.

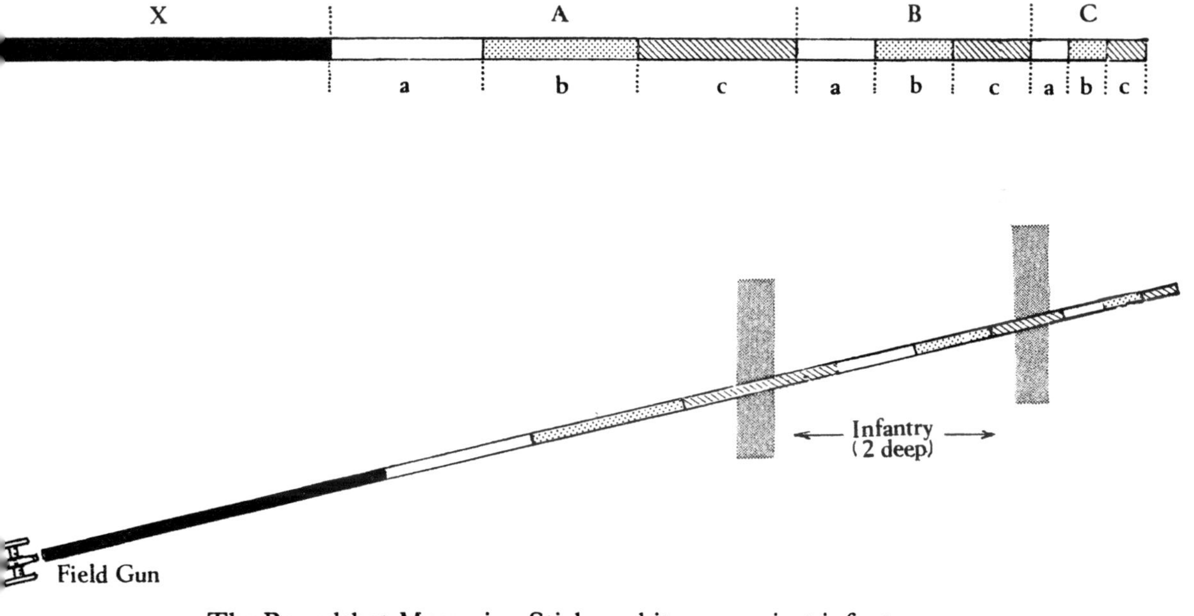

The Roundshot Measuring Stick, and its use against infantry.

This device is somewhat grandiosely referred to as the Roundshot Measuring Stick, is 60″ in length to correspond with the agreed maximum range, and as I use it, it consists of a length of ¼″ half-round wooden beading. It could be made of stout wire, or even a length of string could be used if appropriately coloured, but the stick gives clearer definition and is easier to manipulate. The colour scheme is purely arbitrary and can be altered to suit one's own taste, but it is in effect this: *x* is black,

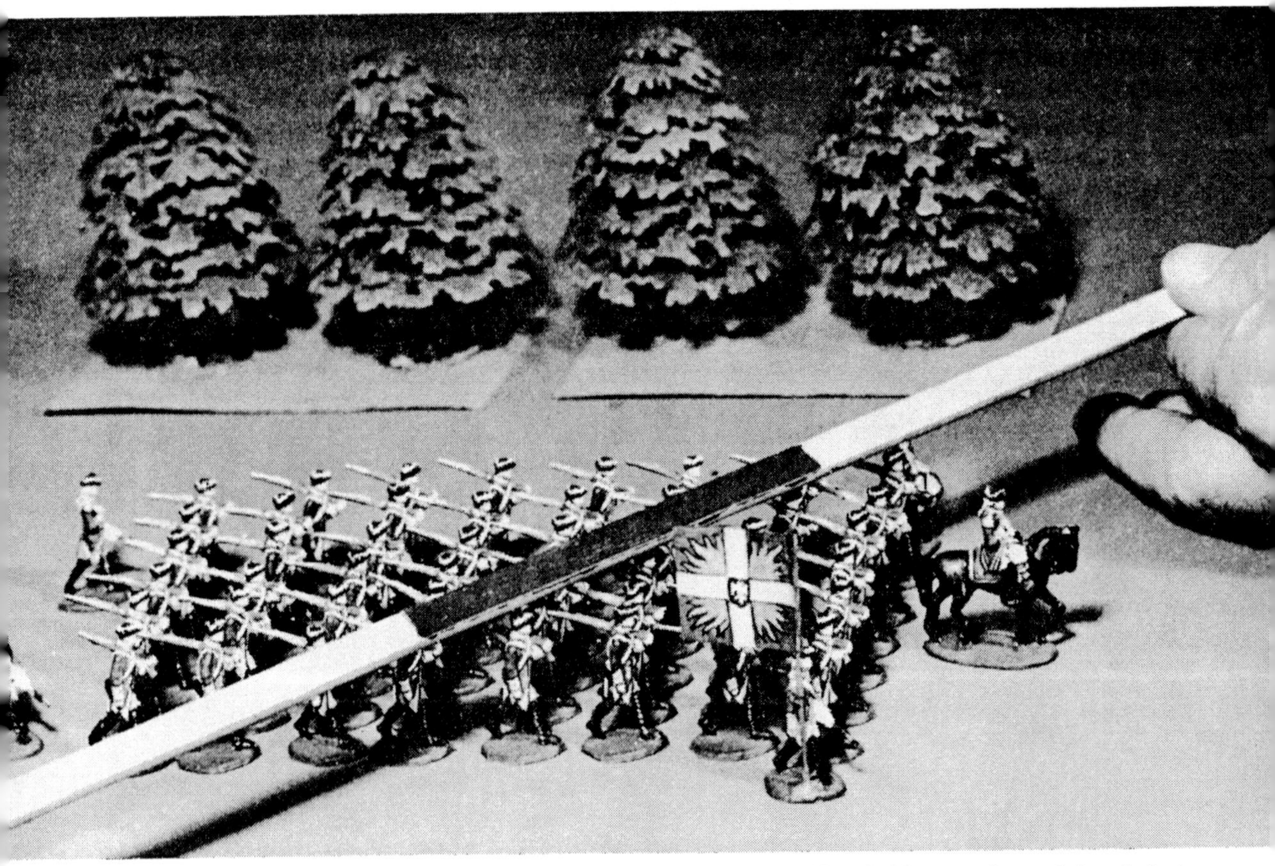

Showing the use of the Roundshot Measuring Stick. The field gun whose firing is being assessed enfilades the regiment rather, and looking down on the Stick as it is held diagonally, it can be seen that three men are covered by the dark section (it is the green section), and should a throw of the three-colour die produce this colour, all three men may be casualties, depending on dice throws.

a, b, and *c* are white, yellow and green respectively, and each group, *A, B,* and *C,* consists of three such sections. Those of *A* are 8″ in length, while *B* and *C* have three 4″ and three 2″ sections respectively. They can be termed the 'near', 'mid' and 'distant' groups in that order. Accordingly, if the roundshot first pitched in a yellow section, *b,* it would again hit in the two subsequent yellows. If the target is not in the first group, the 'near', one assumes that the first bounce takes place in the 'mid' group. It will be seen that each ricochet is half the length of the previous one, and after the bounce in the 'distant' group we take it that all significant velocity has been lost, that the ball is rolling along the ground and will finally come to rest. Before this, however, anything in the line of flight of the ball when it bounced would be in danger, although the further from the gun the less the danger would be.

A second simple device for use with the Measuring Stick is required before our field gun goes into action, this being a three-coloured die, to correspond with the stick, it being similarly white, yellow and green (sides 1 and 2, 3 and 4, and 5 and 6 respectively). It is an easy matter to paint an ordinary die the requisite colours, but it can indeed be left as a numbered die, as long as the numbers are known to correspond with the colours of the stick.

Now armed with the two devices, we shall go through the mechanics of firing a roundshot, taking as the target in our example infantry, ranged in two lines, one in the rear of the other as in the diagram at the foot of page 59.

The stick is placed in position along the desired path of the roundshot, black end to gun muzzle, and the three-coloured die is rolled. Let us imagine that, with the stick as in the diagram, green comes up. At once we see that the ball plunged through the first body of infantry, ricocheted and, by a happy chance for the gunners, has also gone through the second line. If the groups of infantry are two deep, then two men in each group are covered by the stick, and one ordinary die is used for each man to determine whether he is a casualty or whether he was just missed by the cannon ball. The following table is employed and applies equally to cavalry as to infantry:

Near group	3, 4, 5 or 6	kills
Mid group	4, 5 or 6	kills
Distant group	5 or 6	kills

There are other schedules for casualties and damage relating to the effect of roundshot on gun teams, on buildings, field fortifications and so on, but they are detailed later. May I make a last reference to the Measuring Stick? The black section, that is the first 18″ represents point-blank range and normally at this range roundshot would not normally be employed against infantry in the open, almost certainly canister being used in such circumstances, and of this more anon.

IX
Artillery: the Shell

From the solid roundshot we now pass to the alternative—the explosive shell fired from a howitzer, not so widely used, possibly, but nevertheless most effective in suitable circumstances.

The howitzer for field operations was developed throughout the eighteenth century, Frederick the Great being one of its principal exponents, but during the period we are considering it was never used in such numbers as the field gun, which is surprising in some ways. Indeed, as late as the Napoleonic Wars, howitzers were in a considerable minority, and numbered only about a sixth of the guns used by the Royal Horse Artillery at Waterloo for example. Nevertheless the howitzer could be invaluable particularly when the question was one of seeking out enemy troops in dead ground, who could not be reached by roundshot (or only with great difficulty) or when they were behind field fortifications or ensconced in houses.

At this point it might be well to describe briefly what we mean when we talk about the howitzer and its shell. The former as used in the field was a short-barrelled weapon whose calibre varied in different armies, but was usually about 6″ or thereabouts. As for its projectile, it must be pointed out that this was *not* the shrapnel shell as used at a later date by the British Army. Our shell is simply a hollow iron sphere filled with explosive and detonated by a fuse. The firing procedure was something of a hit-and-miss business, I suspect, as the fuse was but a thin tube or quill filled with combustible material and thrust into a hole in the shell, having been previously cut to a length appropriate to the estimated time of flight. The idea was that it, the shell, should explode simultaneously with its fall to earth. The fuse was ignited—it was hoped—by the explosion of the propellant charge (there was considerable 'windage' in the howitzer barrel) and burned down during the passage of the shell through the air. Obviously, this was a pretty elementary sort of technique and doubtless there were many occasions when it soared merrily upwards bearing with it an unlighted fuse.

Another disadvantage was that the shells seem to have had poor fragmentation qualities, i e on exploding, they tended to break up, not into a large number of small pieces giving a high lethal effect against troop concentrations, but into a small number of large ones, reducing their efficacy quite considerably. Against this, though, may be set its moral effect, mainly against mounted troops, the explosions readily causing panic among the horses of cavalry and of gun teams, while roundshot, which in actual fact was probably more deadly, did not have this effect to the same extent. In passing, it is always a source of irritation in the cinema to see cannon being loaded with roundshot which, when fired, appears to explode unaccountably on the target in a cloud of flame and smoke!

Howitzer and field gun were sometimes employed together in mixed batteries, it being presumably tactically advantageous to combine them in this manner. Certainly in the British service this seems to have been the practice, and if I may mention Waterloo again, all the troops of the Royal Horse Artillery, with the exception of Bull's six howitzers, had one howitzer and the remainder field guns.

It will be readily apparent that because of the nature of the shell's trajectory (see the ballistic diagram in the previous chapter), the vagaries of the gunpowder of the charge, possible excessive 'windage' (this being the difference between the diameter of the shell and the bore of the gun) and the shortness of the barrel, it was just as likely to hit any spot around the target as it was to land on that place itself. Allowance will have to be made in our rules for errors all round the target. It may be said here that, in the case of the field gun firing roundshot, no allowance is made for right- or left-hand error when using the Measuring Stick. In practice this was negligible for the field gun, and in any case it tended to be corrected after every round fired, the tremendous recoil necessitating the gun's being relaid after every discharge. One recalls how, in the film of C. S. Forester's story, *The Gun,* grotesquely renamed *The Pride and the Passion,* the firing of this gigantic piece of ordnance, with a bore of what seemed to be at least a foot, simply caused it to rock gently on its carriage!

So if we make allowance for all the factors involved, it seems that the shell, if properly ignited, would land and explode in a variety of positions relative to the point of aim, and the possibilities, much simplified, would produce a pattern akin to that shown in diagram 1.

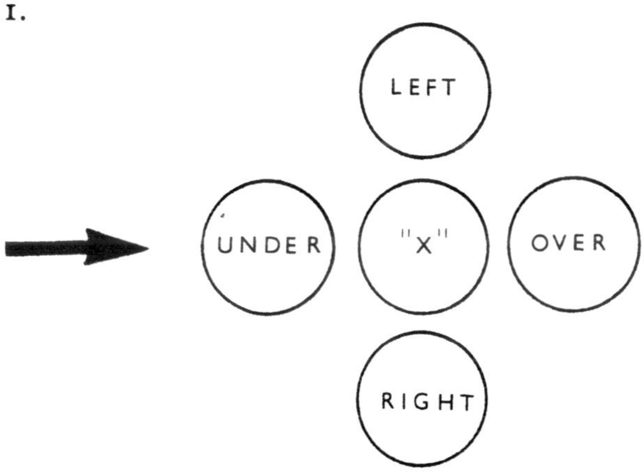

(1) The possible fall of shell from a howitzer.

X is the Point of Aim and a shell bursting there would constitute a direct hit, the circle showing the explosion area. The round could, however, either over- or under-shoot, or it could veer right or left to give the other explosion circles as shown. As suggested above, this is an extremely simplified version of just what could take place, and as we shall see, it will be the subject of still more simplification. In effect, it is a species of burst pattern indicator and we shall use it for estimating the fall of our shell and its subsequent effect.

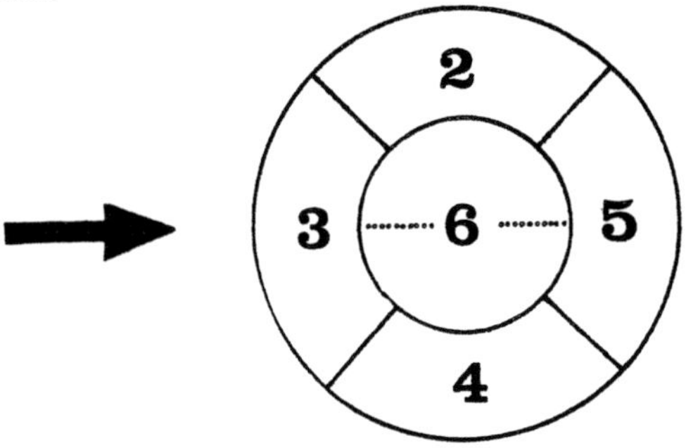

(2) The Shell Burst Indicator.

What we require is some device which will reproduce on the war game table the possible pattern of the fall of a shell, as well as allowing for the initial possibility of a misfire or the failure of the fuse itself. The device should be neither too difficult to construct nor too complicated to use. Ideally it should reproduce the pattern shown in diagram 1, but we shall make do with something a little simpler, this being the Shell Burst Indicator shown in diagram 2.

As I employ it, this device is constructed of thin brass wire, and consists of two concentric circles, joined by the four straight pieces as shown; a fifth may be positioned across the centre circle to show the line of fire but this is not really essential. The whole apparatus is soldered together (it is not of course necessary to include the section numbers), and if the process of soldering is not to the individual taste, the device could be made of acetate sheet or some similar transparent material. It has been found that, when placed in position, the wire shape fits over the troops or other target fired at and leaves no room for doubt as to what is in the lethal area. It is always advisable to avoid any possibility of debate, wargamers being notoriously a contumacious and argumentative lot!

The Shell Burst Indicator is employed along with an ordinary die in this way. When a war game howitzer is fired, the SBI is placed with its centre on the Point of Aim, section 5 being furthest from the gun, and the die is thrown, the figure coming up indicating the section in which the shell has exploded. The missing 1 represents the dud, the misfire, the unignited fuse, the shell which buries itself in soft ground and fails to explode or which has burst prematurely in the air etc. 6 is a direct hit on the intended target, 5 and 3 the over- and under-shoot, and 4 and 2 the right and left hand errors respectively. What it amounts to is that, although the shell may not have fallen exactly where it was intended to, it may nevertheless have exploded where it *did* cause casualties or damage. Insofar as casualties to infantry or cavalry are concerned the process is simple, one die being thrown for each and every man, whether mounted or on foot, in the explosion area, the dead being decided thus:

Dice throw of 1, 2 or 3 = no effect
Dice throw of 4, 5 or 6 = casualty, removed from the table

Similar schedules for the effect of shellfire on buildings and transport exist as they do for roundshot, but these can be detailed later when we deal with counterbattery fire and similar matters.

The actual size of the SBI is obviously of great importance. We take it that we are dealing with a gun of roughly 6″ calibre common to many armies, and a little research shows that the maximum area of the shell explosion was a circle of a little over 20 yards radius. This was the extreme distance of possible damage from the burst,

Cavalry under howitzer fire. The Shell Burst Indicator shows that with the shell coming from the top of the picture, throws of 6, 5 or 2 will give a burst area to include possible casualties.

although owing to the poor fragmentation capability the really lethal area must have been very much more limited. We could make our SBI with areas equivalent to the 20 yards radius mentioned and cut down the lethal rate thereof considerably, but it has been found more convenient in practice to reduce the size of the device and increase slightly the vulnerability of whatever is encompassed in the relevant section. Thus, in the SBI actually in use, the inner circle is of 2″ diameter only, representing 20 yards in our 1″ = 10 yards scale, and the outer of 4″ overall. Rough calculation will demonstrate that although the outer sections do not have the circular shape more like the area of a shell-burst, their area approximates closely to that of the centre circle. The end product, it is hoped, is sufficiently accurate, and the device is easier to construct and operate.

And now for the range of the howitzer. For a variety of reasons, of which its high trajectory is the chief, its range will be shorter than that of the field gun which, it will be recalled, has a maximum range of 60″ (or 600 yards). We therefore give the howitzer a war game range of 50″ (or in the real thing 500 yards). At the same time it will be realised that there is a limit to the elevation of which the piece is capable, and consequently one must specify a minimum range, this being 20″ (or 200 yards). It would be impractical to fire the shell at a lesser distance, bearing in mind the possible errors and also the size of the burst area.

If our howitzer is fired at extreme range, i e with the centre of the SBI on a point of aim 50″ from the gun, and a 5 is thrown, it will be seen that casualties or damage may be caused up to a couple of inches beyond the maximum of 50″, this being the distance from the centre of the device to the outside ring of the 5 section. Conversely, if the SBI is centred on a point 20″ from the howitzer, a score of 3 will bring the area of destruction 2″ nearer than the normal minimum. This is permissible.

Finally, to summarise the above:

Howitzer range	20″ to 50″
Firing procedure	SBI placed on Point of Aim, '5' section away from gun. A die is thrown to show area of shell burst (1 represents misfires, etc). Dice are thrown for effect : 1, 2 or 3 have no effect on horse or man; 4, 5 and 6 kill horse and foot.

X
Artillery: Canister

Having dealt with the rules governing the use of solid ball and explosive shell for long-range artillery work, the third and final type of shot must be considered. This was that used for close-range fire, when the object was not to hit one mark with precision but to shower a whole area with a lethal spray of bullets (as described by R. Glover in his *Peninsular Preparation*), thus simulating the effect of the modern machine gun and having deadly results against the closely-ranked troops of the eighteenth century. Of the two varieties used, grape and canister (the latter also being known as caseshot), we shall limit ourselves to considering canister. Grapeshot was in fact little used by British artillery and in land warfare generally it seems to have been much less popular than canister. It was an arrangement of nine iron balls, varying in weight between one and a quarter ounces and two to four pounds per ball, either bolted together in a sort of framework or strongly corded together in a thick canvas bag. This broke up on leaving the muzzle of the gun, scattering its components, and it was, I believe, more commonly employed at sea rather than on land.

As we are pursuing our policy of simplicity and so ignoring grapeshot, but are going to draw up rules for the use of canister, initially we must get an idea of the construction of a round of canister (or case-shot). To this end we can do no better than quote the following description by Charles James in his *New and Enlarged Military Dictionary* (published in 1810):

> Case shot (or canister) is so termed from the whole charge of the gun being contained in a tin case. The tin case is cylindric, a little less than the calibre of the gun or howitzer. It is filled with iron balls so as to make up the weight of the shot.

The contents were very often musket balls or they could be heavier, depending on the calibre of the gun in question. How true is the time-honoured notion that canister consisted of bits of old iron, nails and such like, I have no means of saying, although I feel that the idea is considerably exaggerated and that in field operations the regulation shot was invariably used but, as always, I am open to correction. Be that as it may, there were at least two varieties of canister for each gun, differently-sized balls being used for different ranges; but once more, to avoid over-complication we shall take one only, one of those applicable to the field gun we considered for the use of round-shot, the very generally used six-pounder. One variety is described in a splendid little work which went through several editions in the early years of the nineteenth century, the nobly entitled *Bombardier and Pocket Gunner* by Ralph Willet Adye, a member of a family distinguished in the annals of the Royal Artillery for nearly two centuries. He says that the six-pounder's canister charge consisted of 34 balls each weighing three ounces and therefore roughly equivalent to the weight of three musket balls. He also gives another type, 12 balls of 8 ounces each, but this seems to have been designed for longer ranges than that really considered appropriate for canister fire, so let us concentrate on the former projectile, the one containing 34 balls.

As with other types of shot the round of canister was attached to the propellant charge and having duly loaded it into our six-pounder we must consider what occurred when it was fired.

When this took place, the round of canister was driven along the barrel of the gun, in the case of the six-pounder five feet in length, and as soon as it emerged from the muzzle, the case broke up, there being an immediate spread of its remnants and of a proportion of its contents up to an angle of about 45 degrees. The bulk of the balls, however, would generally follow the line of fire with a much smaller degree of spread, presumably only those which had been in the proximity of the walls of the container going off at a tangent after being released from the pressure provided by the gun barrel. It should be noted that the charge used in firing canister was a comparatively small one because when it was '...too great, the shots spread out too much, by striking against each other, whereby many of them do no execution' (John Muller's *A Treatise on Artillery*). The combination of the low charge and the fact that the greater the change of direction the greater the loss of speed would cause the balls on the extreme edges of the initial spread to fall off rapidly and lose their lethal velocity. The pattern assumed by the spread of the shot can best be seen in diagram 1.

For long in wargaming the general assumption seems to have been that the firing of a round of canister produced a shot pattern similar to a kind of elongated cone, rather like the triangle *ADE* in diagram 1, despite the fact that, when infantry closed up to the gun, it was apparent by reason of the narrowness of the cone near the muzzle that only the minimum of casualties could be inflicted and that the devastation caused by

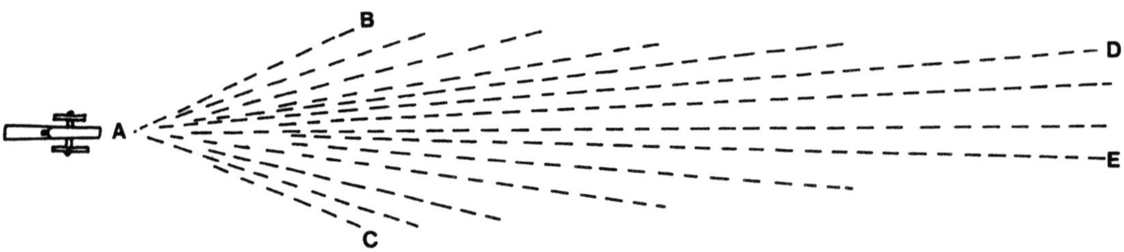

(1) The spread of shot from a round of canister...

canister at very close range could only be reproduced by having at least two guns in battery, with overlapping cones of fire. This applied particularly to wargamers who, like myself, preferred to have an actual device to indicate the pattern and casualties of canister fire in their games. This anomaly may of course be obviated by using dice and adopting various formulae for determining casualties at different ranges, but it becomes rather complicated when one has to assess losses in different formations of infantry, or cavalry for that matter, and I found it easier to use a device. Less calculations were required and one could see at a glance which troops were in jeopardy and to what degree they were vulnerable.

Let us return to diagram 1 and see how we can adapt it for our present purpose. It has been shown that, after the first 45 degree spread, the remainder of the contents of the tin case continued on with slight spread until the balls reached a point where dispersion and drop of velocity rendered them ineffective. The extreme practical range of canister seems to have been about 300 yards and experiments with six-pounders (reported by Adye in *The Bombardier and Pocket Gunner*) took place at this range using a target 6 feet in height by 30 yards long, the latter figure being taken to be the dispersion at 300 yards. Evidently, then, in diagram 1 we can take it that the distance *DE* is 30 yards, and *AD* (or *AE*) is 300 yards. Now, as we have seen already, the initial spread (angle *BAC*) is about 45 degrees and, with the rapid decrease in velocity consequent upon the change of direction, *AB* and *AC* (the distance the bits and pieces are going to travel at the extreme edges of the spread before falling speed and dispersion makes them negligible) are only going to be about a quarter of the distance travelled by those parts of the round moving in more or less a straight line (or so I am assured by a Professor of Physics at a London university). *AB* and *AC* are therefore going to be approximately 75 yards in length.

Thus, by studying the diagram we can get an idea of the lethal area covered by the discharge of a round of canister and thereby obtain some sort of approximation of the shape of the device we shall use in the war game. First of all, area *ABC* is going to be very lethal indeed, combining as it does the main stream of balls travelling up the centre and bits and pieces of the disintegrating canister, plus more balls flying about generally. Of course, right up to the extreme effective range of 300 yards the effect is going to be quite severe within the spread, which at 300 yards would be *DE*. In certain of the tests carried out by Adye with his six-pounder, using the 34-ball type canister against the 30 yards by 6 feet target, he ascertained that one round of canister averaged 10 hits (out of the 34 balls). It need hardly be pointed out that this was a solid target and that for a line of infantry occupying this given length we must, to allow for the intervals between the men, reduce the area by about a half. We therefore have to reduce the effect of the round by this amount, thus giving us 5 hits out of 34 balls, or an effectiveness of roughly one in seven. Bearing this in mind, our wargame calculation of casualties must be based on this as a minimum at extreme range, and we must now construct our canister device, using the scale of 1″ = 10 yards as before.

First of all we shall make an adjustment to the distance referred to as extreme range, to wit 300 yards. That the use of canister was impracticable at anything over this distance infers that something less was desirable. This is a reasonable proposition, I feel, so we are going to reduce the extreme range to a practical one of 240 yards, which translated to our table on our scale equals 24″. This then will be the overall length of our device and so, scaling the pattern shown in diagram 1 down to 1″= 10 yards, we obtain the device shown in diagram 2—the Canister Cone. It is patently not a true cone, but the name reflects the original shape and is used for the very simple reason that I cannot think of another. It will be seen that the distances shown in the diagram 1 pattern have all been reduced as was the 300 yards extreme range.

If this device be superimposed on the pattern shown in diagram 1, one should get an idea of how it duplicates the effect of a round of canister, more realistically simulating the actual wide spread which was missing from the traditional narrow cone. As to the graduation, it will be remembered that at maximum range chances of obtaining a hit on a man were about one in seven, but as we did in fact reduce this range it is reasonable to make the effect in the distant section, that is furthest from the gun, rather more. Besides, we have to use dice to determine casualties and a seven-sided variety is rather difficult to come by! Thus, in the distant portion of the device, a throw of 6 will kill any individual, on foot or mounted. The middle section will be more deadly, and the near one even more so, covering the very lethal area near the gun muzzle; anything therein will have but a fifty-fifty chance of survival. In this near section, then, throws of 4, 5 or 6 will kill, and in the mid section, 5 or 6 will be similarly effective. Thus the pattern is completed.

The use of the device is simple even if its construction is not. Again, as for the Shell Burst Indicator, use is made of thin brass wire, bent and soldered into the correct shape (it really is not too difficult a task), although it could be made from perspex or card. As to its use, it is simply placed in the position shown in the diagram, its centre line in the direction of aim, and dice are thrown for whatever is within its limits, casualties being assessed as in the previous paragraph. This refers to troops in the open and naturally allowance will have to be made for men under cover, behind walls etc.

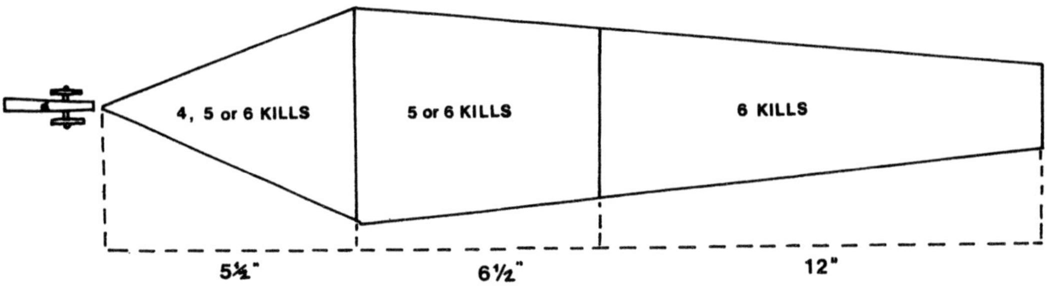

...and (2) the Canister Cone.

The Canister Cone in use, with the Pfalz-Sonderheim Infantry about to take considerable stick, many men being within the centre section where a dice throw of 5 or 6 is enough to cause casualties.

All the theory and practice of canister fire applies equally to the howitzer as to the field gun, the former also being capable of firing canister. Indeed, it is said that the howitzer was more efficient than the field gun, for although it had a shorter range, it also had a wider spread. However, to prevent the rules becoming too unwieldy, my suggestion is that the wargamer takes the same Canister Cone for both weapons; refinements such as a different device for a Cone to suit the howitzer, or indeed to suit heavier weapons, can be worked out by the individual.

XI
Morale

Despite the fact that Napoleon is reputed to be the author of the dictum that God is on the side of the big battalions, he also stated, I believe, that in war the moral is to the physical as three is to one. Without bothering to analyse too closely these apparently contradictory statements, we have to determine how large a part morale is to play in the war game we are organising. Indeed, the introduction of the question of morale is a comparatively recent innovation because for a long time a war game usually ended with the preposterous situation where one of the contending sides was totally annihilated, while the victor had perhaps half a dozen men left standing on the stricken field on their leaden or plastic feet. The use of the very unpredictable human factor is one of the symptoms of increasing sophistication in wargaming today. Among other things, it does go some way towards ensuring that the result of a table battle, in particular one between unequal forces, does bear some relationship to the fact that the tactical ability of one of the players may be greater than that of his opponent, rather than that it should depend upon which player has the most numerous army or the most powerful artillery. What it boils down to is that a player must consider quite carefully the quality of his troops and whether for instance, they have suffered too severely already for them to be able to carry out some new assignment. This is instead of making a strictly mathematical calculation that with, say, forty men, he will inevitably defeat thirty five, because it can happen, and the history of war shows that it frequently did, that a small unit can defeat or even rout a larger. In modern times, and on a grander scale, how else can one account for the result of Wavell's first Desert Campaign and its destruction of an enormous force by a very much smaller one?

It can indeed be explained by one word, morale, and although an entire volume has in the last two or three years been devoted to the subject (*Morale* by John Baynes), it will be enough if we accept a dictionary definition and describe it as 'a state of mind with reference to confidence, courage, zeal and the like, especially for a number of persons associated in some enterprise, as troops'. More succinctly, it has been referred to (Americanese, this) as 'intestinal fortitude', just plain 'guts', or in the old army term, 'umpty poo'.

At various times throughout history, morale of fighting troops has been affected by a multitude of different considerations. Patriotism and religion, for instance, together with the soldierly qualities of training and discipline, have at different times and in different nations powerfully influenced the quality of armies and have caused them to be effective above and beyond what might normally have been expected of them. Wargamers, then, if they wish to make allowance for this in their rules, must have due regard for the period in which they are working and for the nation whose armies they favour. It goes without saying, for example, that the British troops led by Wellington in the Peninsula were infinitely more to be reckoned with than were the forces of their allies; their morale was undoubtedly higher. Sustained by faith in their leader and by religious fervour, Cromwell's Ironsides provided a most formidable fighting force, and we have the case of the Confederates, who at the beginning of the American Civil War were inspired by a most vigorous nationalism. But all things being equal, the well-trained and disciplined soldier, confident in his officers, would generally be far more likely to put up a good show than one who was but a raw recruit, badly led, with no great interest in the cause for which he was fighting. Even within this framework, however, the unlikely and even the near-impossible did happen: a battle-hardened regiment of veterans would suddenly and inexplicably break and run, or conversely a hastily flung together scratch unit would withstand pressure under which it or similar troops would normally be expected to give way. Such events often defy explanation, but war is full of imponderables and of these the human element is the one which makes it an art rather than an exact science and this is something we simply cannot dissociate from our calculations.

Wargamers who sincerely wish to make the correct allowance for morale in their battles or campaigns must consider well the period they are attempting to reproduce because morale varied, as I have suggested, in different times and in different armies. Usually though, if we take the case of a single unit, its state of mind in action will be governed by three things: its discipline, its strength, and its morale, the unpredictable factor. Without a doubt the keen wargamer may well wish to include many other lesser contributory influences, hunger, fatigue, leadership quality, the type of unit involved, whether it be an élite one or otherwise and possibly others, but it will be entirely adequate for our purpose, dealing as we are with the more or less uncomplicated era of the middle eighteenth century, simply to concentrate on the three factors as above. Indeed, they can be used as a basis on which to build a much more elaborate structure to cater for many more aspects of the morale question, but in practice, it has been found that the use of the three are more than effective.

In our period we have neither the complication of 'the nation in arms' nor of 'la patrie en danger'; neither do we have any 'odium theologicum' playing a part, but only the relatively straightforward conditions of professional armies, not infrequently mercenaries of some sort or another, marching and fighting in what might be described as a purely military context. Politicians were customarily many miles away and the people of the country where the fighting was taking place generally apathetic, holding themselves aloof from the brawling in their midst, or at least taking no part in either interest as partisans or guerrillas. So the morale of our troops is going to be found within a rather simple framework, although even so, we shall have to accord its proper due to the element of chance.

Let us, then, set about deciding upon a workable system based on the three elements already specified, one which will not require the services of a computer to operate. These three (in brief, control, losses suffered, and the unpredictable) can readily be assessed for our professional troops and on these variables we base our formula, this being how we obtain it.

Control: This basically is the same thing as discipline, and it will be effective in direct proportion to the number of officers and NCO's of the unit in question actually present with it. Let us start with some kind of an optimum and here I have no alternative but to give as an example my own procedure, which has been found to be both simple and realistic. Briefly, if no fraction of the Control element has been lost, by which we mean that no officer nor NCO has fallen, we say that the figure for this section of the formula is 6. Let me take one of my own infantry regiments to illustrate this point—it has an establishment of 5 officers (of which one is the Colonel) and 48 men. In this set up the 6 is arrived at quite easily—the Colonel counts 2, the four other officers 1 each. I am aware of the anomaly of not using NCO's, but I have none in my regimental system, which took shape over a lengthy period. It just grew in this way—I offer no excuses, feeling that the addition of NCO's would complicate my sums needlessly. So with all the officers present and control at its maximum, the final index, the figure on which the unit's morale is based (shall we call it the Morale Index?) starts at 6 and is diminished proportionately to the loss of officers; eg should the Colonel become a casualty, the Index totals only 4, no longer 6.

Losses in action: Clearly, the more punishment a unit takes in battle and the greater the resulting casualties, the less will be its will to fight. Accounts of troops who fought to the last man are usually pretty exaggerated and an engagement such as Bunker Hill, where the strength of the attacking British infantry was reduced by half, is a very rare thing. Starting then with the premise that casualties have the effect of lowering morale, we say that if one sixth of the rank and file strength is lost, a deduction of one point must be made to the Morale Index, and if the loss reaches a quarter, then the deduction will be two. If the muskets (or sabres) are actually cut down to half the original strength—but this is another story, details of which will be given later. Take once more, if you will, the example of my own infantry regiment of 48 other ranks. If enemy action has reduced the strength by a sixth, ie by killing 8 and leaving 40, then a point is subtracted from the Morale Index. This holds good up to the stage where losses amount to a quarter, that is 12 men, when 2 must be deducted; as will be seen, this is effective up to a loss of 24 out of the 48 men, when the regiment must be considered out of action for the time being.

Finally we consider the *Imponderable.* This is done by a simple resort to chance, by using dice. The player who has to determine the morale of a unit rolls a die, and the result is the uncertainty factor.

The final Morale Index, or the assessment of a certain regiment's morale, is obtained by making a sum of the three factors and is applied after each move during which a unit has sustained casualties. This is done by adding the officers' points and the result of the dice throw and deducting, if applicable, the losses of the other ranks. The total (this being the actual Morale Index) must be 6 or more. Should it be less, the morale of the regiment is bad and it passes out of the control of the commander, for a time certainly. Let me illustrate by example. The Regiment of Pfalz-Sonderheim Infantry—or it may be the Grenadiers de Penthièvre—has moved into enemy musket range in a battle and has sustained certain casualties. Before it can carry on during the next move it must be seen to be of good morale, so the Index must be ascertained, in this way:

1	It has lost 2 officers—1 point each, leaving the Colonel and 2 others.	+4
2	Other rank casualties number 9, that is, one sixth.	−1
3	The dice throw was 4.	+4
		Total +7

As the regiment has the required Morale Index of 6 or more it carries on.

Another example, not so good.

1	Colonel and 2 officers fell, leaving only two officers.	+2
2	OR casualties = 13 men, that is, a quarter.	−2
3	The dice throw was 4.	+4
		Total +4

The morale is bad! The regiment must fall back or must behave as follows:

1 If it is actually at grips, or in a mêlée with enemy, instead of continuing the hand to hand combat, it breaks off the struggle and makes a complete move to the rear (the move being the ordinary move of the arm to which it belongs).
2 If it is advancing, or stationary and firing, it remains halted on the following move and cannot fire.

Once a unit has incurred a bad Morale Index, its morale must be tested on each successive move until it rallies or flees the field, but on each of the ensuing four moves the morale requirement is raised by 1. In other words, on the move after the one during which it was first assessed as bad, the Index to be obtained must be 7, on the second it must be 8 and so on. If these indices are not reached, the regiment continues to retreat move by move, or in (2) above, it begins to move back after the first 'halt' move. If 10 is not attained as a Morale Index on the fourth move, the unit is considered to be completely dispersed and is out of action. If the requirement is, in fact, made during the four moves, all is well and the retreating regiment turns about to meet the foe again. The reason for the increase is plain. It is a fact that unless checked panic increases rapidly: history has many confirmatory examples.

In addition to obtaining the higher Morale Index in order to check the flight of a broken regiment, there is another method by which it may be rallied, but of this more later. As to wargamers whose regimental organisation may differ from that used to illustrate the system, the problem is not insuperable. So long as the officer total can be adjusted to a maximum of six the plan can work; the second factor depends entirely upon proportions (one sixth and one quarter), so actual regimental establishment is irrelevant.

In the second example given above, the bad morale one, it can be seen that with the officer and other rank losses suffered the regiment requires nothing less than a throw of 6 to get the Morale Index required, which seems about right. After having taken such punishment, the chances would certainly be against the unit's having much desire to continue fighting.

All this may seem complex, but it isn't really and certainly in practice the process of determining a unit's morale is limited to a quick glance to see how many officers are present and how many men have fallen. There follows a quick dice throw, a simple sum and there it is: the regiment stands or falls back as the case may be.

Finally, there comes the time when no prompting, inspiration or discipline can make the regiment take further active part in what is going on. Examples can be found, it is very true, of how throughout history bodies of troops have fought literally to the last man. They are few and hard to discover, though, and one does not often come across such events as the fight of the detachment of the French Foreign Legion at Camerone, in Mexico, in 1863. This was a tremendous thing and greatly removed from what we might describe as a military norm of survival. In our war game we have to establish rules which provide for a mean and in this case it is done by the 'Fifty-per-cent Rule', which lays it down that when a regiment is reduced to 50% or less of its muskets (or sabres) it must at once break off the action and proceed to the rear. There, if deemed appropriate, it may be reorganised with other reduced regiments of the same type. The new provisional regiment takes six moves to 'get fell in' and organised. Naturally, the chain of command takes some time to sort out, but the reorganised unit can re-enter the fight when it numbers at least three-quarters of the normal establishment of its particular arm: in the case of a 48 man infantry unit, it would have to have 36 or more. This process cannot be repeated indefinitely, and when a provisional regiment is reduced in its turn to half the strength with which it started, it has to retire and can take no further part in the battle. We do make the concession that if the reduction to 50% takes place on the first move of a mêlée, then the regiment is allowed to complete the mêlée moves before retiring.

Finally, there is one special circumstance which can affect the Morale Index. Imagine, if you will, what happens when heavy cavalry charges a body of infantry; let us take the precise example of a regiment of heavy cavalry charging home against a regiment of line infantry. Having passed through the musket fire of the foot soldiers, some of the horsemen will crash through their ranks, riding down one or more of the infantrymen while doing so, while others will baulk at the bayonets and will simply cut and thrust with the front rank men. The deeper the infantry formation, the more difficult it will be for a breakthrough to take place and chance will play a large part in the matter. Thus it is a rule that when the cavalrymen are moved up in the 18″ charge move to engage foot soldiery, they may under certain conditions break right through, but only if the infantry be less than four ranks deep, otherwise they simply contact the front rank under normal mêlée rules. If less than four deep, this is what happens. One die is thrown for every cavalryman moved up to contact, and if the infantry is in three ranks a 5 or a 6 means that a breakthrough has been made by the trooper concerned. The front rank infantryman is considered to be ridden down and is removed as a casualty, while the second and third rank men are flung aside. They are moved back and aside 3″ to allow the horseman to pass through to the full limit of his charge move and to contact another infantryman if he can. It might be one of those moved back, when ordinary mêlée rules apply. If the infantry is only 2 ranks deep, a 4, 5 or 6 will allow the breakthrough, and the second rank man is moved aside, the front one again being ridden down. It is permissible for cavalry breaking through to veer up to 30 degrees in either direction right or left to make a second contact. *Note :* this applies only to heavy cavalry; light cavalry has no 'breakthrough' capability.

All this leads up to the morale question. Quite certainly, the more breakthroughs which have taken place, the more will the infantry be burst asunder and the greater will be the detrimental impact on its morale. This gives rise to the following rule:

> For every two breakthroughs (remainders ignored) which occur, one point is deducted from the Morale Index that must be ascertained for the infantry before the following move.

An example:

1 Control	Colonel and 2 officers survive.	+4
2 Losses	15 casualties, ie over one quarter	−2
3 Dice throw		+4
		+6
BUT 6 breakthroughs took place		−3

The final Morale Index is therefore +3 and as might have been expected, having regard to what has taken place, the morale of the infantry is very bad, and it will retire on the next move (doubtless hotly pursued!)

When the situation is desperate and extreme measures have to be taken to halt a fleeing regiment and the player deems it wise and advantageous to do so, it can be done in this way. It can be rallied by the presence of a general who is moved on the table to head off the fleeing unit. Once he and it have met, it is considered that his presence will bring it to a halt, this being followed by a dice throw which decides how long it is before the regiment may take positive action again. A throw of 3 means then that on the fourth move, the regiment can get on with the fighting, but there is a rub. The General must remain with the regiment for the remainder of the battle, during which his services are naturally not available to carry out any further rallying.

On the question of generals, my own practice is to have one general per brigade of two regiments, horse or foot. Each is entitled to one aide-de-camp who can be used for courier purposes if such rules are in force. In addition, the army commander is represented by a general figure and he, because of his lofty status, may have two aides-de-camp.

XII
Action!

At this stage of our war game saga it would not be amiss to stage a practical demonstration of how the rules as they have already been established govern an actual war game, and it seems that a blow-by-blow account of a game which took place on the writer's table (for the occasion seven feet by five feet in area) may provide the necessary example. The terrain employed was of the simplest and the forces very limited in number, the whole operation being designed to fall within the framework of the basic rules and to demonstrate that even with such modest beginnings, an exciting and realistic war game could take place. The hope that no situation would arise outside the scope of the rules as they had been considered was almost completely fulfilled, the sole exception concerning the movement of artillery which was not covered in the chapters relating to the arm.

First of all let me name the players, who varied rather considerably in seniority as well as in war game and actual military experience, and who were in fact Lieutenant-Colonel J. B. R. Nicholson, late 18th King Edward VII's Own Cavalry (and editor of *Tradition*, journal of the International Society of Military Collectors), and Senior Cadet Corporal C. S. Grant, RMA Sandhurst. It was hoped that the latter's experience of the war game, conspicuously greater than that of his adversary, would be countered by the former's wide and lengthy experience of tactics and other matters pertaining to the military art, together with such advice on table technique as I, as overseer and umpire, was able in all humility to afford.

Players move their troops simultaneously, each unit the correct distance for the arm and the formation, or less if desired, infantry in column $7\frac{1}{2}''$, in line 6″, and so on. With all the troops in the desired position at the conclusion of the move, casualties are assessed from whatever action may have taken place: from artillery fire, then from that of light infantry, followed by musketry, and finally from any mêlée. This is purely an arbitrary order designed for ease of operation.

The artillery move must also be referred to here. We are employing foot artillery, with dismounted gunners, so the guns will get about at the standard infantry pace, a 6″ move in effect. It takes one move to limber up or to unlimber a gun, field piece or howitzer, and the minimum crew is two, of which one has to be an officer.

The contending armies were almost identical, consisting as they did of two regiments of line infantry, a battalion of light infantry (or jäger), a regiment of heavy cavalry and one piece of artillery (a howitzer for one army and a field gun for the other). The general plan was that each force purported to be the advance guard of a much larger army and, having come into contact during the previous day, had deployed and made ready for battle the following dawn when the war game was due to begin. The period, naturally, is that of the Seven Years War, the armies involved those of that time-honoured pair, France and the Allies, and in detail they were as follows:

France	Dillon Infantry Royal Ecossais Infantry
	Arquebussiers de Grassin (light infantry)
	Allemand Cavalry
	One howitzer and crew
Allies	Ostergotland Infantry Oldenburg Infantry
	Jägerkorps zu Fuss
	Wolfenbüttel Kürassiere
	One field gun and crew

As the infantry regiments each consisted of 5 officers and 48 other ranks, the light infantry battalions of 3 and 24, the cavalry of 4 and 24 and the gun crews of an officer and 4 men, each force therefore numbered 166 officers and men. Obviously a commander and his aide were required and these stout fellows took their places on the war game table: 'General Lord Clare' led the French, while Colonel Nicholson sank his identity in that of 'General Baron von und zu Trinksblut und Eisenessen', and they will be referred to as such if necessary. (With two of her regiments in the field, Her Serene Highness the Markgräfin von Wolfenbüttel-Oldenburg, known to her loyal subjects as 'Tutzi', deemed it necessary to be present, and in fact was in close attendance upon Trinksblut throughout the action.)

And so, with the stage set and the troops in position, it behoves us to survey the scene and this we can do by examining map 1, which shows the dispositions of the contending powers at first light on the fateful day. It needs only to be noted that the French howitzer was in battery position ready to fire, while the Allied field gun was still limbered up, prepared to move off if so desired. Immediate orders for the two commanders were the same: advance, gain control of the crossroads, drive off the enemy and await the arrival of the main army.

We are able to supply the plans made by the generals. They were as follows:

French: Demonstrate on the right with light infantry, and attack the other flank as strongly as possible, the initial aim being to overrun the enemy field gun, while shelling targets of opportunity with the howitzer.

Allies: Hold the left flank by occupying enclosure *B* with infantry; advance on the right, with jäger infiltrating the wood on the north side near the ponds and so threatening the enemy's left flank and rear.

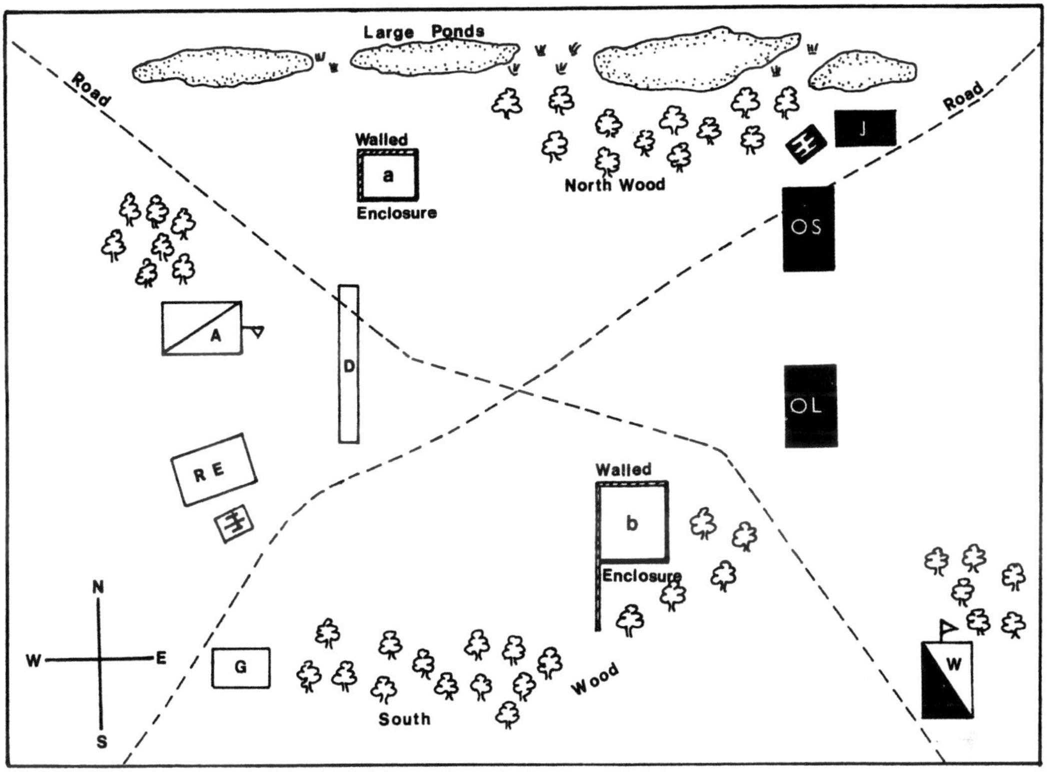

Map 1: the situation at dawn

French		*Allies*	
Allemand	A	Wolfenbüttel	W
Royal Ecossais	RE	Ostergotland	OS
Dillon	D	Oldenburg	OL
Grassins	G	Jäger	J
Artillery	(open symbol)	Artillery	(solid symbol)

So, into battle!

Move I: As planned, French light infantry moved into the South Wood (their move being $7\frac{1}{2}''$ of course), while the rest of the army made a general advance. On the Allied side, Oldenburg Infantry, in two sections, made for enclosure *B*, while Ostergotland Infantry advanced, deploying into a two-deep firing line. On the extreme right the field gun moved up and the Jägerkorps entered the North Wood. At the end of move I only the French howitzer fired, claiming one casualty, an officer of Ostergotland Infantry.

Move II: Lord Clare decided to take advantage of the enemy gun's not being in action and moved forward half the Allemand Cavalry (9″ standard heavy cavalry move), leaving the other half to support his infantry. The Grassins continued their advance through South Wood. Trinksblut, for his part, ordered his gun to unlimber, pivoted Ostergotland to form line with it and pressed part of Oldenburg into enclosure *B*, at the same time starting half his cavalry regiment towards the centre. Dillon, in two-deep firing line, and Ostergotland engaged in the first firefight of the battle, but in spite of both regiment's having the advantage of 'first volleys', little damage was done, each unit losing four men. Oldenburg lost one man to a popping fire from the Grassins, some of whom had emerged from South Wood.

Move III: Coming into extreme canister range of the Allied field gun, which had unlimbered in move II, the first squadron of Allemand lost four men. The Ostergotland/Dillon musketry duel continued, and again there was pretty poor shooting (which caused Trinksblut to give vent to certain salty expressions). Part of Oldenburg was now established in enclosure *B*, the remainder moving round the edge of the surrounding wood. Half of Wolfenbüttel had moved towards the centre, the remainder standing fast in the original position. The Grassins now began to feel the effect of Oldenburg musketry at close range, during this move losing three men.

Move IV: The most dramatic occurrence during this move was the charge by the Allemand squadron on the Allied field gun, and despite losing three men in the charge (to a round of canister) the troopers pressed on to contact the gunners on hand to hand terms. In the mêlée three gunners were cut down, leaving the crew with only one officer and one other rank, the bare necessity for forming an effective gun crew. In the continuing firefight in the centre, Oldenburg lost eight casualties, partly to Dillon musketry but also in part to sniping from the Grassins. The second Allemand squadron took its place in the middle of the French line at this time, facing the Wolfenbüttel Kürassiere, the second squadron of which had followed the first. The Grassins lost four men this move, at the end of which the situation was as shown in map 2.

Move V: The desperate situation of the Allied guncrew, or what was left of it,

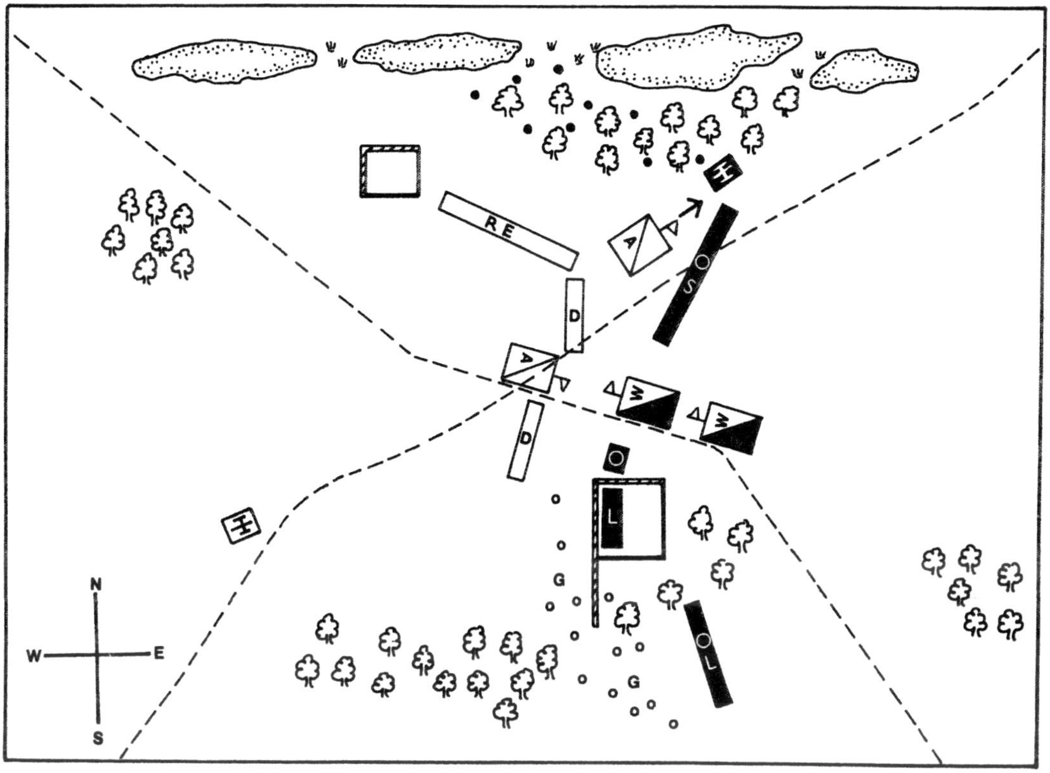

Map 2: the situation at the end of move 4.

was somewhat restored by the advent of some jäger who emerged from North Wood and engaged the cavalrymen (two infantrymen to one cavalryman gives an equal dice throw, with no 'doubling' as in the case of one mounted man versus one man on foot). In this second move of mêlée the Allemand Colonel and another officer fell, and with the subsequent bad Morale Index, the remnant of the party had to flee, the flight taking place on move VI of course. The Royal Ecossais now formed a firing line facing the wood, but the jäger pressed round their left flank and in the move's firing inflicted losses of four men on the regiment. In the centre a mutual charge took place between the second Allemand squadron and the Wolfenbüttel one, with losses to both. On the Allied extreme left, part of Oldenburg closed with some of the Grassins. (Clare should not have allowed this to happen, as a light infantryman is no better in mêlée than his line counterpart, and the more numerous Oldenburgers were able to dispose of several of their adversaries.) All this time, the French howitzer had kept banging away at the Allies, causing steady if not shattering damage.

Move VI: The Allied jäger were now in enclosure *A*, whence they brought heavy fire to bear on the Royal Ecossais. The survivors of the gun crew, with their Allemand attackers in flight, were endeavouring to bring their piece once more into action (an undertaking which, after the gunners have been in mêlée, requires a complete move) and the firefight—Ostergotland against Dillon—continued, with the latter sustained by the right flank of the Royal Ecossais. The second Wolfenbüttel squadron joined in the cavalry clash in the centre, some of the troopers passing through the mêlée and colliding with a section of the Dillon line, which was unable to fire because of the proximity of their own cavalry. Dillon suffered horribly during this move, no less than ten men having to be removed. From its mêlée with the Grassins, and also from fire from those not so engaged, Oldenburg suffered almost as badly, eight men biting the dust. This was a grievous blow, for despite their previous good morale, thrown for when the regiment had had 17 casualties (at the end of move V), now that their strength was down to less than 50% the unit had to withdraw from the action. In spite of losing three men, the Grassins continued to work round enclosure *B*.

Move VII: With less than 50% effective, Oldenburg fell back, the obvious rallying point being within enclosure *B*. The cavalry fight terminated in favour of Wolfenbüttel, who were left with two prisoners. Jäger fire and musketry from part of Ostergotland were concentrated on Royal Ecossais, which lost an officer and ten men. Dillon again fared badly, mainly from that part of Ostergotland not engaged with Royal Ecossais, and losses of ten brought the strength to below 50%, with the inevitable consequences. Royal Ecossais, however, scored a notable success, bringing down the solitary Allied gunner and thus putting the piece out of action; the surviving officer could not work it alone. The situation at the end of the move is seen in map 3.

Move VIII: Ignoring their losses, the Grassins were now pressing right round enclosure *B*, threatening to take Ostergotland in the rear. (The sole exception to the 50% Rule is light infantry battalions, which may be reduced to one third of establishment before having to be withdrawn, it being considered that their normal wide dispersion renders the effect of heavy loss less immediately perceptible as in the case of closely ranked regiments.) To meet this threat, part of Ostergotland was faced about (this being possible because Dillon was now falling back), while the remainder plus the jäger continued to engage Royal Ecossais, whose overall losses of an officer and 21 men had necessitated a morale throw which, as it happened, was a favourable one. Even so, suffering

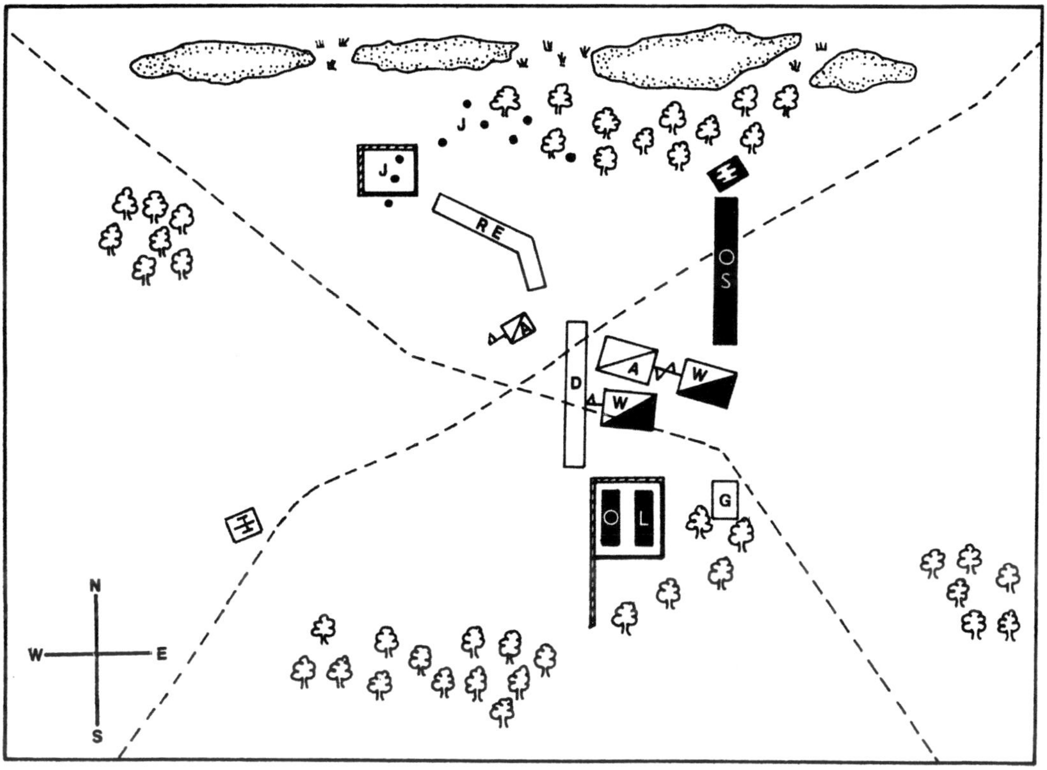

Map 3: the situation at the end of move 7.

further casualties on this move, this regiment also found itself at less than half strength. On the centre Wolfenbüttel Kürassiere were regrouping, preparatory to renewing their advance.

Move IX: The end was now in sight. The Grassins lost three men to Ostergotland musketry; they were now down to a third and their next move would have to be one of retreat. Covered by fire from the howitzer, Dillon and Royal Ecossais were in retreat, following the remnant of Allemand Cavalry.

Move X: The final situation, at the end of this move, can be seen overleaf in map 4. The French are falling back and, after a last round which killed three men from Ostergotland, the howitzer is ready to limber up and move off. On the other side, Ostergotland Infantry and Wolfenbüttel are both fit for action, as is the Jägerkorps zu Fuss, and are getting ready for a leisurely follow-up.

'Twas a famous victory and congratulations were due to Baron von und zu Trinksblut und Eisenessen for his successful tactics.

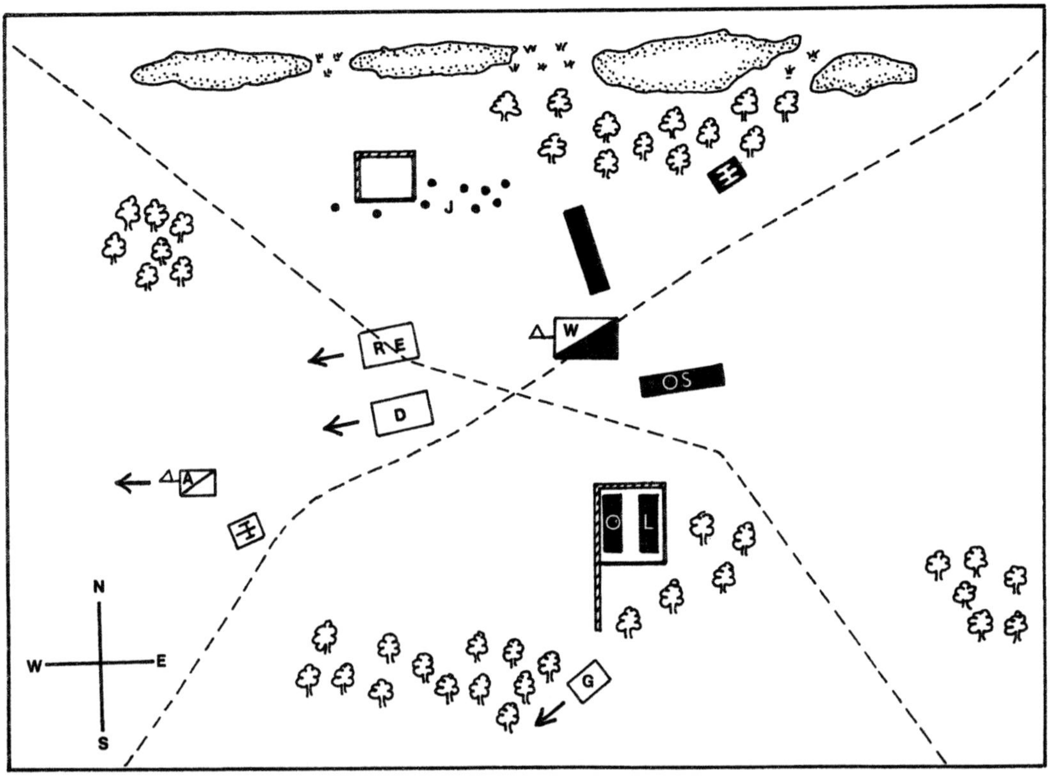

Map 4: the situation at the end of move 10.

Although this was but a small action (ten minutes if one takes the time-move scale, the actual playing time being inevitably longer, in fact some two and a half hours), I venture to suggest that it did reflect accurately the Seven Years War type of tactics. In both cases there was the tendency to use the celebrated oblique approach, and the infantry line was always used in preference to the column, thus demonstrating quite clearly the effectiveness of the former as opposed to the latter.

XIII
Something about Troops

There was a certain amount of rather glib talk in the previous chapter concerning the appearance on the war game table of battalions, regiments, squadrons and so forth, and it seems opportune now to have a discussion about what we mean by these impressive military agglomerations and how many miniature figures will be required to represent, for example, a battalion of infantry. It has been my intention throughout these pages to adhere as firmly as possible to a constant scale of distance, and indeed of time as well, and in determining what will constitute the strength of a unit it is hoped that this scale can be maintained.

Many wargamers choose (and it is entirely their affair) to employ a kind of numerical basis for their organisation representing for instance 20 actual soldiers by one small figure, without much reference to the type and size of miniature involved. A battalion of 600 men would then be represented by 30 figures. To some extent this means that the battlefield, or the ground scale, is governed by the size of the figures; the bigger the miniature, the greater the area occupied by the figures constituting in the player's organisation one battalion. It is better, I believe, to work from the opposite direction, and to say that on the wargame table a certain area would be occupied by such and such a unit (taking an average number for its establishment), and by occupying that area with one's model soldiers to the proper number, lay it down therefore that this number represents in our scale the particular unit involved.

Let me show what I mean. First of all we shall work out what the strength of an average infantry battalion would be and to this end we shall consult the *New Regulations for the Prussian Infantry*, translated from the German and published in London in 1757. This most instructive work states that when a battalion is formed in close order for firing, the 'usual ground' it takes up is 160 paces in length. If we take 28″ as being a pace, the battalion frontage (all muskets being able to be brought to bear) is 125 yards. Not overlooking the fact that this refers to musket-bearing soldiers, if we reduce this in accordance with our table scale (10 yards = 1″) we can see that we have a length of 12½″, and that if we draw up as many of our miniature infantrymen as, standing shoulder to shoulder, will occupy 12½″, then we have the front of a battalion, or certainly the rank and file portion thereof.

It is interesting to see just what numbers are represented by this scale. The establishment of a Prussian battalion (one of Old Fritz's, of course) was 570 private men (ie not including NCO's), so that on the basis of the battalion's being drawn up in the regulation three-deep formation, we have ranks each of 190 men. With every private man in theory being allowed 21″, we can calculate that we have a line of about 110 yards. Adding the smallish intervals between the eight platoons in which the battalion was drawn up (and possibly allowing for a slight increase per man: after all 21″ does not give a fully equipped infantryman much room) we see that we have come pretty close to the 125 yards for which 12½″ was the table equivalent.

We have now made an appreciable step towards organising our army and, when any infantry regiment in the service of my Vereinigte Freie Städte is drawn up in close order for firing, it does in fact occupy a frontage of exactly 12½″. This, of course, is in two ranks of 24 men each; we do not allow firing from a depth of more than two ranks. This gives rise, alas, to an anomaly, the first to whose presence I must admit. In the war game, however, as in grand opera, there are certain conventions which have to be accepted; the perfectly realistic game is an unattainable dream. Historically, the battalion was drawn up in three ranks, but by reason of the fact that model soldiers require bases on which to stand, if they were drawn up in three ranks the depth represented would be something like 2″, or in actual fact about 20 yards. This is palpably much out of scale, so the wargamer must swallow the fact that his infantry must be lined up not in three, but in two ranks when in the 'close order' and all firing position. It is a compromise which has to be accepted. Indeed, even this (about an inch) is considerably more than the three yards or so which would be correct for three ranks. True, with the ordinary sort of bases, the normal 20mm or 30mm figure would be more correct in a single line, in terms of actual depth, but it simply would not look right, would it? This is the sort of pictorial, maybe even aesthetic consideration which players find important when the question is one of using colourfully painted miniatures rather then horrid little blocks of wood shaped to an exact size. Therefore, if we accept all the above, we shall have on a 12½″ front a two-deep line of infantrymen corresponding to the three-deep line of the actual battalion of some 600 men on a front of 125 yards. With both our ranks firing, our unit will produce the equivalent fire power to its parent unit firing on three ranks. This is the best that can be done to achieve verisimilitude without resorting to blocks of wood, and lengthy experience shows that it works with great success.

So far we have really been referring only to the 'muskets' of the infantry unit, and to them must be apportioned the proper number of officers and, if the player desires, of NCO's. I have already indicated that the officer component of my infantry regiment is the Colonel and four other officers, and that I have no NCO's. It might be interesting to investigate what the actual numbers were in various armies at the time with which we are concerned. Again we consult the *New Regulations for the Prussian Infantry* and in it we learn that in the two-battalion infantry regiment there were 50 officers and 220 NCO's to 1460 rank and file. I give round figures only. This is the full establishment for the regiment, of course, and it would almost always be less on active service. Doing a little calculation we can reduce these figures to a ratio of 2:7:48, that is 2 officers and 7 NCO's for 48 muskets. This is quite different from my establishment, but then three officers extra certainly makes up for the seven sergeants or whatever they might be. It is only right to point out that all or almost all the NCO's were musket-bearing and would be included in the battalion front already mentioned. The addition of a further seven men to our scale infantry unit would increase it disproportionately, I think. Finally, should we include them, their number would create some complications in assessing their value for the Morale Index which, as we know, requires a total of 6. Still, we might make another check, this time nearer home. A return of the officers and men in each battalion of the Duke of Cumberland's army at Culloden (*History of the Rebellion in 1745 and 1746*, Aberdeen 1755) gives a slightly different breakdown, which averages out on our scale as 3:3:48, the first two being officers and sergeants respectively. The latter are named particularly, no mention being made of corporals, possibly as they were included in the other ranks category.

So there you have it, three alternatives at least are available, and more would doubtless emerge with further research. First, there is the writer's system of 5 officers and 48 men, then organisations based on the Prussian and British proportions of 2:7:48 and 3:3:48 respectively. The wargamer must make his own choice and indeed he may not want as many as 48 men in his foot regiments. As far as I know, no wargamer has more than 48 and many have less, 20 or 30 being pretty common. I do admit to having one three-battalion elite unit with 4 officers and 24 men to each battalion, this being the Grenadiergarde der Sammlung of Their High Mightinesses the Vereinigte Freie Städte. I would submit, however, that the stronger the regiment the more nearly is realism approached; this is really fairly obvious. Take one case only. The least fraction of its strength that a 20-man unit can lose in one move of action is one-twentieth, or 30 men if we are thinking of a 600-strong battalion, while with 48 men, one forty-eighth is the least, or just over 12 men. It is not going to be easy with a small battalion to simulate the slow and cumulative losses of a prolonged firefight, for instance.

A point about the officers, by the way: one of them will doubtless be the ensign, bearing aloft the regimental colours, and one will be the commanding officer, who will probably be the only mounted officer in the regiment (or battalion), although with the British 3:3:48 system a second officer, possibly the adjutant, might be horsed.

All the above, of course, refers to a system wherein the infantry unit of which we speak (I call it a regiment, although in terms of frontage, it is only a battalion) is the tactical unit. Some players do prefer subdivisions, ie the breaking up of their battalions into companies for independent action. There is nothing wrong with this, in fact it is good practice, but it must be pointed out that there are difficulties with morale if this takes place and obviously adjustments will have to be made when a portion of a regiment is acting in isolation from the remainder. This did not apply in the previously reported engagement when, if any subdivision took place, the components were close enough for an overall morale picture to be made. If one's unit is broken up into companies, say, and one with maybe 2 officers and 24 men, or 1 officer and 2 NCO's and 12 men, was operating at some considerable distance from the rest, the Morale Index could not be based on the system we have gone into, with 5 officers totalling 6 points. Some ad hoc scheme could be arrived at, but it is better to maintain one's units intact and to avoid any sort of fragmentation. This is a personal view—I have a dreadfully tidy mind.

Reiterating the point that what we call an infantry regiment is actually a battalion in terms of frontage we shall carry on to have a look at the mounted arm, the aim being to work out briefly what our cavalry regiment as employed in the recent encounter would represent on the actual battlefield.

A little research makes it quickly apparent that there was not a tremendous amount of uniformity in the cavalry establishments of the various powers taking part in the numerous wars of the mid-eighteenth century and that the strength of the squadron, the basic tactical unit, varied considerably. Shortly after the Battle of Dettingen (1743), Lord Ligonier recommended that in the British Army the cavalry squadron should be increased in number from 120 to 160 troopers, in conformity with Continental practice. It should be noted that in our epoch, brigades, let alone divisions, hardly existed, armies being reckoned as consisting of so many battalions and squadrons without reference to any higher formations. This number of 160 troopers certainly applied to the French Army, and in 1755 Dauphin-Cavalerie consisted of two squadrons each of 160 men, although this included officers (D'Ollone: *Historique du 10me Regiment de Dragons,* 1893). Later in 1776, French squadron strength was established at 7 officers, 12 NCO's and 152 troopers. In contrast, however, round about 1766 the Russian cavalry frequently had only 60 to 80 troopers per squadron (Dennison: *History of Cavalry,* 1913) although this was probably during a campaign when allowance would have to be made for sickness, casualties etc. Turning to Prussia, we find that Frederick's cuirassier regiments had squadrons consisting of 8 officers, 14 sergeants and corporals plus 150 men. All this would suggest that 150 would seem to be a suitable number for the rank and file strength of a squadron of horse. As a campaign progressed, of course, this would be an optimum rarely sustained.

There is no point in being over-finicky, though, so let us accept this figure. Now, cavalry could take up a variety of formations, but as we have already studied the battalion in its customary battle deployment (i e close order for firing), let us do likewise with the squadron. In the early part of the Seven Years War it was found that the best formation for an attacking cavalry unit was a two-rank one, so this is how we shall consider it. Imagine then the squadron drawn up in two lines, one behind the other, with the 150 troopers giving lines of 75 men each. Allowing four feet for each mounted man (it might be just a little less), it is not difficult to calculate that the squadron front would be about 100 yards in length. A quick conversion to our 10 yards = 1 inch scale shows that a squadron of this strength would have a front of 10″ on the war game table. It is a regrettable fact that the cavalry regiments of the Vereinigte Freie Städte have never reached this strength, and the 24 troopers of a cavalry regiment ranged in two lines have a front of but 7″, indicating that the unit numbers only about 105 troopers. Alas, cavalry is an expensive arm to raise and maintain!

However, if the reader does draw up his cavalry and finds it has a front of 10″, he will certainly have an accurate representation of a cavalry squadron as per the Prussian establishment. Even more obviously than was the case with the infantry battalion, the scale falls down when it comes to depth, two ranks being about 4″ deep on the table (depending on the size of figures involved), this being fully twice as much as the actual two ranks plus the appropriate interval. Again as we have to accept this, we can do no less than content ourselves with the correctness of the frontage.

As to officers, my own establishment is 4, again there being no NCO's. Now, Frederick the Great's squadron had 8 officers and 14 NCO's to the 150 troopers, so that in the same proportion I should really have 1 officer and 2 NCO's. I seem to be rather over-officered compared with the Prussian service. This, by the way, is almost identical with that given in detail in the French *Ordonnance* of 1779, which gave 7 officers, 13 NCO's and 154 men (this actually being for a dragoon regiment).

Once more it appears that the wargamer has to make a choice as to how many officers shall ornament his squadron, not that it matters which he prefers in the way of command hierarchy, as long as his Morale Index can be readily calculated. I would point out that the cavalry unit I employ is considered to be a regiment and that the high officer proportion may be accounted for by the addition of the regimental staff, commanding officer, second in command, adjutant and so on. Should the wargamer wish it, he can have two or three such squadrons as we have described, officered on the Prussian model, and add to these a regimental staff or headquarters party; this would certainly be the most correct approach, although most of us, I imagine, would prefer to have two squadrons, each of different regiments, if only on account of the variety of uniforms.

Summarising the above, on the basis of 12½″ being the front of a battalion and 10″ being that of a squadron, it appears that the action described in the previous chapter was one involving on each side two battalions of infantry, a squadron of cavalry (rather weak, with a front of only 7″), plus what we called a battalion of light infantry (24 rank and file) or about half a battalion in the real thing. In round figures, at 600 men to the battalion, we had the representation of 1500 infantry and just over 100 cavalry on each side—as I said, a small though brisk action. Ere long we shall consider something substantially larger. The artillery organisation used will be discussed forthwith, together with additional rules for counter-battery firing, as well as for the effect of roundshot and shell on buildings, etc.

XIV
More about Artillery

As we considered infantry and cavalry in their customary units of battalion and squadron, it would seem logical to do likewise with artillery, and to work out, using our scale of $1'' = 10$ yards, the distance on the war game table to be occupied by the number of cannon we calculate will represent an actual battery drawn up in firing position. Before we do our sums, though, there are one or two points to be considered.

Obviously the size of miniature guns we use will govern to a large extent the number we employ, and once again, unless the wargamer goes to the extreme length of fabricating his own pieces, he is at the mercy of the commercial manufacturer. As far as 20mm and 30mm guns are concerned, his lot is very far from being an unhappy one, there being on the market a splendid variety of guns in these scales ranging from the heaviest to the lightest, and in the proper place I shall make it my business to detail those available, their manufacturers and their prices. These cannon are usually of very constant and reliable scale, and this is significant, particularly in the important dimension of hub-to-hub measurement. It is this vital statistic which has the greatest bearing on the number of guns filling a given battery frontage. This width of the artillery unit when formed in battery is the next consideration, but it must be pointed out en passant that in our period the battery as a tactical entity was not the rather rigid thing it later became; it did not consist of a stipulated number of guns, four, six, or what you will. This concept seems to have come along at a much later date. So with some justification we can allow ourselves some latitude as to the number of pieces of ordnance we assemble into an artillery unit.

As for the actual frontage for a given number of guns drawn up in firing position, some research shows this to have been a rather variable quantity, and it is certain that in action, guns drawn up in haste would not necessarily adhere to parade ground intervals. In particular, if a very large number of guns was involved, intervals would naturally be kept to a minimum for maximum concentration of fire. Furthermore, the question of control is important: the further away the gun the less direction the artillery commander can exercise. So, the investigation carried out on this point shows that the frontage occupied by a battery, which we shall initially think of as

A battery of field guns in action. It is assumed that the supply of ammunition is carried in the limbers.

comprising six guns, varied between 60 yards and about 110 yards, these figures being obtained at different stages of the research, during which enquiry was made inter alia of the King's Troop, Royal Horse Artillery, and of the author of a recent and most authoritative work on the campaigns of Napoleon. Ever advocating the spirit of happy compromise, may I suggest that one splits the difference which, if my calculations are accurate, will give 85 yards as the length of ground occupied by six guns ranged in battery position, or converting this to the war game table, a distance of 8½″.

How many pieces of artillery, then, are going to occupy this space in a manner appropriate to their function, allowing a reasonable gap between each cannon to permit the 'matrosses' to go about their business? A 1″ interval between the guns seems to be just right; it represents 10 yards in actual distance. Taking a typical miniature field piece, one with an axle of 1¼″, and setting four of them in position, it is found that 5″ are taken up by the guns, and with 1″ between them, the sum total for the front is 8″, or close to the actual length we decided upon as battery frontage for six actual guns. Therefore, should we decide to have an artillery unit of four guns (they can be field pieces or howitzers, or a mixture of both) it will represent the front of and should provide the fire-power of a six-gun battery on an historic battlefield. In the service of the Vereinigte Freie Städte, the artillery unit consists of two guns, so in fact it appears that it may equate to something like half a battery in the later nomenclature.

As to personnel in the war game, this can be determined as a proportion, as we did with infantry and cavalry. To be brief, let me say that my two-gun battery is serviced by three officers (one of whom is mounted, although this fact does not prevent him, in extremis, from taking a hand with the business of firing) and eight other ranks, that is an officer and four men per gun, plus the mounted commander of the unit. I should point out, too, that my artillery consists of six-pounder field guns and medium howitzers. Heavier pieces such as twelve-pounders would require more numerous crews.

One other thing, and I suppose this partly concerns the personnel of the unit and partly the battlefield scale. As with infantry and cavalry, the latter falls down rather badly when depth is considered, particularly so with the guns. The cannon I am considering, the one I use myself, is about 2″ long from the muzzle to the end of the trail, or no less than 20 yards in terms of our ground scale. This is just something we have to accept, the actual length being probably not more than three yards, but the point does arise here as to how we move the gun about? What about the gun team? This is one of the very many points which have to be left to the individual and is, I feel, largely a matter of the look of the thing. Some players do not bother to have a horse team for their guns, simply taking it that they are limbered up to and unlimbered from an imaginary gun team. I don't think I should be particularly happy about this and feel that as long as tactics and military results are not affected, then appearance should count for something. I prefer my own system which involves the use of a four-horse team. This at once means that the limbered-up gun is going to be hopelessly out of scale, so much so that it is really pointless to calculate the discrepancy. As to the real thing: the length of a gun plus six-horse team is about 20 yards, so a six-gun battery in column of route (and excluding caissons and other necessary vehicles) would extend, allowing for intervals, to something like 150 yards. As one of my guns with its team measures some 6″ overall, the four cannon, which in battery represent an actual six-gun battery, would have in column, and again allowing for intervals, a length of about 27″ or more—or 270 yards. This is almost double the length of the parent unit. These figures are approximate only, and it is not really necessary to be accurate to the individual yard. If the player wishes actually to unlimber and limber up his guns, he will have teams; if not, he will dispense with such niceties. It is, I repeat, a matter of taste and of the importance one attaches to appearance. There is the point, of course, that the use of teams does away with any doubt as to what any specific cannon is doing—no evilly-disposed opponent can allege that it fired when in fact it was on the move. With teams present it is simple. If the gun is unlimbered, it can fire; if limbered up it cannot, and there's an end to it.

Still very much on the subject of artillery we have to consider a point which did not arise during the course of the little action we reported earlier, this being the question of counter-battery fire, that is when opposing guns fire directly at each other. In the day and age of our choice, this was not a thing much used or greatly encouraged and indeed, considerably later, the Duke of Wellington passed some severe strictures on certain of his gunners for firing at enemy cannon rather than enemy troops. This is not difficult to understand, really, bearing in mind the lack of accuracy in eighteenth century artillery, and also the obvious fact that round shot had to pretty well pinpoint its target in the way of an enemy gun to be effective. It was much easier to send a ball ploughing into a mass of infantry or cavalry, and it was almost bound to inflict casualties. One might also say that it took a direct hit on the barrel of a gun to put it irreparably and immediately out of action, by knocking off a trunnion for instance. It was a comparatively easy matter to replace a shattered wheel or a damaged trail, and the chances of a roundshot's hitting a truly vital portion of a cannon's anatomy were not tremendous.

War game rules must reflect these conditions and practice to the extent that counter-battery fire, while by no means being completely out of the question, is in normal circumstances rendered much less profitable than firing at enemy personnel. This is especially important when we set about fighting larger scale battles than the one already described, as we shall do before long. It would be unreal if by phenomenally good shooting (which may be translated as a series of inordinately lucky dice throws) one could destroy the whole of an enemy's artillery which might be representative of a great number of batteries. This rarely occurred in major battles, and if an instance of such a thing be quoted at me I shall claim it at once to be the case of the exception proving the rule, thus giving myself the opportunity of repeating that *these* rules are designed to cater for a mean of what might take place. The unusual is certainly allowed for, but it is preferable that events should fall within the framework of the reasonably possible than that of the highly improbable.

We shall not then establish our counter-battery rules on the basis of one fortunate

A howitzer battery about to go into action. The frontage is more than the minimum laid down for efficient operation, but there is adequate room available to spread out a little.

shot's striking a vital part of the target cannon and knocking it completely out of action in one fell swoop (by throwing a 6 for instance). We shall adopt a cumulative system of damage, rather as though the gun were being subjected to a number of lesser hits, maybe a wheel knocked off or the barrel temporarily dislodged from its mounting and both having to be replaced; each occasion cuts down the efficacy of the piece and its rate of firing until finally it is so badly battered that, in a manner of speaking, it gives up the ghost and is no longer serviceable.

The system operates in this way and mathematically is the same for roundshot as for howitzer shell. Let us take the former first. The Roundshot Measuring Stick is laid across the enemy gun it is hoped to hit and the three-coloured die is thrown. Suppose that the gun is covered by the nearest green section, and the die comes up green as well. Then an ordinary numerical die is thrown for effect. Actually the two might be thrown simultaneously, and if the colour is wrong the other die is ignored; it's always a good principle to save time. Let us imagine that the second die gives 3—this is the beginning of the total of hits which will ultimately, it is hoped, put the gun out of action, the total required for this being 20. The rule may be formulated thus: when the gun has been hit a number of times by counter-battery fire and the total of such hits has reached 20, the gun is out of action for the remainder of the battle. Indeed, in a campaign, it is considered to be beyond repair and is noted as destroyed. Before 20 is reached, though, it has partially suffered to the extent that when the total is 10, the gun may be fired only every other move, indicating that damage of increasing severity prevents the repairs being done quickly enough to allow fire as rapid as before. It takes that much longer to keep the weapon firing.

The book-keeping which is necessary is minimal. The record may be kept thus:

Move	1	2	3	4	5	6	7	8	9	10
Hits on gun	–	3	–	2	5	–	2	3	3	4

This is very rapid destruction, but it will suffice to show what is meant. In the case quoted, the gun was reduced to firing on alternate moves after move 5, and on move 10, when the total of hits reached 22, it became completely out of action. The same numerical system applies when a howitzer is firing. The Shell Burst Indicator is placed on the target, and if the dice throw shows a hit has been made on the section containing the gun, a second die is thrown for effect. The adding procedure is as above.

There is one point which will occur at once to the percipient reader, and that is the reduction in the effect of roundshot as it loses velocity with successive ricochets. Simple! If the target is in the 'distant' section of the Stick, a reduction of 2 is made to the effect die; if it be in the 'mid' section, 1 is subtracted, and if in the 'near' section, no deduction is made, the actual throw being used in the totalling process.

Finally, if the player did not use horse teams, the following does not apply. If he does, however, they can also be subjected to enemy artillery fire, and the destructive process is as for guns but with a total of 10 being necessary only. Horses are pretty vulnerable and casualties not easily replaced.

XV
Buildings in Attack and Defence

Before going on to any sort of discussion on the tactics of attacking or defending built-up areas, and eventually on how buildings are affected by artillery fire, we shall have to digress a little into the field of war game terrain, the reason being that we shall have to make it quite clear what we mean by a house or a building. The reader will be well aware that, whatever the size of his troops, it is virtually impossible to scale down a building in keeping with the size of one's miniature soldiery and at the same time give it the relative military importance of the original. If we recall the ground scale of 1″ = 10 yards which we use, and think of the smallest commercially made buildings on the market, we might get the surprising concept of a cottage with a length of about 40 yards, while larger buildings are even more absurdly out of scale.

I would point out in passing, though, and once again the theory of the 'look of the thing' raises its head, that it is pleasant to see nicely-made and realistic-looking buildings occupying their places on the war game table, realistic-looking especially from the period point of view. It jars a little to see a modern semi-detached about to be stormed by a column of eighteenth-century grenadiers. Let us not make too much of this, however, and if a building has to be defended, the functional may well take precedence over the merely decorative and the player might quite happily pile his musketeers into an engine shed and think none the worse of himself for doing so.

Still, if he has a little time coupled with the inclination and only the veriest modicum of skill, in a very short time and without much effort he can produce all manner of simple or complex buildings with a sheet or two of balsa wood, of say, ⅛″ thickness, plus a sharp knife and some balsa cement. For the sake of the actual wargamer, it is as well if he can do this, because by making his own buildings in the manner briefly detailed, he will get the effect of action in built-up areas (house to house fighting in effect), and can more satisfactorily see the results of his skill or luck with his field guns and howitzers.

What is really wanted is a building which, in addition to being used as a defensive position by troops, can be juggled about to show, for example, that it has been hit by round shot. At the same time we do not want to build a lot of permanent ruins, than which there is nothing more depressing.

Two examples of houses or built-up areas. The one above, the ecclesiastical edifice, is of the composite type, which can house twice as large a garrison as its smaller fellow can.

First of all it might be a good thing to establish just what size our buildings are going to be and, if we construct or purchase a church or cottage, exactly what it represents on the war game table. As I have said, it is not possible accurately to represent any complex of buildings either to scale with our figures or even with the ground scale we employ.

We make or acquire a building and put it on the table. Perhaps it occupies an area 4″ by 2″ and thus covers, using the ground scale, 40 yards by 20 yards, quite an edifice in fact. What this boils down to, though, is that we are not considering a single house (or whatever it might be), but that amount of built-up area it includes. In principle, this somewhat resembles the theory of the infantry occupying a frontage of 120 yards, the figures taking up a front of 12″ in the correct formation being representative of a battalion. In the same way our building represents a number of buildings, not just one. We shall have then perhaps half a dozen miniature buildings which, as regards the area they cover, represent maybe a small village. To keep the record straight it will be incumbent upon us to assess the number of men who can comfortably occupy this or any other given built-up area.

A simple war game house.

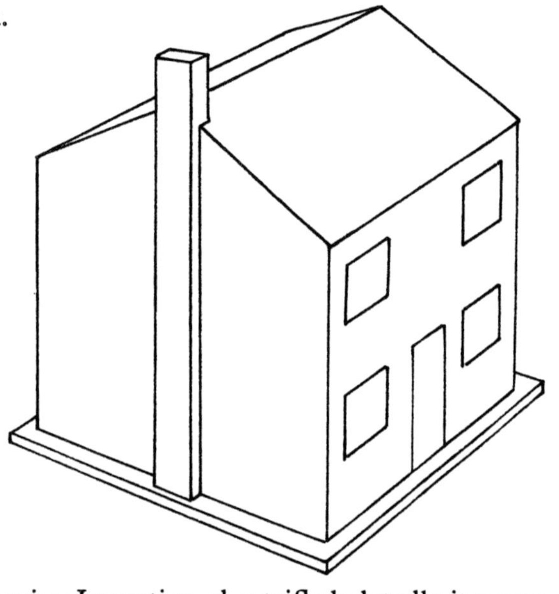

Now, let's get on with the digression I mentioned, a trifle belatedly it seems. It is a fact that much pleasure can be had from making one's own model buildings if one feels so inclined. They can be of the simplest type, a species of box with the doors and windows painted on or cut out of the balsa. They can, though, be something a little more elaborate and in keeping with the architecture of the period being considered. For us, it would naturally be the eighteenth century or earlier, and one can really go to town here, particularly if some pictures of what is wanted are available. Travel brochures frequently have coloured photographs of what is required, and those for the Rhineland or Bavaria are most prolific in this respect. I'm not suggesting that the enthusiast should set about recreating Neuschwanstein Castle (it is not eighteenth century, anyway) or even one of the Loire Châteaux. I would suggest that the typical white-washed, red-tiled South German house or mediaeval Burghaus are not too difficult to represent in simple fashion. Of course, as with many of the details of the hobby, it is a matter of taste.

What I shall describe, then, will be the bare bones of the thing, and I can best illustrate what I mean with the aid of the simple diagram opposite, which is basically one single house.

This, I hope, will be seen to be the least complicated structure, consisting of only a few pieces of balsa wood, an eighth of an inch thick, with the external details painted on in a rudimentary sort of way. Although on a base, it is not permanently attached thereto, and when the house itself is lifted up, the result is something like this:

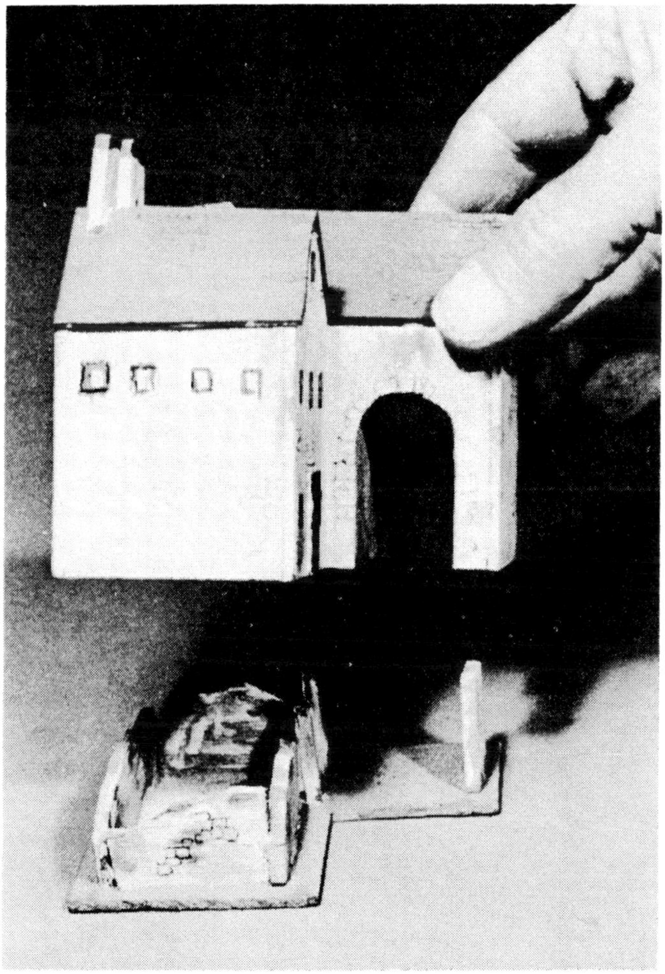

The shell of a house is removed, leaving its ruins.

This demonstrates the basic idea. In the diagram the building was in its normal unscathed condition, while the photograph shows its functional use. Having now been destroyed by artillery fire the house itself has been removed, leaving only its ruins. These are also made from balsa wood, shaped and painted to represent a shelled building and once again I show only a very simple version. It must be borne in mind in constructing the ruin that enough floor space be left therein for the troops it is intended to have as a garrison. Another point is that the more snug the fit of the house over its ruin, the more secure it will be on its base; it won't flop about. It might be suggested that the ruin be made first and the house then constructed around it. Myself, I make as simple a ruinous outline as possible, large enough for the men I intend to station inside it, when its shattered walls will afford them a high degree of protection. The whole question of just how elaborate terrain features may be does not concern us at the moment, since we are more interested in dealing with action involving our houses.

To start with, we shall consider the rules necessary for governing the attack and defence of the built-up areas we have made.

I must point out that these rules are necessarily based upon the idea of a standard house, by which I mean that every building used is of one size, or each covers the same area as do the others. The height is immaterial, and they can be fitted with towering steeples or can be squat barns. The reason for the standardisation is that we ensure that the correct number of soldiers may garrison each building, or built-up area as it really is, and that there is no unreal over-crowding. It would obviously be totally incorrect to cram a whole regiment into one house; this would mean that the troops would be in a situation worse than that endured by Clerembault's battalions at Blenheim, when they were so tightly packed that the individuals were unable to raise their arms from their sides.

Considerable experiment, amounting to much trial and error in a vast number of war games, plus a deal of research and calculation, shows that infantry will garrison a number of houses in a posture for defence in a certain proportion. Reducing this to our war game scale we find that seven of our infantrymen would occupy one of our standard houses; seven of our five officer/forty-eight man regiments, that is. Our regiment represents, it will be remembered, a single battalion, and such a unit will be capable of defending, by itself, an area covered by seven of our standard houses (with four men left outside as a reserve).

Into one house then we can put seven men. Ordinarily this would be an officer and six men, although seven of the latter are permissible, and the houses themselves are shown in the photograph. In point of fact, though, the right hand effort is what I call a composite building: a noble edifice made in two sections. It has advantages. It was interesting to make (having an actual counterpart) and it is useful in that it can play a dual role, being usable either as two separate entities or, placed together, as a whole. In the former case, each section will have seven men as garrison, while the whole

Infantry defending a ruined building. It accommodates seven men, the same number as it would do in an undamaged state.

thing will be defended by fourteen, thus preserving the proper numbers. The idea is a reasonable one; a building such as a Town Hall occupying a considerable area would accommodate a number of troops equivalent to those of smaller houses taking up the same area.

At this point, a brief reminder about the firing rules for infantry might be in order. It will be recalled that volleys are calculated in groups of six men. There is no difference when men firing from houses are involved. It is assumed that all muskets in the houses can be brought to bear, through windows, loopholes etc, and no account is taken of the number of doors and windows which have been painted on the walls of the houses. The muskets available, and naturally within firing range, are counted and divided by six, the normal calculations for casualties being made.

I don't have to point out to the military-minded reader that as in the case of an infantry attack on field fortifications, it is a rugged business to assault defended houses. Street fighting is an expensive and bloody affair. We can picture the defenders substantially protected and blazing away with their muskets at the attackers, who will be feeling pretty naked in comparison, although doubtless making every use of available cover as they approach. Those who succeed in coming up to close quarters will make a final rush to bring themselves right up to their goal, and they will fling themselves at the doors and windows in an attempt to force their way in and engage the defenders. If they are lucky enough to do so they will fight the latter on fairly equal terms, but if they do not, they will be at a great disadvantage vis-à-vis the chaps within who will still be under cover.

This is what happens on the war game table. Let us imagine that we have a house defended by seven infantrymen, and it is under attack by about a dozen enemy foot. The latter advance, doubtless taking casualties from the defenders' fire, until they are at a point from which the next move will actually bring them into contact with the building itself. Here they are rushing forward at speed to get right up to their objective and the players thereupon throw dice to determine whether the defenders are able to fire a final volley as the assault troops close. The high throw is the winner, of course. If the defending general wins, his men fire and casualties are removed. The attackers are then moved up to the doors and windows, or as many of them as can do so within the limits of the proper move distance. One point to note: irrespective of the details of the building and how many doors and windows are shown, it is enacted that as each is a representation, all shall be considered to have a standard number of these modes of entry. These are six in number, two on each long side, and one at each end of the building.

With as many of his troops in position at the doors and windows, the attacking player throws a die for each soldier seeking to force an entry to decide whether on the initial 'crunch' he can force his way inside. If the dice throw be 4, 5 or 6, then he has done so and the man is placed inside. There he fights on equal terms with the defender posted to cover that particular entry, normal combat rules applying. On the other hand, if the throw is only 1, 2 or 3, his initial rush has failed and he remains outside to fight with the defender still comfortably positioned behind the door or whatever. His disadvantage is obviously considerable, and the defender adds 2 to his dice throw to allow for the protection he is enjoying. (eg: attacker throws 2; he cannot enter, and both players throw dice. The attacker scores 4 and defender 3, but he adds 2 to this, making a total of 5, and he wins the encounter, the attacker being smartly removed from the table). If a window happens to be undefended in a house otherwise garrisoned, a throw of 4, 5 or 6 will obtain entrance, and the attacker fights within on the following move with whoever might be available.

Let us follow succeeding events, and an example will best show what happens. Suppose that two men of the original force gained an entrance and won their fights. At the end of the move we have in the house 5 defenders and 2 attackers, with more of the latter about to move up to the doors etc. It is up to the defending player how he disposes of his men for the second stage in the affray, his primary aim being doubtless to liquidate as quickly as possible the enemy troops who have gained entry. Possibly he will depute two of his five to engage the intruders, leaving himself with three to cover the same number of windows and having no option but to leave the other three unguarded. Still, it is only after all a fifty-fifty chance or not whether the attacker, despite his being unimpeded, can in fact clamber through a window or smash his way through a door. Again the individual fights are decided with dice throws and casualties are removed, all this presupposing that morale is everywhere unimpaired.

Fighting inside a building, when the combatants are most probably totally ignorant of what is going on outside the confines of its walls, is rather special in that it is fought out to the bitter end in the war game, by which I mean that there is no withdrawal after two moves of hand-to-hand combat, as would happen in the open. The fight is carried on until one side is no more. This is so even though, outside, the regiments to which the men belong are reduced to half strength and in consequence are retiring. This, incidentally, applies to a house which might have been occupied without a struggle by some unit or other; if the remainder has to retire by reason of a 50% overall loss, those in the house may remain as garrison, if the general so desires.

XVI
Final Points Concerning Artillery

All we have to do before entertaining the reader with a second battle report (something rather more ambitious than the small action described in Chapter XII) is to round off the rules for artillery fire and, for practical purposes, we can do this by dealing with the effect of roundshot and explosive shell on buildings.

Basically, the procedure involved in bringing any sort of building under artillery fire and either destroying it or rendering it untenable is similar to that discussed in Chapter XIV, where we dealt with counter-battery fire and the system of putting a gun out of action by the cumulative effect of a succession of hits. The destruction of a building, ie one of the standard houses already described, is carried out in exactly the same way. Let us see first what happens when roundshot is being used.

What takes place, then, when a solid roundshot hits a building? It can penetrate, cause casualties and damage the building, then depending upon its velocity and the stoutness of the walls it had to go through, will come to a halt or will carry on through the edifice, more slowly of course, although it can still be travelling at a lethal speed and can cause some considerable pother in its course. Accordingly, we go about the business in this way, using the time-honoured Roundshot Measuring Stick and the corresponding three-coloured die.

The Stick is used normally, placed with one end at the gun muzzle, and the other across the building being bombarded. The three-coloured die is thrown. If the colour which comes up is that covering the target house, an ordinary numerical die is thrown for effect. Obviously, at different ranges, the roundshot will have varying degrees of effectiveness. At long range, or even occasionally at close quarters, it will not penetrate but will simply bounce off. Even if it does break through it might be slowed up to such an extent as to be brought to a halt. If, on the other hand, it does go clean through, it might hit another target, either troops or a building, in the corresponding colour of the next ricochet group, and dice will have to be thrown for casualties and damage as in the previous hit. Possibly a glance at the Table of Immediate Effect will give some sort of idea just what is intended.

Roundshot on Buildings—Table of Immediate Effect

	Dice Throw				
	1 and 2	3	4	5	6
Near group	Does not penetrate	Penetrates kills 1 stops	Penetrates kills 1 stops	Penetrates kills 2 goes on	Penetrates kills 3 goes on
Mid group	Does not penetrate	Does not penetrate	Penetrates kills 1 stops	Penetrates kills 2 goes on	Penetrates kills 2 goes on
Distant Group	Does not penetrate	Does not penetrate	Does not penetrate	Penetrates kills 1 stops	Penetrates kills 1 stops

A practical example will best illustrate the idea. Let us say that the target building lies in the green section of the medium-range colour group of the Measuring Stick. The die is thrown and green comes up. A numbered die is then thrown for effect and the result, is let us say, a 5. Consulting the table, it seems that the roundshot penetrated the house and caused 2 casualties to the troops therein (if indeed there were any inside) and continued on right through. Now, suppose that a couple of infantrymen were covered by the green section of the distant group of the Stick. They would naturally be possible casualties and if, instead of the men, another building happened to be in the same 'distant' green section, dice throws would be necessary to decide the fate of men or house, as the case might be. In the case of the latter, if perchance 5 was again the effect throw, it would cause but one casualty, as can be seen from the table.

Now, all this above relates to the immediate effect and the dice throws are effective as they come up, 5 in the above example and so on. However, when totalling the hits which relate to the eventual destruction of the building, the same deductions for long and medium range are made as they were when guns are put out of action by artillery fire, that is 2 and 1 respectively. So, in the example quoted above, the 5 would be reduced by 1 when a note was made of the hit points for the destruction total, making it only 4. The number of hits required for a house to be completely demolished is in fact 10. In practice, then, when this total has been reached, the shell of the house is removed, leaving the ruin starkly exposed.

So much for roundshot; with howitzers firing shell the procedure is as previously related. The Shell Burst Indicator is placed on the target house, if it is within range of course. What will almost invariably occur is that a direct hit (the 6 of the inner circle of the device) will be required, although in the case of a composite or double building, with one portion of it in the 6, the other will be in one of the outer areas. If the initial throw shows that a hit has been made, a second is thrown for both immediate and cumulative effect, but before giving details of these, it must be pointed out that shell has a somewhat different effect from the impact of a solid shot in that it may quite possibly set fire to the construction in or on which it explodes, as well as knocking it about by blast.

To simulate this process in the war game we rule that when the house has taken a certain amount of punishment from shell fire, the odds are that it would be in flames. We therefore rule that, in the same manner in which roundshot destroys a house when the total of hits has reached 10, when howitzer hits upon the building have reached the same total it must be taken to be well and truly alight on the succeeding move, and all troops therein must be taken out and moved away an appropriate distance.

Now, in considering the length of time the house remains in flames, we have to consider just what has happened. This is no small blaze, easily extinguished, but rather a full-blown conflagration; we are not thinking of small fires which can be easily beaten out with a coat or a blanket. That sort of thing we can ignore. What we are concerned with is the fire which will involve the burning down of the building and this, without doubt, will last some little time. This we must take to be at least a quarter of an hour (in practice it might well take very much longer, but it is advisable, for tactical reasons, to reduce this time somewhat) and this, by our time-move scale, will be 15 moves, one move taking a minute to complete on the table. So, we rule that the house is actively burning for 15 clear moves, at the end of which the shell is removed, leaving the ruin, which can be entered and defended.

While the 'burning' moves are in progress, troops cannot enter the house on fire or indeed approach within 3″ of it. So, when two houses on opposite sides of a street are both in flames, they form a pretty impassable barrier for troops who want to get through. This is but reasonable as anyone who has been close to a fiercely burning building will testify, the heat generated being intense. Another point concerns the composite building we have spoken of earlier. Initially only the part actually hit is burning, but there is the obvious possibility of the second portion's also taking fire. The rule to cover this is as follows:

> On each of the 15 moves of 'burning', a die is thrown to decide whether the second section of the building also takes fire: 3, 4, 5 or 6, it does not; 1 or 2—it does. In the latter case, it will burn for 15 clear moves, as in the case of the original building. It must be evacuated during this period.

The question is now of how the player wishes to indicate when the building is actually ablaze. This can range from simply putting a coloured counter on it to show that it is ablaze and out of bounds, to something a little more graphic, such as putting a few tufts of cotton wool to represent smoke on top. This suffices, but to my prejudiced eye it's not quite enough, and indeed I like to see a little symbolic flame about. This, like all the other ingredients going to make up a pictorial effect, is one for the

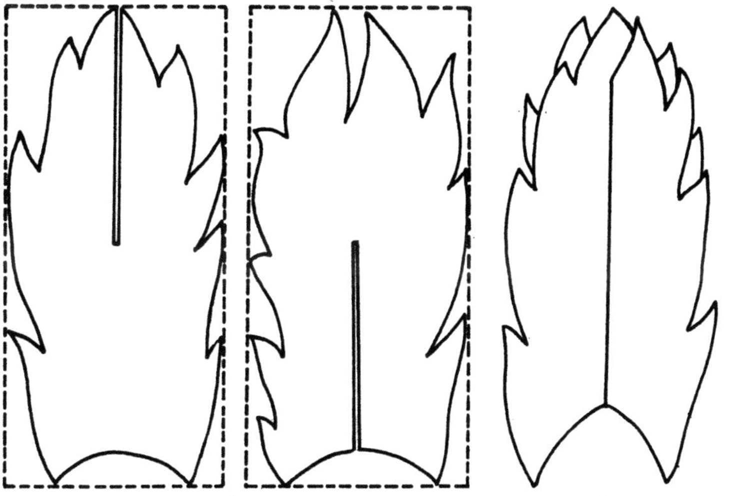

1 2

A simple method of making 'flames'.

player's choice, but for what it is worth, here is my own idea. It does involve a small do-it-yourself operation, and the reader may not think it worth while. Still, it does not take a lot of effort, and the explanation is in fact rather more complicated than the actual construction. All that is required are two pieces of card; postcard thickness is adequate, and indeed a couple of plain postcards provide the means to show a splendid conflagration. On the cards are drawn jagged outlines, to represent leaping flames, and then these are cut out to form the shapes such as are shown in diagram 1.

These are then painted in as fiery hues as possible—it is quite remarkable what an effect results from generous dollops of red, yellow and orange, and by applying these colours with a certain gay abandon, the result can be rather spectacular.

The keen-eyed reader will doubtless have noticed the slots in the two 'flame sections' of diagram 1, one from the top and one from the bottom, and he will readily deduce what they are for; one card is slipped on to its fellow and the result, looked at from the top or bottom, forms a cross, and in elevation is something like the contraption shown in diagram 2.

The use of this device is quite apparent. When the dice throws have reached the incendiary total of 10, it is placed on the building to indicate that the latter is on fire, and the whole result can be seen in the photograph with which we illustrate the procedure. The building shown to be on fire is a composite one, one portion of which has already been destroyed. We can take it that fire has already put paid to the left hand section, and that the right still burns. The photograph gives but a pallid indication of the gloriously technicoloured original! When the 'burning' moves are completed, the flames and the building are removed, and the ruin revealed.

As with roundshot, in addition to the long term effect, there is an immediate one as

Fire! A composite building in flames, the left-hand section having already been reduced to ruins.

regards casualties. It is again related to the actual dice throws and operates in the same way as in the case of roundshot. When a hit has been registered on a house by a shell, casualties are caused to the occupants, thus:

Dice throw		
1, 2, 3	=	no casualties
4	=	1 killed
5	=	2 killed
6	=	3 killed

The 1, 2 and 3 are, of course, added to the destruction total although they caused no casualties. It will be noticed, too, that range has no effect on the dice in the case of shell fire, the range having no effect on the explosion.

XVII
The Battle of Mollwitz

The first occasion on which Frederick the Great commanded an army in battle, at Mollwitz on 10th April 1741, at the beginning of the War of the Austrian Succession (or, if you like, the First Silesian War), was not a happy one for him, and indeed it had a certain 'opera bouffe' quality which in later life he was glad to erase from his memory. This was for a commander the dreadful situation when, early in the fight, he decides that the day is lost and flees the field, leaving a subordinate, in this case Marshal Schwerin, to win the battle in his absence. Historically, though, the engagement is an interesting one, not by reason of its Frederician tactics (they were non-existent) but as being the first demonstration of the fighting power of the Prussian infantry, a power which was to have such a profound effect on the battles of the succeeding twenty years or so. Mollwitz was, in fact, a good ding-dong sort of affair, and is particularly suitable for refighting on the war game table, this being obviously the reason for my choosing it as an example of what I call a 'big battle' in contrast to the small action previously related.

Before starting on the details of Mollwitz as it was fought out on the table, it might be in order to sketch in very briefly the background, for although it was for all intents and purposes an encounter battle, it might be a good thing to have some idea of what it was all about. Near the Fortress of Brieg the Austrian forces were surprised by Frederick, who came up most unexpectedly in their rear but not sufficiently rapidly to prevent the Austrians being able to wheel about and present a solid front to the bluecoats. Due to the complicated evolutions of the time, though, this was not quite as simple as might first appear. In round figures, the Prussians fielded some 21,000 men, the Austrians about 19,000, although these figures vary (they always do) depending upon which authority is consulted, and both armies deployed traditionally, infantry in the centre, cavalry on the wings. The Prussian artillery, which as we shall see was much more powerful than their opponent's, was quickly in action, but by successive charges of the splendid Austrian cavalry, the Prussian horse were driven from the field. It was at this point, voluntarily or otherwise, it does not seem possible to say with certainty, that Frederick went off, leaving his infantry to save the day, which they did in great style. As Christopher Duffy writes (in *The Wild Goose and the*

Eagle, published by Chatto and Windus in 1964):

> The whole army marched in perfect step, like a machine propelled by a single spring, the Brandenburg platoon fire flaming from platoon to platoon towards the centre of each battalion until taken up again on the wings, the noise merging into a continual roar of thunder.

This was all too much for the Austrians, who saw fit to make a retreat under cover of darkness.

These are the barest of bare bones of the course of the actual battle and we shall now unveil the story of what took place when Mollwitz was refought under the 'Grant rules for mid-eighteenth century war games'.

When this event took place, the opponents were on the one side myself, assisted by Andrew Green, and on the other, two formidable adversaries, Brigadier Peter Young, DSO, MC, then Reader in Military History at the Royal Military Academy, Sandhurst, and, acting as his Chief of Staff, Charles Stewart Grant, Senior Cadet Corporal at the same institution. Despite the expertise and experience of the opposition, I generously (and doubtless ill-advisedly) offered them the choice of sides. Having looked at the terrain and the troops arrayed in the initial situation, and having ordered me to withdraw pending deliberations, they opted, as I might have guessed, to command the Prussians, attracted thereto, I have no doubt, by the preponderance of infantry and artillery. The contending sides were as follows (culled by me from *Der Erste Schleschische Krieg*, an official publication of the Great General Staff of the Imperial German Army, consulted in the War Office Library):

Prussia 31 infantry battalions (of which 8 were grenadiers)
30 cavalry squadrons
3 hussar squadrons
37 field and 16 heavy guns

Austria 16 infantry battalions
14 grenadier companies
11 cavalry regiments
2 hussar regiments
19 field guns

The sapient reader will quickly observe that the Prussians were indeed much stronger in infantry as well as in artillery, while the Austrians had the more powerful cavalry. There is no great point in detailing the process by which the actual numbers were converted to their war game equivalents, but basically, one takes the map of the battlefield and reduces it to the size of the table available, and then the armies are fitted in as far as possible to correspond with the situation desired. The idea is to deploy the greatest number of troops and at the same time to allow sufficient room for them

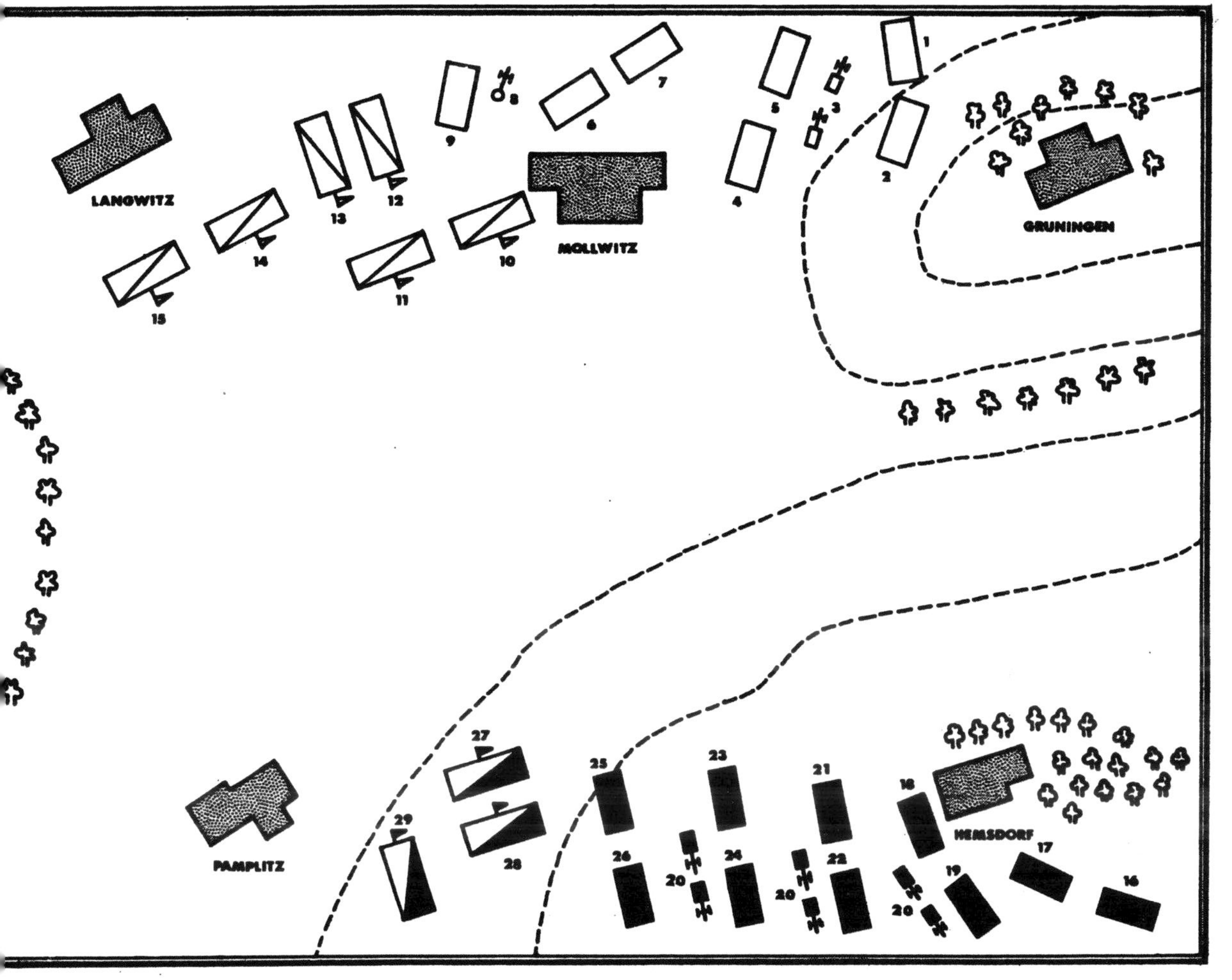

Mollwitz, map 1: before the battle.

Austria

1. Normandy Infantry
2. Picardy Infantry
3. Field gun battery
4. Bulkeley Infantry
5. Dillon Infantry
6. Royal Ecossais Infantry
7. Navarre Infantry
8. Howitzer
9. Grenadiers de France
10. Bourbon Cavalry
11. Cuirassiers du Roi
12. Les Mousquetaires
13. Gendarmerie du Roi
14. Lanciers de Saxe
15. Chasseurs de Fischer

Prussia

16. Vastmanland Infantry
17. Livgarden Infantry
18. Schaumburger-Lippe Infantry
19. Oldenburg Infantry
20. 3 field gun batteries
21. Ostergotland Infantry
22. Pfalz-Sonderheim Infantry
23. Löwenstein-Oels Grenadiers
24. Knyphausen Grenadiers
25. Butyrsky Infantry
26. Sobieski Infantry
27. Hohenzollern Kürassiere
28. Ahlefeldt Kürassiere
29. Von Ruesch Hussars

to manoeuvre if so desired. So, after a little trial and error, the battlefield finally had the appearance of that shown in the Plan of Battle, which also depicts the armies at the beginning of the action. As can be seen, the terrain is pretty flat, and although contours are shown, the slopes they indicate are so gentle as to have no effect on movement one way or another. There seems to have been a fall of snow, but it does not seem to have had any slowing-down effect either. Away off the map to the lower right is the Fortress of Brieg, held by the Austrians, and with which it was necessary or at least desirable for them to maintain communications. One might say that the raison d'être of Mollwitz was that the Austrians should at least hold their position, or better still drive off the Prussians, and for the latter, that they defeat the Austrians and drive them away from their fortress.

After some juggling with and adjusting of figures, it seemed that the following reflected the actual strengths of the contending armies as nearly as could be:

Prussia
- 2 regiments of grenadiers
- 8 regiments of line infantry
- 2 regiments of heavy cavalry
- 1 regiment of light cavalry
- 3 batteries of field guns (6 pieces in all)

Austria
- 1 regiment of grenadiers
- 6 regiments of line infantry
- 4 regiments of heavy cavalry
- 2 regiments of light cavalry
- 1½ batteries of field guns (actually including one howitzer)

It will be noted at once that the 3:1 superiority in guns enjoyed by the Prussians has been reduced to one of 2:1. This was done for two reasons: first, I did not want to make the artillery disparity so devastating (even 2:1 was bad enough, as I found) and second, I believed that this was a justifiable reduction, feeling that some of the Prussian heavy guns were not likely to have come up in time to take part, at least in the initial stages of the battle. Should I be wrong, I must plead wargamer's licence.

Another point the student might observe is the absence of light troops, jäger and the like. This I also found mildly surprising, but after all, it was the first of the Frederician battles, and neither side might at this early stage have raised any of the jäger forces which were such a feature of this and the succeeding wars. At any rate, the very detailed Order of Battle for the armies as given in *Der Erste Schleschische Krieg* makes no mention of such units, so one must assume none took part in the engagement. Incidentally, should the German work daunt the reader, the English historian, C. T. Atkinson, has a good account of Mollwitz in his *History of Germany 1715-1815*.

Yet another fact which will not have escaped attention is the presence on both sides of grenadiers. Now, the day when it was the task of these people to lob cumbersome grenades at the enemy was long past, but the fact that the men chosen for this particular duty were the strongest and best trained was later the reason why they were considered as a sort of élite force. Each infantry battalion included a grenadier company and a number of these were frequently grouped into a separate battalion, a practice frequently met with in continental armies, and used as assault troops. This military philosophy persisted up to and including the wars of Napoleon, as for example, in the case of Oudinot's division of grenadiers. So, having grenadiers in the contending armies, and as they were rather special troops, we have to give them qualities commensurate with their ability. Three points cover this contingency:

> Musketry: grenadiers fire in groups of four, instead of the usual line infantry groups of six. A volley from a full grenadier regiment consists then of 12 groups as opposed to the 8 of ordinary infantry, this giving increased firepower.
> Mêlée: in hand-to-hand combat, the throw for a grenadier is always increased by 1, substantially increasing his fighting capability in close combat.
> Morale: no reduction to the Morale Index for rank and file casualties is made until the losses have reached 25% (ie until 12 men have fallen), when 1 is deducted from the dice throw for morale.

I did contemplate allowing a grenadier regiment to suffer up to two-thirds other rank losses before it was compelled to withdraw from the action, but on second thoughts, it seemed that even for élite troops this was asking too much, and in any case, the special qualities provided above ensured, as we shall see, that grenadiers were a most potent force at Mollwitz.

As to the actual troops taking up their positions on the war game table, their numbers can be worked out from previous discussion of my own organisation. It may be recalled that infantry and cavalry regiments comprise 5 officers and 48 men, and 4 officers and 24 men respectively (light cavalry having one less officer), and an artillery battery 3 officers and 8 men. With these as the strengths of the units engaged, it can be calculated that the Prussian Army fielded 530 infantry, 83 cavalry and 33 gunners, the Austrian totals for the same arms being 371, 166 and 17 respectively. This seemed to be a reasonably close comparison with the historical numbers of combatants taking part in the actual battle. For my own satisfaction and information (and possibly to provide a species of alibi) I worked out a sort of 'power ratio', allocating points values to the different types of troops and the various artillery pieces. By dint of some prestigious calculation, this showed that, all things being considered, the Austrian force was 92% as powerful as the Prussian one. So, all in all, although the 'dark blues' did have a slight edge, it was not sufficient to frighten me—or at least not much. In point of fact, although the bulk of the Prussian Army was indeed in dark blue and was vaguely Germanic in regimental nomenclature, it was nothing less than the flower of the army of the Vereinigte Freie Städte (a sad thing for me to command against my own men!) and by some kind of military metamorphosis

The opening stages of the Battle of Mollwitz. In the distance the Prussian columns advance towards Gruningen and in the immediate foreground the Austrian light cavalry are pushing forwards on their disastrous move towards the Prussian left.

the Austrian commander had in his ranks, instead of his normal forces, a number of French stand-ins, these being provided by the Grand Duchy of Lorraine. These being mainly clad in white, however, it might be held that they did resemble the Austrians as far as the uniform was concerned. All this should explain why, should I refer to a particular regiment in the narrative, it need not necessarily appear in the historical Order of Battle of the army to which it belongs.

General officers and their suites, naturally, were in addition to the above totals, each two-regiment brigade having its commander assisted by an ADC, while each army commander had two such, plus his personal standard. The Austrians, having regard to the heavy metal of the opposition, deemed it wise that Count Fritz von Tarlenheim, Marshal-General of the Vereinigte Freie Städte (doubtless an ancestor of him who played such a part in the affair of *The Prisoner of Zenda* over a century later) should take the field. At the head of the Prussian chain of command was one General Graf von Grunt, this being something which caused no little surprise. In a

General Graf von Grunt, commanding the Prussian Army at Mollwitz.

previous campaign (the great and victorious one waged by the Vereinigte Freie Städte against the Electorate of Teutoburg-Althaufen) this individual, while concealing himself in a cellar during the bombardment of a strong place he purported to command, had been struck upon the cranium by a piece of flying masonry. This mishap resulted in his prompt demise, but strange to relate, it was later reported that he had been seen alive and well in the Teutoburg capital, and it was put about that he had made a miraculous recovery. The rumour ran, though, that the fact of the matter was that his corpus delicti had been transported to the capital, there subjected to expert taxidermy, and that the resulting effigy had been carried about the Electorate in a sedan to encourage the citizens during a period of severe reverses to the forces of the Elector, who was popularly known throughout the VFS as the 'Teutoburg Troll'. Be that as it may, it was certainly one bearing the likeness of Von Grunt who could be seen leading the Prussian Army, albeit from a position well to the rear of his troops.

There remains but to note that the war game table used for the major engagement was nine feet by seven, about twice the size of the one involved in the previously reported action. This is about as large as a war game table can conveniently be,

Commanding the Austrian Army at the Battle of Mollwitz: Fritz von Tarlenheim, Marshal-General of the Vereinigte Freie Städte, with two orderlies.

anything wider making it difficult to move troops in the centre. The long style of table, by which I mean something say 8 feet by 4 feet, I don't care much for, feeling that it tends to give a rather stereotyped sort of game. One seems more inclined to manoeuvre on a table nearly square, but this is a personal impression only.

Finally, if the reader cares to scan the initial disposition of the two armies in the Plan of Battle (noting, in passing, that both sides had taken slight liberties with their cavalry, the Prussians massing theirs on their left, the Austrians holding part of theirs in the centre) he may judge the efficacy of the plans made by the two generals. These were as follows:

Austrian: The left flank of the Prussian Army is to be attacked by the entire cavalry, with the object of preventing him bringing all his artillery into action, and at the same time of driving off his cavalry and forcing his infantry back towards Hemsdorf. Our infantry will occupy the line Mollwitz–Gruningen, as it will be almost certainly in this direction that the enemy will launch his major effort. If he is able to form a strong front with artillery support to face our cavalry, the cavalry attack will not be pressed home. The mounted troops will in this case form up to the right of Mollwitz, to await events.

Prussian: Part of the infantry, with strong artillery support, will form a front facing north-west to contain the Austrian cavalry, should it attack. The remainder of the infantry will advance and seize Gruningen, then swing westwards towards Mollwitz.

There it is, then: with the armies in position and straining at the leash, we await the command to advance (in both cases, presumably, it would be 'Vorwärts') and the account of the battle, which follows.

XVIII
Mollwitz: the Narrative

With the armies arrayed as already described, and a fine sight they were, the battle began. At the outset it was a pretty grim affair, the silence broken from time to time by a laconic 'Finished? Right, next move, then'. Initially, the movements of the armies were exactly as planned by the generals. From the Austrian side of the table could be seen the expected oblique move of the Prussians towards their right flank, columns of infantry passing on both sides of Hemsdorf, their obvious intention being to throw themselves against Gruningen, while cavalry moved gingerly forward to form a line on their left, the light regiment (Von Ruesch Hussars) actually entering the village of Pamplitz. This unit was withdrawn on move 3, when it became evident that following orders, the entire Austrian cavalry was advancing against the Prussian left. Meantime, Von Grunt's guns were moving forward with the aim, it seemed, of forming a huge battery about his left centre: a mass of ordnance which Von Tarlenheim viewed from his position near Mollwitz with no little concern.

My own, ie the Austrian, moves were also taking shape. Mollwitz was garrisoned with infantry, the Royal Ecossais regiment, while a brigade consisting of Picardy and Normandy infantry advanced towards Gruningen, the Irish Brigade (Dillon and Bulkeley) linking them up with Mollwitz.

It must be admitted that, all this time, I was by way of being on the horns of a painful dilemma, the problem being whether to dash all the Austrian cavalry against the Prussian left and to take the chance of striking a shattering blow (chiefly by destroying the enemy horse, if possible) or whether the cost of such a manoeuvre would be prohibitive, especially if the Prussian artillery, or part of it, unlimbered and came into action in time to catch the mounted troops in their charge (a truly horrid prospect).

It was plain, furthermore, that a strong infantry attack on Gruningen could not be long delayed, as the columns which had passed Hemsdorf were now in full march for that crucial point. One brigade (Sobieski and Butyrsky infantry regiments) had moved to its left to protect the Prussian guns, which were now drawing together although somewhat outdistanced by the infantry moving $7\frac{1}{2}''$ in column to the $6''$ of the guns.

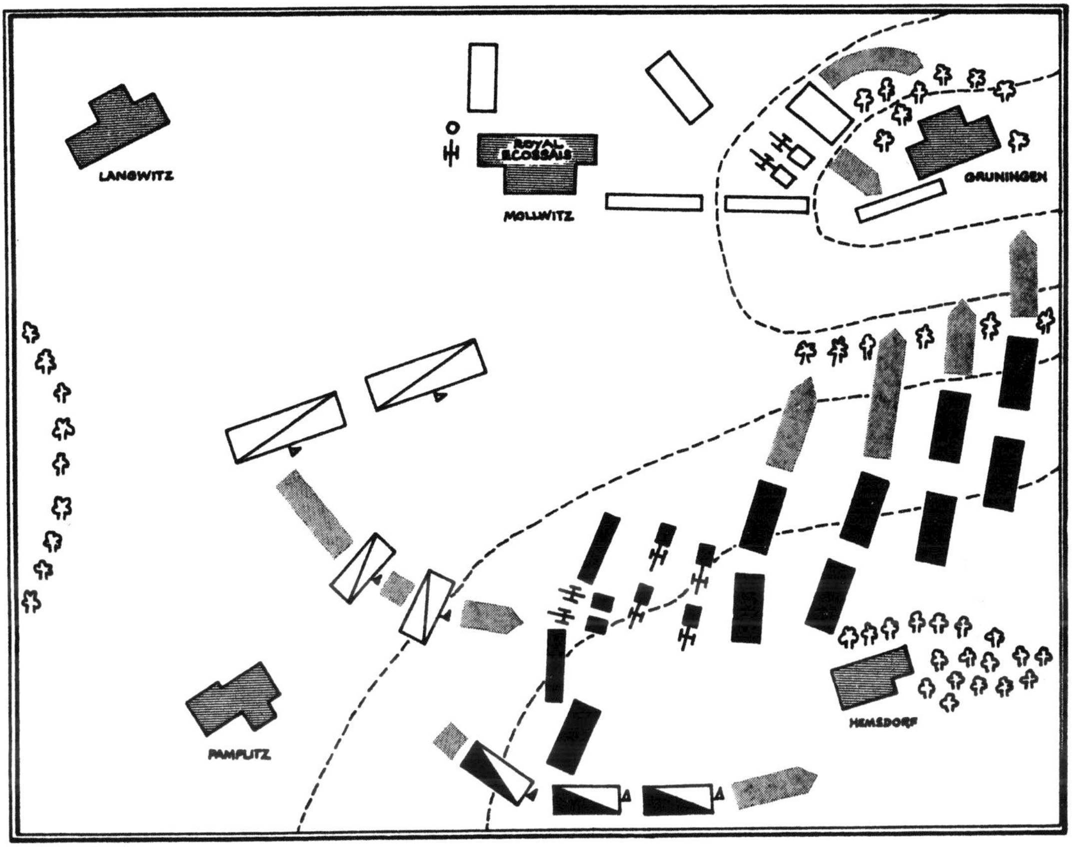

Mollwitz, map 2: the position after move 5.

For my part I maintained the infantry advance towards Gruningen, and directed my field battery in that direction as well, the idea being to bring it into action at a point just south-west of the village, to enable it to sweep the approaches thereto. The howitzer, the only one, was quickly in battery position to the west of Mollwitz and on move 5, both howitzer and field guns opened fire, drawing first blood: the former claimed three casualties from Sobieski Infantry.

The overall situation at this point, move 5, may be seen in map 2, with the Prussian cavalry about to disappear behind their infantry, part of which has now formed a strong flank guard with two guns also coming into line, and the Austrian light cavalry (the 12″ move, of course) pressing forward, having left the heavy regiments well behind.

These heavy cavalry regiments, having been moving since the beginning of the action, had had no opportunity to build up a reserve of 12″ 'battle' moves and the gap between the two types was unavoidable. Even so, it began to appear that all three regiments of the Prussian cavalry had well and truly reached the protection of their infantry and guns and the chance of catching them in the open was gone, probably for good. Momentarily, however, it did appear that the Austrian light horse might be able to drive home and wreak havoc among the artillery, not in action as yet and in fact still unlimbering (a complete move for this operation, it will be remembered). So, throwing discretion and, I suppose, better judgement to the wind, and with many an inner qualm, I allowed the two light cavalry units to press on regardless—a true 'death ride' it turned out to be, the details of which are explained in the diagram.

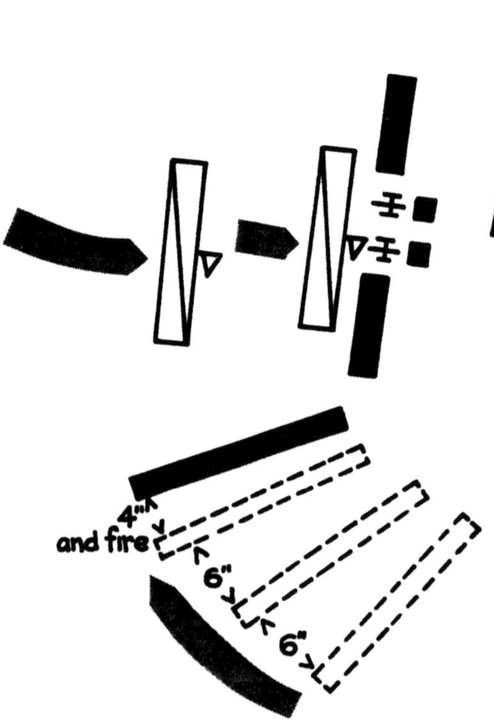

The charge and defeat of the Austrian light cavalry at the Battle of Mollwitz.

What it really amounted to was that the light cavalry having been pushed so far, a decision had to be made pretty quickly as to whether to withdraw them somewhat ingloriously, or to take the chance that they would hit the guns before the latter could get into action, and do some good by disposing of as many gunners as possible, thus going some way towards cutting down the Prussian artillery power. It was not expected that much would be accomplished against the infantry, as the wargamer will remember that light cavalrymen have no break-through capability when charging infantry as do their heavy brethren. In the event, it seemed that I had reckoned without mine hosts and their excellent tactical sense and timing. Already in line (close order for firing) on both sides of the battery, Sobieski Infantry had the Butyrsky regiment on its left rear. As the cavalry came up (Chasseurs de Fischer in the lead followed by the Lanciers de Saxe), Butyrsky advanced in line, pivoting on its right, for two 6″ moves, followed by a 4″ one, during which it fired as the cavalry passed in full cry for the guns. The Austrians had already been relatively unscathed by a long range volley from Sobieski and an ineffectual round of canister, but the discharge of Butyrsky's muskets (a first volley as well it should be pointed out) did tremendous damage, the Lancers losing an officer and 12 men, half their strength, and the Chasseurs also being badly mauled. The latter, however, were able to make contact with and cut down several gunners as well as some infantrymen, but, reduced to half strength at one blow and without even having made contact, the Lancers had to turn about and make off on the next move—in accordance with the fifty-per-cent rule.

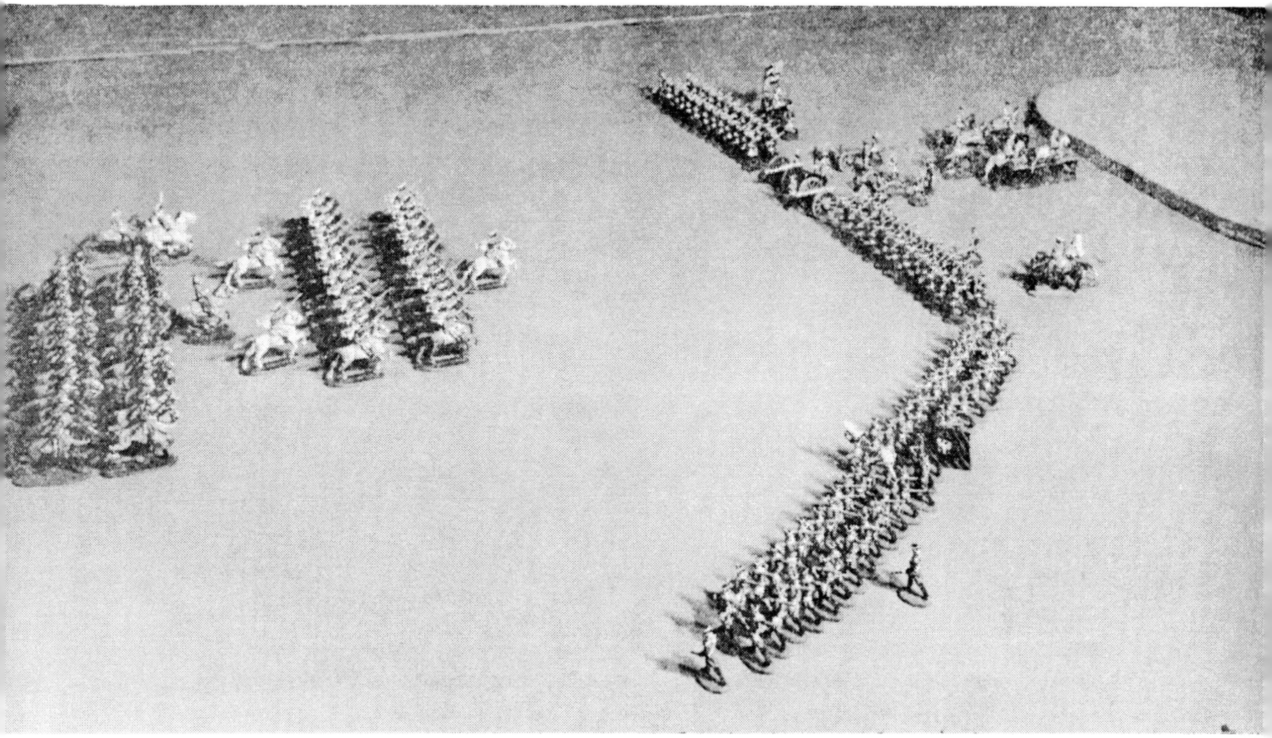

Mollwitz: the Austrian light cavalry on the point of being shattered by musketry. The Butyrsky Infantry, the nearer of the Prussian regiments, are about to make a 4″ move and fire into the flank of the charging horsemen.

With such losses a dice throw for morale had to be made at once, and it was still good, though only just. They were therefore able to retreat in good order instead of bolting. It was sad that they were unable to cross lances with the enemy bayonets, but they were immediately followed in their retreat by the Chasseurs, now reduced to a virtual handful but still, surprisingly, of good morale.

In retrospect, this seems to be the turning point of the battle. Caught off balance,

Mollwitz: a view of Hemsdorf with the Prussian infantry in full march towards the attack on Gruningen.

it must be admitted that I had in effect flung away two whole cavalry regiments to no purpose at all, and there was more to come. Already, on the other flank, the Prussian infantry were pressing against Gruningen, in front of which, on move 7, Picardy infantry, having made a normal 6″ move in line and being unable to fire, suffered a first volley from a line of enemy infantry, the Livgarden Regiment, which had made only a 4″ move. Another mistake, this—it certainly was not a day when the Von Tarlenheim star shone with any brightness. Picardy was at once withdrawn into the village, whose houses it filled and prepared to defend, while Normandy Infantry came up through the woods to the east, in which area another threat was developing. At the same time Bulkeley Infantry was moved closer to Gruningen.

Before this, however, it had been seen that with six Prussian infantry regiments plus two grenadier units in support in full march for Gruningen, it was imperative to get reinforcements there. Accordingly, the heavy cavalry brigade composed of Les Mousquetaires and La Gendarmerie du Roi had by move 6, or just before the light cavalry débâcle, been started off towards the left to support the infantry about the village under assault. The Grenadiers de France were also moved in this direction where, by move 10, frequent, indeed almost continuous exchanges of musketry were taking place. In these, Picardy Infantry, ensconced in the houses of Gruningen, was taking heavy toll of the enemy to such an extent that, on move 11, Livgarden Infantry was so reduced that it required a morale throw. To the general satisfaction of the Picardy men, this was bad, so back the enemy had to go, although there was, unfortunately, more than enough enemy foot to take their place.

A little earlier, on move 8, all the Prussian guns, in addition to those involved with the light cavalry, had come into battery position and had opened fire, bringing a prodigious amount of roundshot to bear on the Austrian field guns south-west of Gruningen. By move 10, one of the latter had been reduced to firing on alternate moves (as the total of hits built up) and the succeeding move saw it completely out of action, a sad event due to the concentration of fire and partly to some exasperatingly good dice-throwing by Von Grunt's Chief of Staff. The one field gun remaining to the Austrians kept firing away at the flank of the Prussian infantry attacking Gruningen, as did the howitzer, which had been sited in a position which afforded immunity from the Prussian guns. It will be remembered the Prussians had no howitzers.

The fighting round Gruningen was now becoming quite desperate (what Marbot would have called 'un combat acharné') with the Prussians assailing the houses and striving to force a passage round the east side of the village. The arrival of the Austrian cavalry reinforcements came not a moment too soon. It had also been deemed necessary to bring the Irish regiments up to Gruningen and the Grenadiers de France had also been drawn thither. It was on move 13 when, with Normandy locked in a fierce mêlée with Oldenburg Infantry about the eastern end of the village, the Mousquetaires, coming round the north side, charged home and flung back Oldenburg with crippling losses, at only slight cost to themselves. Simultaneously, on the other side of Gruningen, the Gendarmerie du Roi charged the Löwenstein-Oels Grenadiers, but this operation was not so successful as that of the Mousquetaires, the volleys of the grenadiers (12 groups of 4 instead of 8 of 6) taking a heavy toll of the advancing cavalry, and in this and the subsequent mêlée, the Gendarmerie regiment was pretty well destroyed, while the grenadiers remained in fighting condition, having lost only 11 men to the 17 of the cavalry (most of these having fallen to musketry during the charge). True enough, to the musketry of the grenadiers, which included a first volley as well, had been added fire from supporting infantry, but even so, the Gendarmerie had been well and truly put out of action, and the situation about Gruningen was growing increasingly serious. At this point, move 13, the state of the battle, which can be seen in map 3, showed a definite disparity in the losses suffered by the two sides. Although not tremendous, the advantage was certainly with the

Mollwitz: the Prussian attack about to be launched against Gruningen, where the Picardy and Normandy Infantry are hastening to take up their positions.

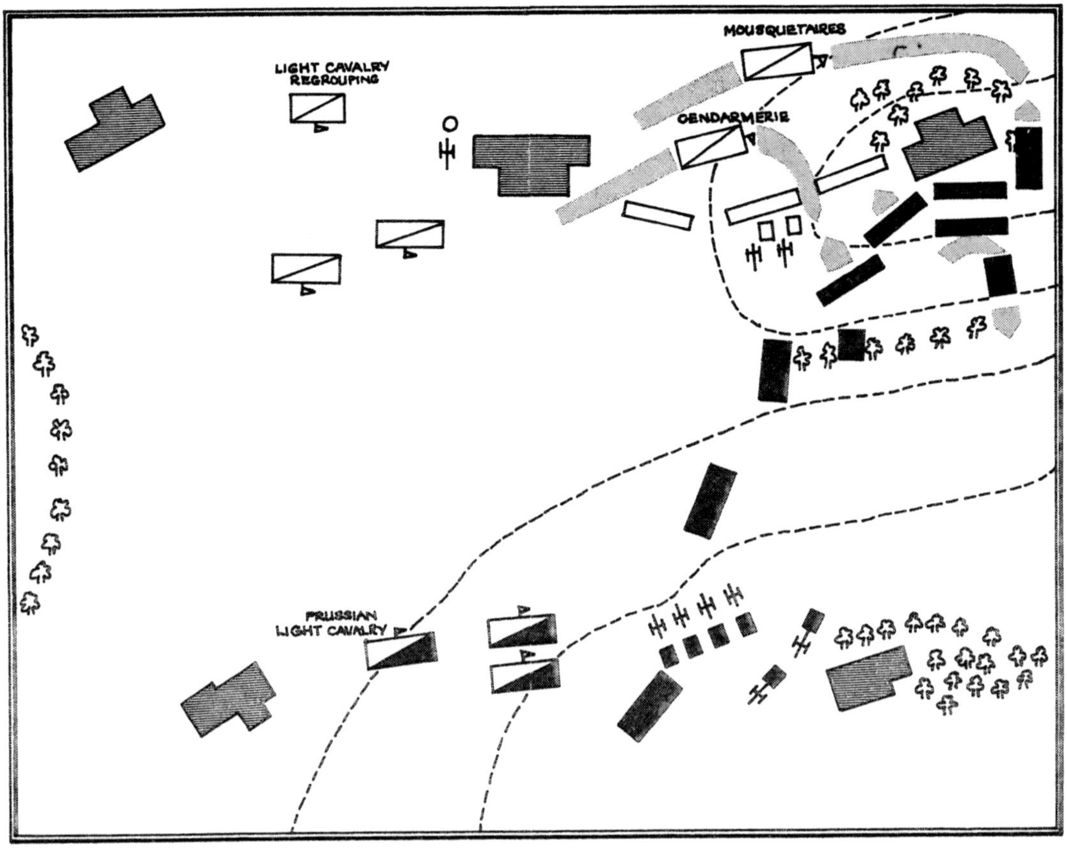

Mollwitz, map 3: the position after move 13, with place names omitted for clarity.

Prussians, the losses at this stage being actually as follows:

Prussians	Infantry	116
	Cavalry	1
Austrians	Infantry	104
	Cavalry	56

One Austrian gun had also been destroyed, and quite obviously the overall picture, especially that part relating to cavalry casualties, was something to afford considerable satisfaction to the Prussian commanders. The latter, with their great superiority in foot, were very much better off as a result of the fighting so far, while the loss of so many cavalrymen, plus a gun, was a problem to tax the Austrian commander most severely.

Indeed, it was evident here that the Prussians did in fact feel that the battle was going well for them, for a red and inflamed visage, bisected laterally by enormous moustaches and crowned by a tricorne heavily laced with gold, could be seen peering from the fringe of trees surrounding Hemsdorf. This belonged without a doubt to the egregious Von Grunt who, up to this moment it appears, had been sampling the strong liquors purveyed at a hostelry in the town (the 'Elector's Head') and whose spirits were now sufficiently fortified to cause him to view what was happening about him.

In fact the destruction of the first Austrian gun was followed by another calamity, the loss of the second, which, subjected to concentrated fire from the massed Prussian artillery, was destroyed on move 15.

About half of Gruningen was now in Prussian hands, although this success had been dearly bought (it has already been made clear how difficult it is to assault defended houses). The Royal Ecossais still garrisoned Mollwitz, but only one regiment was available to cover the area between this town and Gruningen. This was Navarre, behind which the remains of various regiments, both horse and foot, were busily regrouping. (In an individual battle such as this, such reorganisation is permitted.)

Faced with all this, the Austrian commander had reluctantly to admit that the situation was irretrievable and that the only course open to him was to save the remains of his army by a general withdrawal. This was decided upon forthwith, the Royal Ecossais infantry, covered by the remaining cavalry, the Cuirassiers du Roi and the Bourbon regiment, was to hold Mollwitz during the retreat. However, the cavalry was not left long in idleness, the Cuirassiers being fiercely attacked by the Prussian horse, Von Ruesch Hussars and Ahlefeldt Kürassiere. Although suffering almost 50% losses, the Cuirassiers most gallantly drove off both enemy units, and thereafter the Prussian troopers maintained only a discreet watching brief.

Although the remaining shreds of Picardy and Normandy had to be abandoned in Gruningen, there to hold up the Prussian infantry, the rest of the Austrian army was able to make an orderly withdrawal, Navarre and Royal Ecossais continuing to show a bold front. The howitzer continued in action until the last moment before it limbered up and made off. It took the enemy some time to pull himself together and follow up and on move 20 the situation was as shown in map 4 (overleaf).

Only a few more moves and it was all over, the Austrian army quitting the field (ie marching right off the table) and the Prussians, following historical precedent, being too knocked about to give effective chase. It had been a very hardly fought battle, casualties on both sides being heavy. They were as follows:

Austrians	Infantry	216	
	Cavalry	87	
	Gunners	1	(plus 2 guns destroyed)
Prussians	Infantry	180	
	Cavalry	19	
	Gunners	4	

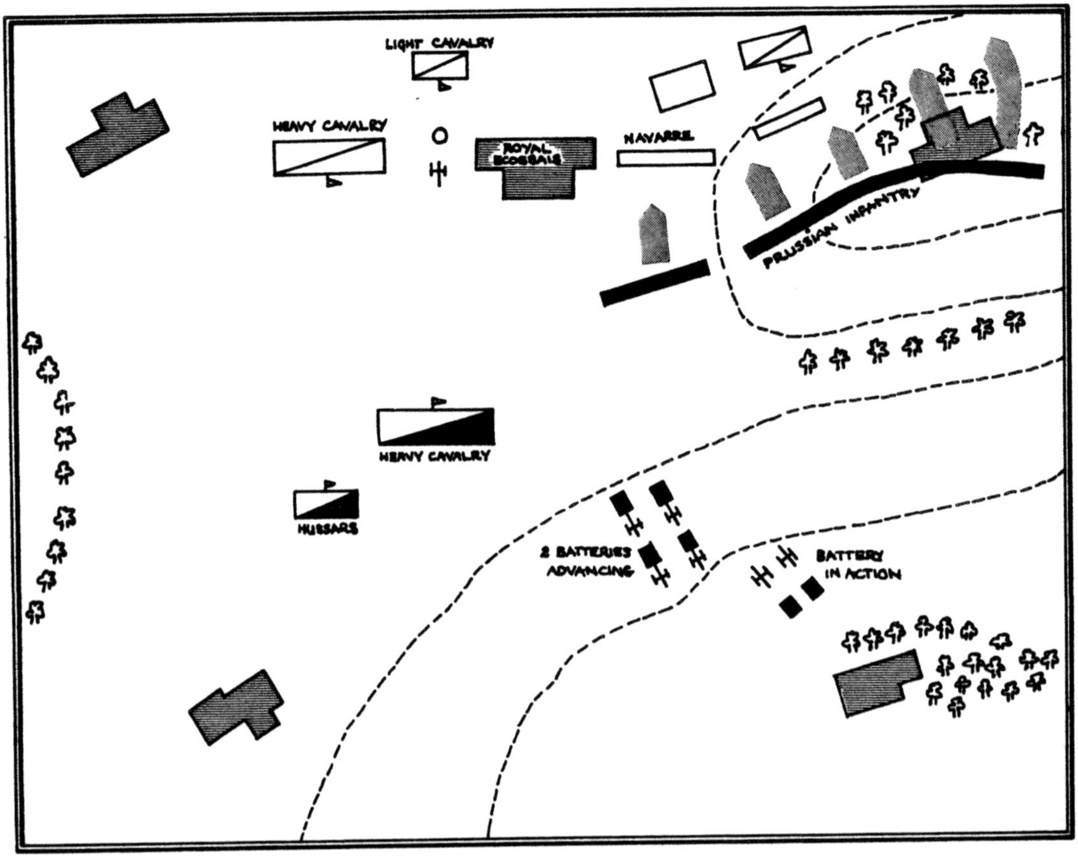

Mollwitz, map 4: the position after move 20, with place names omitted for clarity.

This has been a purposely brief account of a long and most exciting battle and I have given only the gist of what took place. The fighting about Gruningen, for instance, was complicated as well as hectic, but it would be tedious to expose the reader to a blow-by-blow account of the numerous firefights, the charges in the streets and the to-and-fro swing of the fighting in the houses. What has been given is a general picture of the main events.

XIX
Afterthoughts on Mollwitz

Now that we have described what, by normal wargaming standards, might be considered to be a 'big' battle, some profit might be gained from a discussion of certain points which might require clarification and from a description of some of the mechanical details involved in the playing of such a game.

First of all, while I hope I was able, in the narrative of the encounter, to give some idea of the tension and excitement which were produced during the fighting of Mollwitz, it might be useful to enlarge a little on some of its more mundane features, such as how long the battle lasted, and how, although a considerable number of miniature figures had to be moved during the course of each game move, the action was such that time did not drag in the least. On the subject of time, the battle of Mollwitz was actually fought over a weekend, midday Saturday to early afternoon on the Sunday to be exact, and in actual playing time it occupied from start to finish just under eight hours. In all fairness it should be pointed out that the troops had already been set out in their initial position (*vide* the map in Chapter XVII) when the generals, or three of them at least, first set eyes on the battlefield. Fighting, naturally enough, was not continuous, the necessary breaks being made for food, drink and similar necessities. Round about eight hours must be considered to be pretty good going when one thinks that the troops are not on multiple stands, but are all moved about individually. This leads us to the first point, a practical one which, like so many others, the player will have to decide on for himself.

This is the question of whether, for the sake of speed and convenience, the wargamer is to mount a group of maybe three or four figures of the same unit on some kind of common base, the idea being to cut down the fifty or so individual actions required in moving a regiment of infantry to about a dozen or fifteen, depending on the size of the groups mounted on each common base. It should be noted that a number of figures would have to be left as singles, to enable odd numbers of casualties to be removed when necessary. This system is a perfectly valid one to which, generally speaking, no great objection can be raised. Indeed it is very suitable when the wargame rules in use are of the type which entails the making of decisions on a group basis. By this I mean, if I might offer an example, the case of an infantry regiment's colliding with another, and the method whereby the conflict is decided. If the issue is decided by a single dice throw by each player, multiplied perhaps by the number of heads involved on the two sides, due allowance being made for charge impetus, or for the type of troops involved, élite or otherwise, with the winner being the player whose comparison total is the greater, then this multiple stand system works well. Assessment of casualties is included in the original throw if desired, or can be decided by a second dice throw. However, when one's rules are not of the type allowing for this formula result, each single combat being decided on a man-to-man basis, and where an effort is made to duplicate the unholy turmoil and confusion of such a fight (we are still considering the mêlée) then the system suffers from a considerable degree of inflexibility. As I have tried to show, in a hand-to-hand combat the neatly dressed lines rapidly break up and the mêlée becomes a completely mixed-up affair. It is much easier to simulate this and to obtain a truer result with single figures than by the use of groups of three or four men, as the case may be, where one tends to have two precisely arrayed lines staring each other in the face for a couple of moves or so, with occasional casualties being removed as the fighting goes on and the dice are rolled, until numbers or lack of morale tell and one side or the other has to give up and retreat.

The practice of mounting troops on multiple stands also encounters difficulties when the defence of buildings is considered. It will be found difficult to place such groups in the type of house we have described, and much the same applies when they are passing through woods, where formation has to be broken and the men have to get about with some little distance between the individual soldiers. There are times, naturally, with units advancing over a flat surface (this will usually occur in the early stages of a game) when it might be an advantage to have the figure placed, not actually stuck, on some sort of moving tray. This could be done by using a sheet of thin card, of the same dimension as the area occupied by the unit. If a small handle or 'lug' projects from one side of the card to assist in pushing or pulling it, it can be moved along until the regiment on it has to change formation or deploy, in which case the troops are taken off the stand which is then discarded. On a purely irrational principle of aesthetics, I prefer not to use such a device, but can appreciate that when time is limited and a decision has to be reached, speed is essential and these little trays become a regrettable necessity.

In the case of Mollwitz with, for the greater part of the time, two players on each side to move the troops, this part of the operation did not appear to be over-tedious and a high level of interest was maintained throughout the battle. One factor which probably did facilitate the movement part of the game was that the troops were plastic and not of metal. It will be found that it is much easier to move the former: one can take liberties with plastic figures impossible with their leaden brethren, which are usually more detailed and certainly more expensive, particularly in the 30mm size. If a couple of 'plastics' happen to collide through the player's haste or clumsiness no harm is done, but with metal models on the other hand, paint is liable to flake off and small details break if they are involved in such an accident.

Another point which may arise in connection with the mechanics of the war game is the order in which the contending players move their forces. The question is whether both players should move simultaneously, or whether the move should be alternate, ie when one player moves all his troops, or all he wishes to move, and then is followed by his enemy, who does the same. This is followed by combat, firing, mêlée or whatever it might be. The problem is one to be solved by local or individual preference. Some wargamers choose the alternate move method, deciding upon which player moves first by some arbitrary means, the roll of dice or the draw of a card. This system has one obvious disadvantage, in that the player who moves first at once gives his opponent prior knowledge of what his intentions might be, and an enormous advantage when it comes to carrying out his own move. The system, it would seem, also tends to slow down a game in that the moving part takes twice as long, and furthermore, it causes the player who wins the choice of move order (should this be the result of a dice throw) to opt to take second place in the move order; it seems to create a defensive sort of attitude, I feel. The disadvantages of this method of moving are very apparent and no amount of juggling can obviate the anomaly. Thus it would seem that the simultaneous move is the answer, but this is itself rather imperfect without certain elementary safeguards. On the one hand, if a player moves his troops more quickly than his opponent, simply because he is nimble-fingered, his forces will be in position before those of his slower enemy, giving the latter considerable advantage. Although such behaviour is rare, it is not unknown for players to be deliberately slow in their moves with the fell intent of obtaining some slight benefit: in the heat of action even the most honest of wargamers tend to develop an immunity to scruples or to qualms of conscience! Or indeed, one might unashamedly ask 'What is that regiment going to do? If it does so-and-so, then I'll do this and that.' This is unreal, not to say unfair, and is a situation which can only be coped with by written orders.

In this system, each of the players writes down briefly but clearly just what each of his units is to do on the following move, or for a number of moves, if an extension of the one move idea is required. This eliminates any ambiguity or argument, for your Knyphausen Grenadiers, during the move for which orders have been written, must, if they have been instructed to do so, advance 6″ without firing. This despite the fact that, when you look again, your opponent has cleverly moved a regiment of cavalry on to your flank and on the next move will be able to roll up your line with a tremendous charge.

In a big game with a considerable number of units participating, it is as well to be equipped with some prepared order sheets with regimental titles already entered, which can quickly be filled out with the relevant orders, thus saving a great deal of time. Naturally, this can be done only with such an engagement as Mollwitz, where considerable preparatory work was done in laying down the regiments engaged. In these enlightened days it is even possible to purchase pads of printed order forms, with spaces for different moves, types of formation adopted, and so on.

Actual orders need not be other than brief, certain conventions readily coming to mind: SF for Stand Fast, F for Fire, Adv for Advance, and so on and so forth. The direction of a certain movement can be indicated with reference to the points of the compass, or by drawing a directional arrow in the space provided on the order sheet. In regard to artillery, an indication would have to be made when firing was taking place, and very important, the ammunition being used, roundshot or canister. To give an example of what an order sheet can look like, one from the Battle of Mollwitz is reproduced, a document of rare historic value, I don't doubt. Directions are seen to be simple and unequivocal, which are important points if an umpire is in charge of the game and decides whether certain orders cannot be carried out because of lack of precision.

An order sheet from the Battle of Mollwitz

Austrian Army Move No. 10

Unit	Orders
Grenadiers de France	Deploy into close order for firing (2 deep)
Picardy Infantry	SF Fire
Normandy Inf.	1st 18 men charge straight ahead Remainder adv 6″ in support
Bulkeley Inf.	SF
Dillon Inf.	SF
Royal Ecossais Inf.	SF
Navarre Inf.	Adv 7½″ in col south-east
Gendarmerie du Roi	Adv 9″ to psn in rear of Gren de France
Mousquetaires	Move 9″ due east
Cuirassiers du Roi	SF (5)
Bourbon Cavalerie	SF (5)
Chasseurs de Fischer	Adv 12″ north
Lanciers de Saxe	Adv 12″ north
La Fere Battery	Fire RS
Howitzer	Fire Shell

N.B. The figures after two of the cavalry regiments indicate the number of 12″ battle moves they have accumulated.

Behind all the above is the aim to make the conditions in which the generals guide the course of the battle as realistic as possible, and with this in mind we might examine the number of troops in action at Mollwitz. This should afford some indication of the magnitude of the affair.

Taking the Prussians first, and referring to the unit strengths we dealt with in Chapter XIII wherein, in our wisdom, we decided that what we called a regiment of infantry, 5 officers and 48 men, was equivalent to a battalion of some 600 men, and that a cavalry regiment could be likened to a squadron of approximately 105 troopers, we find that they (the Prussians) fielded the equivalent of 6,000 foot and 315 horse. The Austrians, with seven infantry and six cavalry regiments, had 4,200 foot and 630 cavalry. The numbers engaged mean that our battle was really a fairly substantial engagement, and it took place in an area of 9 feet by 7 feet or, using our scale of 1″ to 10 yards, 1080 yards by 840 yards. From first to last, when the Austrians had completely left the table, the game occupied 23 moves, or by our time scale of one move to the minute, 23 minutes in all. Now, a battle involving something like 11,000 men, while not in the same league as the great encounters of the Seven Years War, with up to eighty or a hundred thousand men taking part, is not to be sneezed at and would hardly have been over in just over twenty minutes. Here we come to a sort of invisible time factor, one which has to be allowed for in considering the time of the war game move. What it amounts to is that the actual action depicted on the table, the movement of men, the firing and the mêlée, really occupies a minute in the time scale, but to this should be added a period during which command decisions are made and the time it takes to implement them. Taking this into account, the move might well be brought up to the equivalent of ten minutes, although this is purely speculative. One might say, if accepting this theory, that one move occupies ten minutes, nine for organisation and communication and one for actual physical action.

Another way of looking at this type of battle, the sort which endeavours to recreate an historic one and where the actual terrain has been reduced to the size of the war game table, is to take the area of ground occupied by the fighting in real life, and to compare it with the scale size of the table. In the case of Mollwitz, such a calculation demonstrated that 6″ on the war game table represented not the 60 yards of the normal scale distance but rather the equivalent of 420 yards. Therefore instead of the normal 6″ infantry move equalling 60 yards it did in fact represent 420 yards. Consequently the time occupied in traversing this distance was not a minute but seven and the move time was actually seven minutes. So the battle which consisted of 23 moves lasted 7 × 23 minutes, or an hour and 41 minutes. This is far more realistic as to time, but the idea falls down on the fact that not only has the relative move distance been increased, but so have all other measurements, making the 180 maximum musket range a prodigious 1260 yards! This rather puts paid to the idea and it is probably better to stick to the original one, where our ground scale is accurate, and we can assume that the action takes up about a tenth part of the overall time involved for the move.

Let us try to solve this problem in a more down-to-earth way and attempt to make the actual table time element a little more realistic. First of all, at the beginning of the engagement, the orders can be committed to paper not for just a single move but for a number of them, units being given specific tactical objectives. These orders would have to be carried out by a player irrespective of changing situations elsewhere on the table. Instructions contrary to the original ones would have to be carried between the army commander and the unit by a figure representing a courier travelling at the normal speed for the type he is (such a courier would almost invariably be a cavalryman of some sort). A situation report from the unit CO to his commander would also have to be communicated in this way and sufficient time would have to be allocated for the appreciation of the missive and the writing of new orders etc.

This would seem to be the most effective solution to the problem and it would tend to reduce the unrealistic effect of the instant view of the entire battlefield enjoyed by the wargamer in contrast to his real-life counterpart, whose knowledge of what was happening out of sight was dependent upon the information received from his subordinates. In any case, when orders for a number of war games moves have been written down, it is essential that an umpire of weight and authority should be in charge, to ensure that there is a strict adherence to the letter of the written orders, and that the correct allowance be made for either the time for an actual figure representing the courier to get from *A* to *B* and back to *A* with a change of orders, or the simple calculation of the number of moves required for the double journey, not forgetting the time it takes for the assimilation of the contents of the dispatch and the writing of fresh instructions. If an umpire is not available, or indeed if the whole process appears too complicated, one can forget it, and carry on with the single move orders as was done with conspicuous success at Mollwitz. After all, if occasionally one player is able to take steps to foil an enemy move more quickly than he would have been able to do in an actual battle with the expected time lag, then his opponent before long will certainly get a similar opportunity and the two will tend to cancel each other out. This is not a tremendously scientific approach, but experience shows that this is so.

The estimation of a war game, however, will depend in the final analysis upon just what the feelings of the players might be when it is over, apart from those of despair or self-satisfaction. If there have been no tactical anomalies, if nothing has occurred outside the context of military probability, and in fact if the feel of having directed a battle is present, then success has without doubt been achieved.

XX
The Construction of Terrain

In neither of the engagements already described did terrain have any very appreciable effect on the course of the fighting, both encounters taking place conveniently, as it happened, on practically flat ground. This indeed was not an unusual thing in eighteenth-century warfare, as the complicated process of drawing up an army in battle order was far more easily carried out on a flat stretch of ground rather than on one which was irregular or broken by hills, woods or streams. This is not to say that a great many actions did not take place on rough or uneven ground, and indeed in many cases some topographical feature was of the greatest importance during the action and often played a vital rôle therein. The ridge at Rossbach which concealed the Prussian cavalry, the marshy course of the River Nebel at Blenheim, and the Wood of Barry which, together with the Arquebussiers de Grassin, protected the left flank of the French at Fontenoy; all these come to mind in this connection. As these features influenced the course of the actual battles, so must we make rules which allow them to have a similar effect, in a practical and realistic way, on the war game table.

Probably it might be as well to start with a consideration of hilly or rising ground, and our first aim will be to deal with its material representation before going on to consider its tactical effect, and this will apply to all the terrain features we are going to discuss; a few descriptive hints on their actual construction followed by the rules relating to them.

First, then, let us take the question of hills, from the point of view of the player who tends to favour the 'dioramic' treatment, for so it might be termed. He will wish his hills to be as realistic and attractive as possible, and if his wish is granted, he will certainly have a war game terrain which will have a most splendid appearance, comparable to the scenic layout of any model railway, although it will have certain functional disadvantages. Nevertheless, let us suppose that this is what is wanted. It will quickly be found that the making of such terrain pieces is by no means a difficult task. To begin with, it is supposed that different sizes of hills will be required, that is hills covering different ground areas, so the bases for these will be of different sizes. Briefly, one sets about the job thus: the first requirement is a sheet of hardboard, a square being suitable, or any rectangle for that matter; the idea of having straight sides is that they can be easily placed together to make a continuous stretch of hilly country. To the hardboard are glued odd blocks of wood of various heights, then numerous strips about a couple of inches wide are cut from ordinary newspaper and thoroughly soaked in office glue. These strips are then draped across the hardboard, beginning at one side, carrying the strip over one or more of the wooden blocks and finishing at the other side. This is done with as many glued strips as possible, all criss-crossing in different directions, until the whole affair is completely covered, and you are left with something like the shape of the desired hill. In section, it might be rather like the example shown in the diagram.

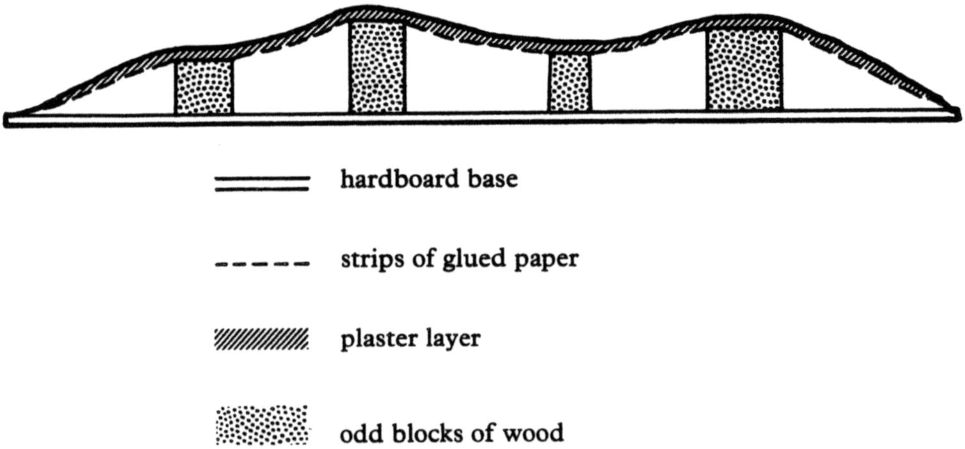

Section of a home-made plaster hill.

A point to be noted is that it is as well to let the strips sag a little between the edge of the hardboard and the first wooden block when sticking them, as during the process of drying there is a tendency for the paper to contract and one might find the edges of the hill being pulled up rather disconcertingly. Once they are dry, however, the resulting shape is quite firm, but not really strong enough for the purpose in mind, something stouter being required to take the weight of numbers of miniature soldiers, especially if they are of metal, so it is used as a base for additional reinforcement. A layer of plaster of Paris or of one of the proprietary brands of cellulose 'fillers' on the market is spread over the paper shape in a continuous layer up to a depth of about an eighth or a quarter of an inch, bearing in mind that it does represent a hill and the surface can be as smooth or rough as the player wishes, depending upon what he had in mind. I shan't, by the way, go into the technicalities of preparing the plaster, since they can be easily learned if not already known. When the whole contraption is dry it forms a pretty tough surface which will stand up to a fair amount of wear and tear, although it needs reasonably careful handling, and inevitably tiny fragments will quickly begin to flake off. They always seem to make their way on to the floor, to be trodden into carpets, to the justifiable wrath of the housewife.

There is an even easier way of preparing such hills as I have described, and this is by purchasing ready-prepared plaster-impregnated bandage (it can be obtained in strips or squares), which after being treated with water can be applied direct to the wooden blocks without the necessity of building up the shape with the glued paper strips. Even so, I feel I should like to have a few strips in place to provide the initial skeleton for the hill. It would make it sturdier as well. Anyway, once constructed, the hill can be coloured to taste and ornamented, if desired, with lichen bushes, granite chips to represent rocks etc, and in fact considerable artistry can be lavished upon it—it's up to the wargamer.

So far so good, and certainly when made and painted with a little care, a few of these hills will give quite a colourful appearance to any battlefield, but it is fair if we consider their drawbacks. From my own experience I know that they do exist. When one is making such terrain pieces there is a tremendous compulsion towards creating the most dramatic type of scenery, precipitous and awesome crags and so forth. I recall creating such a piece, a peak which soared something like 18″ from table level, the whole complex including a subsidiary pinnacle only slightly less than the first in height, with a pass between them and a road winding down the lower slopes of the larger hill. It looked absolutely splendid. The trouble was, of course, that when it was employed in a war game the players seemed to feel it was a pity not to use it if at all possible, and it became the focal point of some quite extraordinary and irrational fighting, the most terrible battles being waged for no good tactical reason up and down the pass itself and around the slopes. On the latter the inclines were so steep that the troops simply could not stand on their bases, having to be moved about in a highly unsatisfactory recumbent position, and this is by way of being the main disadvantage of this type of terrain. To show any sort of gradient at all, the slope must be such in our ground scale that troops even with fairly wide bases (and above all metal ones which are appreciably more top heavy than their plastic fellows) so easily topple over, usually bowling over the next in rank until the whole regiment ends up in an ignominious heap at the foot of the hill up which they have been so bravely advancing. Within the confines of the war game table it must be accepted that it is more than a little difficult to reproduce at once the appearance and functional qualities of a hill by the method just described.

One has to abandon, then, with possible regret, the spectacular in favour of the more mundane method of using some sort of contour to indicate rising or hilly ground, and this, in fact, is the method I make bold to recommend, justifying myself on the ground that it has been well tried on numerous battlefields and has always provided the tactical realism required. This I hold to be the prime necessity. All that is needed in fact is a sheet of 1″ thick insulation board or blockboard; I prefer the former as it is lighter. From the sheet can be sawn as many irregularly shaped pieces as desired, some large, some small, all can be used. They are placed as desired on the war game table whereon they perform exactly the same function as contours on a map.

Used as such they have an additional advantage. The individually-made, scenic-type wood and plaster hill is complete in itself, and there is little that can be done about altering its shape or height, so that if a number of battles are fought, or more particularly, if a campaign is in progress with successive engagements requiring frequent changes of terrain, then each new hill will have to have its table counterpart to represent it. With insulation board contours the answer is easy.

The contours can be juggled about, placed end to end and so on, and as to height, the same applies as in the case of the contours of a map: one shape is placed on top of a larger one and there you have a hill twice as high as that of a single thickness. Not only that, but the steepness of a hill can be determined by the closeness of the contours—as on a map. If the contours are close together, the indication is that the slope is steep, and if the edges of two contours coincide, giving a height of 2″ (if 1″ board is used, of course), it can be assumed that the slope is so steep as to be unclimbable. We shall discuss the rules governing this and allied questions a little later. Nor do I think that the contours themselves need be wholly inartistic. For example, instead of making the edges perfectly vertical, one can shape them a little with a sharp knife, giving them some irregularity, or at least the suggestion of a gradient, and when painted (a quick coat of basic green works wonders) they can look not at all bad, again if trees or shrubs are strewn here and there. In the photograph it can be

Showing the use of inch-thick blocks to represent contours, each indicating a height of 50 feet. The summit is crowned by a patrol from the Lanciers de Saxe. The trees are the commercial type referred to in the text.

seen that one can have a fairly realistic appearance which, combined with other features, is not unattractive, even to the most dioramically minded wargamer.

One final word on the subject of hills is that yet another sort of material can be used, as indeed it can for general terrain as well. This is the stuff used for making ceiling tiles, expanded polystyrene, which can be obtained in slabs of varying thickness. These slabs can be carved into all sorts of shapes, shallow valleys, watercourses and so on, and can be naturally coloured. The material is not cheap, however, and again when in constant use it tends to crumble, and does not have the lasting properties of the insulation board, which I prefer for this reason.

In passing, by the way, I should really point out that although my remarks on terrain apply fairly generally to all periods of wargaming, they do so in particular to those set in the eighteenth century. For more recent times, where cover is used to a far greater extent than in the era we are thinking of, the wargamer might well find that some other type of terrain would be more suitable, possibly that made from polystyrene slabs with which very close country could be represented, giving greater and more realistic scope for the modern tactics of infiltration, concealed approach, hidden anti-tank guns and so on. In our period, however, with masses of troops being moved about in orderly ranks with the emphasis on precision and accuracy of movement, then practice demonstrates most certainly that the contour system works exceedingly well from the point of view of war game mechanics and, as we shall show, from that of ensuring the tactical accuracy of the rules relating to it.

The next feature we have to reproduce, and very important from the tactical angle, are rivers and streams. In thus differentiating between the two I deliberately put them in these two simple categories: one large, the river, and one small, the stream, because the respective effects on war game tactics are materially different. One will, for instance, hold up the passage of any army for a longer period than the other, will take longer to bridge, and will be more difficult to ford. Once we have got to making the streams and rivers we can determine the interesting and vital statistics concerning them, but first a look at the material preparation of the features themselves. I am not going to devote much time to the home-made variety because the commercially produced article is so good and may be purchased so cheaply that it is a waste of time to make them oneself. However, the dyed-in-the-wool do-it-yourself man can, if he desires, prepare river sections from lengths of hardboard about 9″ in width. Having decided on the size of the stream, he paints its course on the hardboard in blue, green and white, lavishly mixed with thinner to a good, runny, consistency. When this has dried, on the painted river can be glued transparent cellophane, previously crinkled to give the appearance of waves or ripples, which makes it more realistic. The same method can be used to create small lakes or ponds. The river banks can be built up either with strips of hardboard glued to the base, or with the ubiquitous plaster of Paris. The latter gives a more natural appearance but it does have the disadvantage of easily coming loose from the base board, although it can

Commercially produced terrain. River sections, walls, trees and a bridge with the Royal Ecossais Infantry about to cross the last named.

be glued back in place should its own bond be insufficient. However, if the reader examines the photograph showing an infantry regiment making its way along a river bank and over a bridge, he will see that the commercially produced article has a highly satisfactory appearance. It is the stream which is depicted, the river being wider. The banks are painted in natural colours, and one can establish certain conventions, for example to suggest the existence of a ford. This can be shown by an expanse of muddy brown to indicate the point at which horses and vehicles approach and enter the river to make a crossing. When one fights an engagement over a river or where a river has an important bearing on the battle, it is of the greatest importance to know just where any fords are to be found.

This is as much as we need say concerning rivers in the present context, and this leaves but one feature to discuss, namely woods. Again these can be made by the wargamer, or as in the case of the river sections, they can be purchased easily. In the first instance, to make a tree is simple, albeit a pretty messy business, and it is carried out thus. Four or five lengths of wire, say about 5″ long or thereabouts, are twisted together for about half their length, leaving $\frac{1}{2}$″ free at one end and about 3″ at the other. The short ends are splayed out flat to provide the 'roots' and the others irregularly, these being the branches. The central part, the section twisted together, is covered with plastic wood, as are the branches, and when this has dried and hardened, the foliage is applied. This consists of odd pieces of rubber sponge roughly shaped in a representation of clumps of leaves, soaked in liquid glue and stuck on the branches as appropriate. Best of all, the branch can be poked through the piece of sponge. The tree is fixed to a base, a small square of plywood, by covering the roots with plastic wood, which is smoothed down to the base itself. I would advise against covering a square of plywood with a number of trees set close together, no matter how good the finished product looks, as it will be found more convenient for the trees to be arranged in rows—three or four, or even more, as illustrated. To organise a wood is easy, by simply arranging a number of tree rows to form its circumference and popping one or two individual trees into the middle. It is not a good idea completely to fill the area, because it will be found to be the devil's own job to move troops therein; it is better to leave room to handle one's soldiers without getting one's fingers tangled up with branches, and rules for dispersion can be just as easily applied without the need to fiddle one's way through a heap of overturned trees.

With the commercially produced article the same applies: the wood is again represented by a ring of trees of the shape desired, while a small copse can be shown by about three or four individuals arranged together. Trees can be obtained in various sizes and species, three of the most popular being the alder, seen in the photograph, the poplar, and the fir. These are of soft plastic and as such can be knocked about with impunity. Take care though, because if not attached to a small base, they can bounce along merrily and cause considerable havoc to one's carefully set out regiments.

Now it remains to show how the rules ensure that the presence of these terrain features is catered for in the war game.

XXI
The Effect of Terrain

Inevitably some degree of standardisation will be found necessary in drawing up rules to cater for the effect on war game tactics of the various terrain features whose construction has just been discussed. If we take the first, the hill, it is apparent that within our terms of reference, it is not possible to make a rule to cope with every sort of gradient or slope, at least as far as laying down a single rule is concerned, and something of a general nature has to be adopted, although it can be used as a basis for more detailed rules. Hills come in all sorts of shapes and sizes, ranging from the completely unsurmountable, particularly to men in line or in column, to the gentle incline which one's troops can ascend with barely a perceptible quickening of pulse or breathing rate. The latter can be discounted for the moment, and since there is no immediate point in postulating a rule to cover such an eventuality as infantry having to scale something like the Heights of Abraham, as Wolfe's men had to do prior to the Battle of Quebec, we have to opt for something in between (being fully aware that from the general rule, the particular case such as the Heights of Abraham thing can always be deduced or calculated). In considering then just what we shall make our hill, we shall assume it to be of a steepness which will not cause marching troops to break formation, but which will nevertheless be of a nature sufficient to make their upward progress appreciably slower than a similar movement on level ground.

It may be in order to point out that the following has been arrived at by a judicious combination of both theory as drawn from drill manuals and similar works and from a simple process of trial and error by myself. The picture of the writer flogging up and down various slopes with a stop watch is not far removed from the truth.

Since we have already decided that the best method of reproducing hills on the war game table is the use of 1″ thick insulation board contours, it is on this type that we shall base our deliberations. Generally speaking, the majority of British maps of the Ordnance Survey type use 50 foot contours, ie the difference in height between two adjacent contours is 50 feet; so let us say that one of our 1″ contour hills indicates a height of 50 feet above the level of the table, with two contour blocks, one on top of the other, obviously giving a hill of a hundred feet in height. To get the complete effect, this has to be considered in conjunction with the slope or gradient we referred to above, the one which will slow down marching troops to an appreciable extent. Again we have to adopt a standard from which, if wished, rates of ascent for slopes of different gradients can be calculated. What we do is to take the slope we have already briefly described which, while retarding the rate of movement of men in formation, is not sufficient to cause any breaking in the formation, although it should be noted that to the steepness of the hill as a factor to be considered in cutting down the speed of an ascending unit will be added the reduction due to the increased difficulty in maintaining formation and dressing. The experiments I have already spoken of show that a gradient of 1 in 10 is a suitable one for our purpose as it seems that it takes about twice the time to climb such a slope as it does to cover the same distance on the flat. I repeat that this is the result of my own somewhat exhausting personal experiments, but it will be found to be accurate, I believe.

Now, this means that during a war game, infantry in line will, if mounting such a slope, move only half the normal distance, or 3″ instead of the usual 6″. We have to express this in terms of our terrain and we can best do this by enacting that on the move wherein a contour is actually crossed, in an upward direction naturally, the move is reduced by half, of whatever arm and in whatever formation the troops might be. For example, infantry in column moving at the regulation 7½″ per move will have that reduced to 3¾″ when actually crossing the contour. Say, for instance, that the head of the column arrived on a certain move at a point 2″ from the contour, on the next move the leading rank will be placed 1¾″ beyond it. The penalty applies to the column as a whole, of course, not to every individual as he comes up or is moved forward. Diagram 1 (overleaf) shows a hill, or the contour as it is used on the war game table, together with what it actually represents; it will illustrate what the foregoing is all about.

Progress down the slope merits no penalty since it is insufficiently steep, but it does provide certain advantages in combat. Men charging down such a slope will clearly have an advantage provided by the acceleration imparted by the downward gradient. The rule resulting from this is a simple one. Troops charging an enemy down a slope, that is when the charge move takes them downwards across a contour edge, are given an impetus bonus for the contact move. This applies to infantry and cavalry alike and consists of the addition of 1 to the dice throw for every figure which has carried out the downward charge. This applies to the charge move only, the impetus being lost for subsequent mêlée moves.

A second and equally important tactical consideration concerning high ground is its effect on visibility, it being apparent that what is on the other side of the hill is beyond the ken of troops at ground level, and in view of the use of contour boards to represent such hills, we have to decide on how to work out a system to give our contour boards which, in effect, appear to be low plateaux, the tactical effect of what they represent. In actual fact a man, ie a figure, placed close to the contour would be concealed from a similar individual standing on the contour and a couple of inches

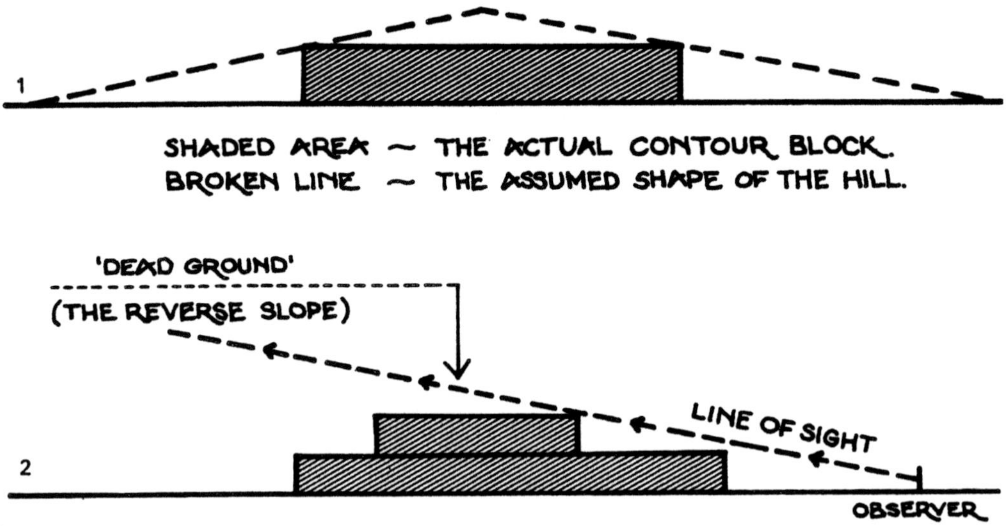

The effect of the contour block on visibility.

in from the edge. We ignore this, however, for our conception of what we are using rationalises this contour into a slope (one in ten, as we decided) and consequently, to a man at ground level, visibility extends all the way up the slope to the summit. It is when we are looking at something beyond the summit that it disappears from the view of us at ground level, down the reverse slope as it is called.

This is the tactical situation so dear to the heart of Wellington, whose ploy it was to garnish the crest of the hill with skirmishers and to deploy his forces on the other side, the reverse slope, so that their strength, disposition and composition could not be discerned by the enemy.

The thing is that we have to determine what constitutes the reverse slope in terms of our contours. This may be quite easily done by placing a second and smaller contour on top of the first, as in diagram 2, which illustrates what this is all about. The same will apply, even though no second contour be used. We can stipulate that, as in diagram 1, the contour represents a rounded eminence with a summit roughly in the centre. If our contour/hill be considered to have a round base, then its centre is the summit and can be marked as such with a blob of paint or some terrain feature such as a tree or bush, which we would accept as indicating the actual peak. Whatever then is on the side further from the observer at ground level, ie beyond the tree or other marker, is invisible and militarily, the observer will suffer from this fact.

Many of our hills, though, are going to be of irregular shape and will not have perfectly rounded bases, some being elongated into ridges. Again, if one contour be used, the length of the summit of the ridge can be shown by drawing a line on the contour, and beyond this troops in numbers may be concealed.

A few words may be in order concerning reverse slopes. Basically, they afford excellent protection to troops taking proper advantage of them. Attacking infantry advancing up the forward slope cannot fire their muskets with any effect, since they would be firing blindly into the air, with nothing in sight save the odd skirmisher. The same applies to field guns firing roundshot. Howitzers firing shells have the opportunity of using plunging fire and could indeed have the chance of doing some damage, the greater in proportion to the density of troops on the hidden slope, but this business of 'firing blind' is pretty much of a wasted effort unless it were known that a very considerable body of troops was in a position known from a previous report, and lavish supplies of ammunition were to hand. One could, it might be supposed, throw shells at random in the hope of panicking cavalry and artillery horses, but I feel that at this moment it is better to make the rule that troops on a reverse slope cannot be fired at, although if infantry advance up towards the crest and reach it, their new field of vision will take in the entire downward reverse slope. If the defending general decides to move his men forward to the summit to fire on the attackers he will naturally have revealed his position to them and will have to take whatever medicine is coming.

This would seem to have covered in general terms hills and their tactical effect, and we shall go on to treat woods in the same way. Pursuant to our policy of standardisation, we specify, not really surprisingly, that our 'wood' is an area of trees spaced fairly densely together. This is no sparse sort of copse we are dealing with, something offering little or no impediment to movement, but something sufficiently thick to inhibit the passage through it of men and vehicles.

First, we enact that cavalry, artillery and transport vehicles cannot negotiate a wood unless by way of specific roads or tracks therein. Infantry, on the other hand, may do so, although not in formation. To pass through a roadless, wooded area, formation has to be broken and line infantry will move as independent individuals. In addition, they must be at least 1″ apart to do so, thus reproducing their having to pick their way round trees, past clumps of undergrowth and so on. Not only would they be somewhat scattered, but because of the difficulty of the terrain, their progress would be slowed down considerably and for the normal 6″ move one of 4″ must be substituted.

We know of course that musketry from line infantry is effective only when the men are firing shoulder to shoulder. The chances that a number of isolated infantrymen, busily engaged in groping their way through a wood, would be able to co-ordinate their efforts and produce a reasonable volley would be remote, so it is ruled that line infantry have no fire power inside woods. However, they may line the edge of a wood and fire from this position of vantage, benefiting from the cover provided by the tree trunks.

For light infantry, however, things are very different. They are much in their element in woods and forests. Trained to operate individually and in the eighteenth century being mainly foresters, poachers, mountaineers and possibly bandits, the light infantryman (or jäger, depending on your army) can get about as easily in difficult country as he can in the open. So light infantry movement is not restricted within woods but remains at 7½″ as always. They must, however, continue to adhere to the dispersion rule for their arm, and operating as light infantry they must be 3″ apart.

Even so, the range of his fire would be reduced within woods, the density of the trees doing this, so his maximum range comes down to 9″, and when he fires, he requires a 5 or 6 dice throw to account for any individual within that range. No firing into the brown is possible, as even line infantry, as we have seen, are fairly scattered when passing through woods.

Should it happen, by the way, that opposing troops meet in hand-to-hand combat in woods, normal combat rules for the mêlée still apply.

Finally, there is the question of rivers, and this can be dealt with quite rapidly. At the moment we are not concerned with bridging operations, but rather with how troops can, if possible, cross a river where no bridge exists, that is by plunging in and fording it. If the war game in progress when the problem arises is a refight of an historical one, or is on terrain forming part of an actual map, the fords are possibly shown, and as the game progresses, crossings may be made at the actual points indicated. If the battle, on the other hand, is an ad hoc one, an encounter battle maybe on imaginary ground, then we have to decide on how crossings can be made in the absence of a bridge. We have to standardise yet again, and say that certain watercourses can be forded, some cannot. The simplest solution is to have two classes, thus: rivers, which cannot be forded by reason of depth, width or rapidity of current, and streams, that is the little chaps. These, we rule, can be forded by all troops, infantry, cavalry or artillery, although some might prefer that the last should be excluded, this being a matter of personal preference. The crossing can be made as the players decide, either anywhere along the stream or at previously designated points only. The time involved is important, as the fording operation will not take place at the same rate as troops cross dry ground. It has been found that infantry and cavalry are sufficiently handicapped if they take two complete moves to cross a stream, while artillery and wheeled transport, which would take appreciably longer, require four moves to make the crossing. After all, eighteenth-century guns, limbers and so on, were cumbersome things, hard enough to manoeuvre on firm ground, let alone whilst sliding about on the muddy bed of a stream.

XXII
The Use of Maps

Sooner or later there comes a time when the wargamer, at some crucial moment in the battle he is fighting, has to face a situation where he must make a quick decision as to what he is going to do—whether to take a chance and press on regardless with some course of action, while realising that what he is about to do is a pretty risky undertaking, one from which a general in real life would shrink as being far too uncertain a thing to contemplate. This 'It's only a game—let's have a go' sort of philosophy is not calculated to increase the realism and authentic quality of one's war game, but is almost inevitable in the sort of battle we have described, whether it be the small, quickly-organised skirmish or the reconstruction of some actual battle which has involved study and research. It is to be supposed that our main idea is to make the war game as realistic and correct both tactically and strategically as we can, so what we have to create then is some sort of background which will cause a general to think twice or even more often before committing his miniature armies to any manoeuvre which would, in the real thing be a patent improbability. In other words, some sort of political backdrop is necessary, so that a battle is not fought *in vacuo* but rather as part of a campaign, wherein its result would have an actual bearing on future strategy and events.

To organise properly, a campaign will require some little preparation. Many things are involved which we do not meet in an individual battle, and a certain amount of book-keeping becomes essential to keep track of troop movements, to note intelligence concerning enemy activity, to maintain parade states of units which have suffered in battle and so on. This additional work is well worth the trouble, and no wargamer who has taken part in any sort of campaign ever regrets the clerical work required. As to the nature of the campaign the choice is wide indeed: it can be between two small states, coalitions can be formed, territory seized or liberated according to the point of view, and certainly in the middle eighteenth century the wargamer can light upon more or less anything he fancies in the way of campaigns; they are of every type. Innumerable states were involved in the most complicated wars, but apart from this, a totally fictitious set of nations may be created, all at odds one with the other. This sort of fictional set-up I believe to be preferable, as one can decide exactly on the sort

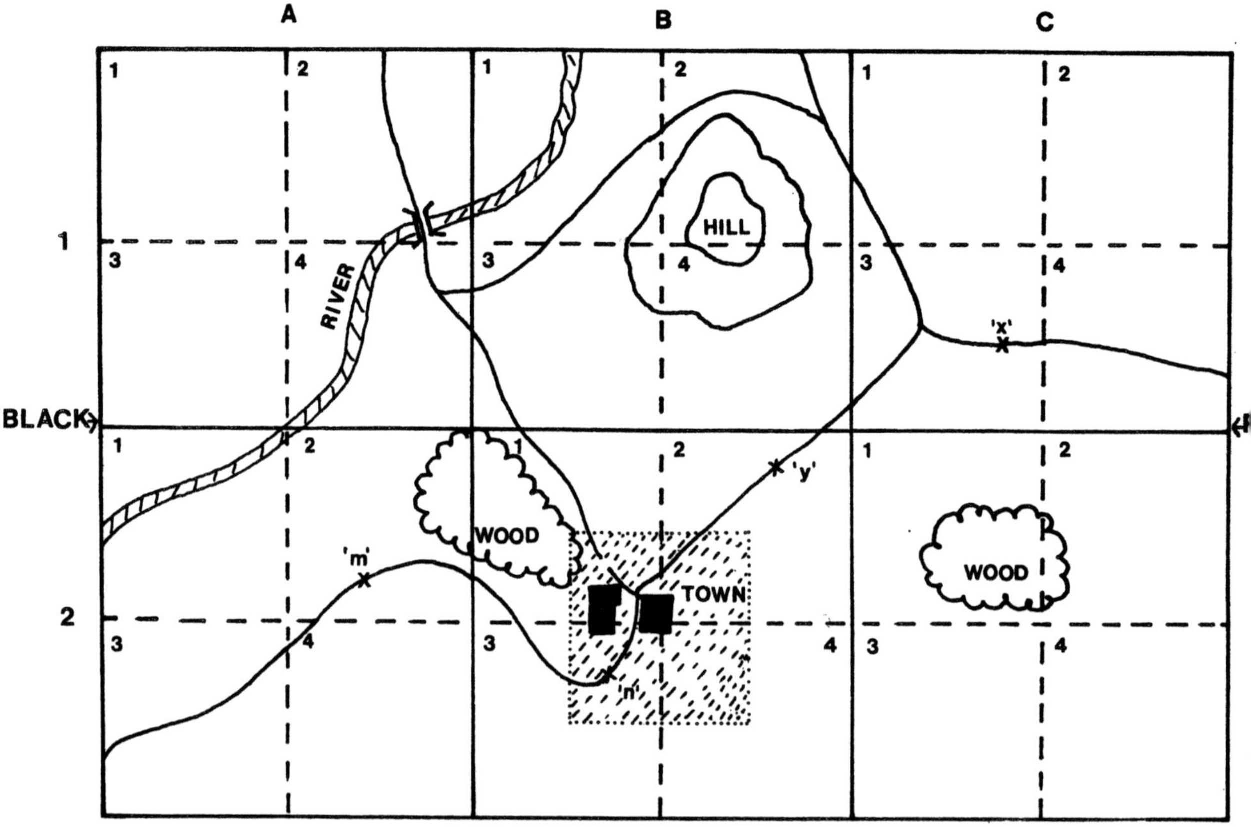

The elements of map-moving.

of campaign desired and can organise the political background to personal taste. There has to be another country, of course, to provide a frontier which can be violated, or possibly between the frontiers can be located a smaller and neutral area which can function as a battle ground as did the Low Countries during a great part of the eighteenth century. It is an easy matter for two wargamers to provide themselves with such a debatable land over which the planned campaign may take place.

This leads us on to what is the primary requirement, this being a map of the campaign territory. Now, suitable maps of countryside over which one can move troops to simulate warfare of the eighteenth century and of a suitable scale are hard to come by, the modern map being usually far too complicated for our period of war-gaming. After all, in the time with which we are concerned, good roads were few and far between, and the country was not built up to anything like its present extent, even in the most rural areas. The alternative to groping one's way through the complexities of a modern Ordnance Survey map, trying to ignore railways, overhead cables, motorways and so on, is to create one's own. This at first sight might seem to be a fairly formidable task, but this is really far from being the case. Just as we did in our study of the individual war game, in which we progressed from small action to major battle, we begin by drawing a small map, familiarise ourselves with the use of it in a war game, then proceed to something more ambitious, in which greater forces may be controlled. First then, a few words may be devoted to the way in which we use the map we have drawn, and principally, just how troops are moved on the said map before getting down to actual action.

In the same way as on the table, troops proceeding from point to point have a certain number of moves to cover a specific distance so, when using maps, the players have equivalent map moves, during which various sorts of units will cover certain distances according to the scale of the map. According to this scale the lengths of the moves may be calculated. At the moment we need not concern ourselves with the map scale, but can simply lay down a series of moves for different types of troops which, although correct relative to each other, can always be altered in proportion if the scale of the map requires it. The basic moves for the map we can deduce from the table moves for infantry, cavalry and so on which, quickly recapitulating, are: infantry 6″ (we shall use this rather than the 7½″ column move, since the route march was not normally carried out at this speed, allowance having to be made for periods of rest etc), heavy cavalry 9″, light cavalry 12″, and guns and transport as for infantry 6″. Without going into a lengthy discussion of how the map moves were calculated, experience shows that for the purposes of showing movement on maps, the various arms are most advantageously given the following moves: infantry 1″, heavy and light cavalry 1½″ and 2″ respectively, while artillery and transport move at the same rate as infantry, 1″ per move.

With these moves in mind we can set about showing how they are used with the map. Let us assume that we have decided to use a synthetic map, that is an imaginary one concocted by the players, and that two forces, in this case both of heavy cavalry, are moving towards each other in some previously unreconnoitred countryside. The diagram shows the area in question and it can be seen to be a pretty uncomplicated piece of terrain, but it will be enough for our purposes. As can be seen, there is a system of gridding, each of the larger squares within the continuous lines being easily identifiable, the top left square being A 1, for example. Each large square is sub-divided by a second grid line, the dotted one, into four smaller squares, or sub-squares for convenience, and in each case the four are numbered 1 to 4 in the manner shown (as long as the system of numbering the sub-squares is maintained, they do not have to be numbered on the actual map). Squares are used here for convenience, and certainly when one uses graph paper to make one's map the construction is rendered easier, but ideally each sub-square should represent the area of the war game table, although this is by no means obligatory. Most tables are rectangular rather than square anyway.

Let us follow then the movements of the two opposing generals, one advancing onto the map from the left or west side—he can be Black—and one from the right, or east, and he can be Red. For the purpose of the exercise let us postulate that each is feeling his way through a stretch of unknown country, using for the purpose as suggested above a body of heavy cavalry whose move on the map is, as we determined, 1½″. The sub-squares, by the way, are 1″ square.

As I have earlier propounded, simultaneous moves are preferable while fighting on the table, but on the map, alternate moves seem to work better, as it is just possible when moving simultaneously to get into situations which are not really feasible, through no one's fault I hasten to say. As I hope to show, alternate map moves are quite foolproof if carried out correctly and should provide the necessary realism, particularly in respect to the well-known phenomenon, the fog of war. Using alternate moves then, we proceed, and let us suppose that Red has first move. To carry this out he moves his scouting party of horse or dragoons the correct distance for the move, this being 1½″, from his starting point on the right hand side of the map where the road actually starts. By so doing, his party has reached point *x* on the road. Having done so, and this in the present circumstance being his complete move, he declares to the enemy his presence in square C1. Black is now provided with some information, not a lot, but sufficient to indicate enemy activity in a given area, although precisely where and in what strength are unknown at the moment.

Black's primary objective is now to see what his foe is up to, so he makes his own move, this of course being his part of the first game move; remember that although the move is alternate, the two are in theory simultaneous. Black's cavalry moves onto the map its normal distance, reaching point *m*, and to Red he announces that he is in square A2. Red is not immediately affected, although doubtless aware that this adversary is seeking him out, and he makes his second move, bringing his cavalry to *y*. To Black he gives his new position as B2. He omits C1, thus indicating that his force has passed through and that C1 is now devoid of troops. Had Red been more cunning he might have left a party there to confuse the issue and leave Black guessing even more. If infantry were involved, for instance, they would not have been able to quit C1 on the second move, and Red would have had to maintain the C1 declaration.

Black, however, carries on with his advance, his second move taking him as far as point *n* and to Red he states that he is now in B2. The confrontation cannot be long delayed, for as Red has already given his position as B2, Black has to be more specific and, in addition to giving the large square as his location, he has to declare the sub-square as well. His full statement then must be that he is in B2, 3 and discovery is imminent. In point of fact he has also to specify B2, 1 as well as B2, 3, having passed through the former on his way to his final position. Red must now decide on his course of action, whether to push ahead or await the enemy move. He chooses the bolder alternative and as his patrol is a fighting one and ready for action, he causes it to move forward, first through the town into B2, 2 and then into B2, 3, where he meets the enemy. As Black did, Red discloses the sub-squares corresponding to his progress, first B2, 2, then B2, 3. It is only when he moves into the second sub-square that Black brings him to a halt with the magic word 'Contact!'

What happens next depends upon the intentions of the players and what forces they have available. In the present example we have simply a couple of cavalry patrols looking at each other and wondering what to do. Both would be roughly of the same strength, possibly an officer, a sergeant and half a dozen troopers, so a resort to the arbitration of a fight would, in ordinary circumstances, be profitable to neither side. The most sensible and logical thing to do would be for each to note the numbers of the enemy, what type of troops they were, and to try to identify them, by uniform details and so on, in order that intelligence of their presence and regiment could be relayed to headquarters. If, on the other hand, one side was appreciably stronger (if it were half a squadron, for example), it would be likely to press forward, driving the weaker force back, until the latter bumped into reinforcements and decided to call a halt to its withdrawal. In any case, sooner or later comes the time when both sides dig their heels in and action must result, with consequent recourse to the war game table. Experience shows that on the great majority of occasions the contact may be settled by discussion without actually having to set out one's troops on the table and make up the terrain corresponding to the map. It must be said, however, that either player may at any time he chooses, in regard to any contact, decree that there may be a set-down. He might well have something diabolical up his sleeve in the way of an ambush, for instance.

When the crunch does come, though, we have to decide just what amount of terrain we should set up on the table, how much of the map is necessary to reproduce for fighting purposes. If, as I said above, the campaign map has been gridded so that every sub-square represents the war game table, the answer is easy. The terrain of the sub-square is simply transferred to the table—rivers, hills, woods, houses, the lot. This may not be completely satisfactory, however, since the centre of the contact may be at the extreme corner of a sub-square, leaving one of the parties with no room for manoeuvre. It would therefore be more suitable in such a contingency to reproduce parts of more than one sub-square, and this can be achieved thus. Have a piece of perspex or acetate sheet, transparent of course, cut to the scale of the table relevant to the map, and pin it thereto so that the centre falls on the exact spot where contact took place. In the example we have just worked through, the contact was roughly at the town in the lower right hand corner of B2, 1. The lightly shaded area shows what would, if it came to a set-down, be the most logical part of the map to transfer to the table, this, of course, if the sub-square were scaled to the actual size of the table. It is important to note here that such a set-down could be of advantage to one of the parties providing that he had a follow-up force located, possibly, in B2, 2 (this would be Red's in the situation detailed), his small vedette being possibly in advance of a couple of regiments of cavalry. If the position of these regiments was such that they had to be revealed when the set-down took place, this would be a stroke of luck for Black, whose patrol would lap up this intelligence with gusto. On the other hand, if the cavalry force was at the extreme north-east corner of B2, 2, then it would not appear in the set-down and Red would have to decide whether to bring it on to the table in due course, or to leave it concealed. Again, if both sides displayed a strong body of horse, then they would have to make up their minds whether to fight or to sit tight and await events. This would depend on the campaign context in which the event took place, but now that we have learned the basic mechanics of map moving, the refinements will follow.

XXIII
More about Maps

It will be obvious that the operation detailed in the previous chapter was really simplicity itself, but it should be pointed out that it concerned but one individual scouting action carried out by a small body of cavalry on each side. Now, multiply this by any number you like and you will get something in the nature of a cavalry screen, a wide-ranging curtain of groups of horsemen probing into the enemy position, obtaining information, determining the lines of his advance, and getting any information concerning his movements and composition. Now the question can be asked as to what might have happened had the few men in the scouting party been replaced by a much more powerful body of troops, moving fast and carrying a considerable punch as well. What I am proposing to do is first to illustrate at the same time just what can happen in such an operation when a much stronger force is involved, and second, to give a more general picture of how maps are used in a campaign.

This, I might say, is an account of something that really did happen in a campaign in which I was one of the protagonists. The narrative does not in any way cover my strategical sense with glory, but notwithstanding this, I shall relate it just as it happened, the details being taken from the War Diaries of the generals who took part. I have to stress that in the tapestry of the whole campaign, this is only one small section of embroidery, but it did have an effect, actually and morally, although only a comparatively small number of men were concerned. Although I was on the receiving end in that I was hurt more than was my enemy, the whole thing gave me a tremendous boost, a pleasure I always get when in a battle or campaign something happens to indicate that the Rules and the manner in which they operate do provide a high degree of realism.

First, if the reader will be good enough to study the map overleaf, I shall try to put him in the picture, beginning with the initial background information that he finds himself in the middle of one of the campaigns which have bedevilled relations between the Grand Duchy of Lorraine and the Vereinigte Freie Städte for some years. The map shows a small section of the frontier between the warring powers, the Vereinigte Freie Städte being that part enclosed within the loop of the River Schwarzwasser, Lorraine

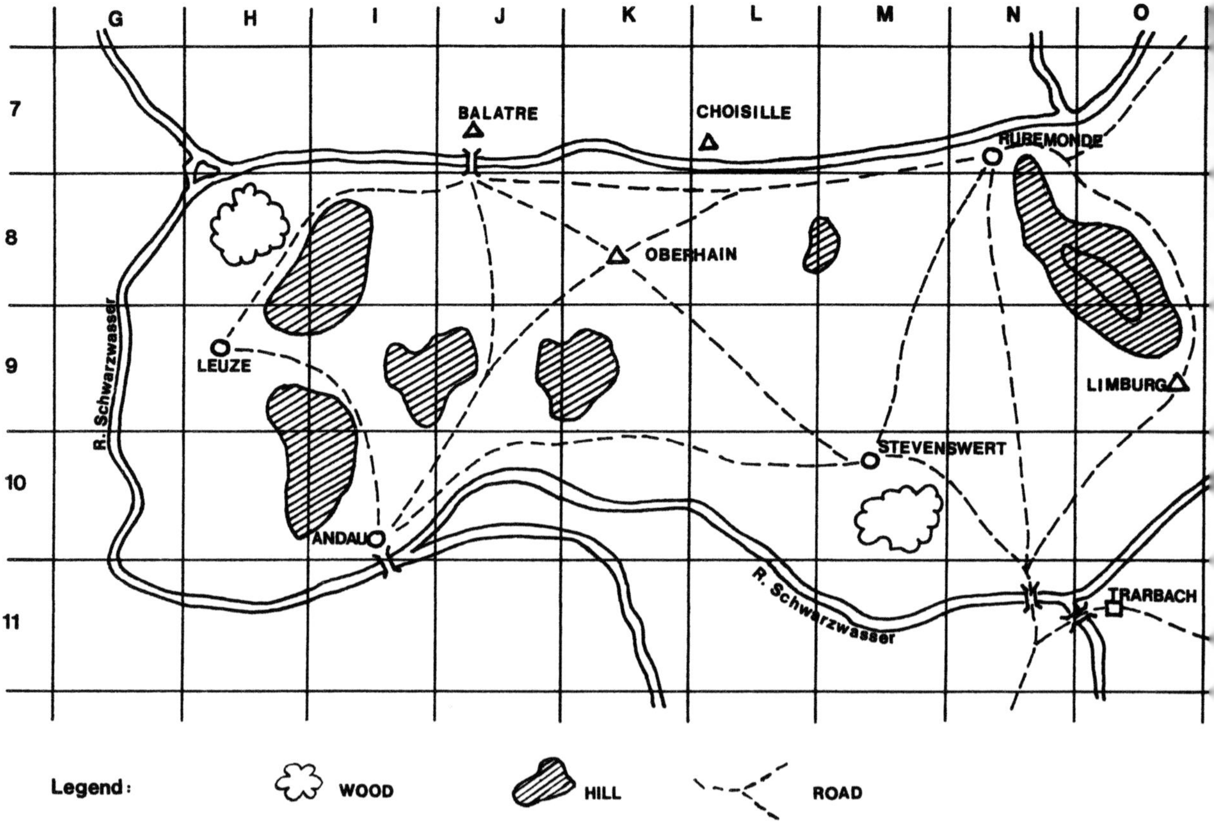

Map to illustrate the 'Andau Raid'.

being on the further or west bank thereof. At the time with which we are concerned (towards the end of July, the campaign having started, traditionally, on 1st April), a considerable amount of manœuvring, marching, countermarching and so on, was taking place in the northern theatre of operations (off the map, that is), but in the area shown, the VFS forces (if I may use the abbreviation) had already crossed the river and seized Balatre, garrisoning the place with infantry and guns. This was opportunely done, as when we join the action a powerful army of Lorrainers had appeared from the north and west and was preparing, it seemed, to launch an all-out attack to regain the captured town. The date, in fact, was 19th July.

The details of the forces engaged in the Balatre battle are not important in our immediate story, and what must be remembered is that a large scale encounter was raging there for the following two or three days. The troops with which we are concerned on the VFS side are relatively few in number and are as follows: just south of Balatre, over the river from the town, stood a reservé regiment of heavy cavalry, the Ahlefeldt Kürassiere, stationed there as it was of little use in defending the town. At the road junction, reference J9, and under orders to join the first named regiment, was another heavy cavalry unit, the Kronstadt Dragoons. The two were normally brigaded together. At the provincial capital, Trarbach (O11) was a battalion of light infantry or jäger, the Feldjägerkorps, in process of mustering and not due for final activation until 24th July. Mark this well, for it was an important factor in what was to follow. Finally, at Andau (I10) was stationed a company of militia whose function will appear as the tale unfolds.

Before starting the actual narrative, a few words on the mechanics of map moving, some of the details of which we know already, such as the moves for heavy cavalry being 1½″ and for infantry 1″. The map, as reproduced, is for clarity gridded only in the large squares, the sub-squares being left out. As we have said, moves are alternate, and as it happened it was the Lorraine commander who was first to move and to read out his list of map references. The scale of the map is also important; each square has 2″ sides, and by trial and error over the years it has been established that a day's operations can be encompassed by four map moves. This is not the best method of formulating a rule, but many campaigns with a variety of players have failed to produce any system better than this representation of a day's activity by the four map moves mentioned. This seems to be as much as is necessary of background detail, so with the Grand Duke of Lorraine ready to give voice, and the Marshal General of the VFS all agog and awaiting his enemy's list, we shall get on with the operation (ignoring the numerous contacts not directly connected with it).

Listening to the map references given for move 1, 19th July, the first thing to make the Marshal General prick up his ears was a contact for N7, there having been nothing there during the previous day, 18th July. However, thinking that this might be concerned with enemy movement north of the river, not a great deal of attention was paid, the attention being focussed mainly on the fighting at Balatre. Nevertheless, when the same reference was given for both move 2 and move 3 of the same day, it was felt that it might be worth looking into, and it was recalled that some time previously Lorraine barges had been seen in the left hand branch of the Schwarzwasser (that extending over the north edge of N7). So, with the thought in mind that it might be just as well to make sure nothing was amiss, Kronstadt Dragoons were ordered east from the junction at J9, to make an investigation. At this stage Ahlefeldt Kürassiere stood fast. With move 4 the N7 reference was still there; something was definitely afoot in this region, although it was briefly considered whether it might not be a bluff to draw troops away from the operations at Balatre.

On move 1 of 20th July, Kronstadt reached Oberhain (K8), and simultaneously came confirmation that a crossing had taken place, enemy references being given for N8 and O7. It now seemed that whatever had crossed had started to spread out (no doubt now that a crossing had been made—those confounded barges, of course!). This was enough and it was boots and saddles for Ahlefeldt Kürassiere south of Balatre, and at the same time Kronstadt was urged forward. Throughout the day the enemy continued to give N8 and O7 and by nightfall, that is move 4, Kronstadt was at the south-east corner of M7 (on the road south of the river) and Ahlefeldt, starting later of course, had just entered L8 and was on the river road due south of Choisille. The Brigade Commander, one Von Seydlitz, was riding with this regiment. Whatever was taking place about Ruremonde, the enemy was not in any hurry. Could they have seized the town with the aim of holding it? This was not thought likely, with the lack of communication a problem, barges not being very reliable from several points of view.

On the following day, the 21st, it seemed almost certain that a visual sighting would be made, but move 1 showed that there was no longer an N8 reference, although once more there was an N7 (the Ruremonde square) as well as a new one, namely O8. However, the VFS cavalry pressed on, and the sighting came at last on move 2, when Kronstadt entered N7, for arrayed solidly in front of Ruremonde was a full regiment of enemy horse, quickly identified as the Gendarmerie du Roi, resplendent in scarlet and gold. (It was never clear just how a Grand Duke happened to have a regiment so entitled, but be that as it may, there it was.) The fact that it was at full strength of 4 officers and 24 men quickly indicated that, as another reference had been given, there was something additional in the offing, the question being what was it? With Ahlefeldt coming up behind, the commanding officer of Kronstadt decided to await its arrival before attacking, since it is never a very profitable undertaking for a cavalry regiment to mix it with another of approximately equal strength. At the end of move 3 Ahlefeldt appeared, just entering N7, whereupon the Gendarmerie fell back through Ruremonde and round the northern extremity of the hill south of the town. During moves 3 and 4 the O8 reference persisted, as it had done on move 2. This was something of a puzzle and the Marshal General was beginning to be somewhat exercised about it, wishing that the jäger battalion being raised at Trarbach was more nearly ready for action. Caught in two minds, in fact, and with his eye really on the Balatre encounter, he split his cavalry and on 22nd July directed Ahlefeldt south-west, while Kronstadt, after standing fast at Ruremonde during move 1 of this day, set off after the Gendarmerie which had moved south-east into O8.

The move during which Kronstadt had remained at rest increased the Lorraine horsemen's already considerable start and at the end of the day, when Kronstadt had reached a point close to the southern edge of O8 (on the road, of course), the enemy contact (one only) was O9. Evidently the Gendarmerie had united with whatever force had preceded it; how the Marshal General wished he had some troops at Limburg. On move 4 of the 22nd, Ahlefeldt had almost reached Stevenswert (actually on the south edge of M9), whence it was hoped that the enemy could be intercepted if heading for Trarbach. The conclusion was being reached that it was indeed that town which was the objective of the invaders, the aim being probably to divert troops from other theatres; the fighting was still going on about Balatre, up to this point inconclusively.

On 23rd July, with still a day remaining before the jäger battalion was due to be activated at Trarbach, tension in the VFS headquarters was mounting considerably. Meanwhile the pursuing (or intercepting) regiments of cavalry pressed on, the Kronstadt Dragoons entering Limburg on move 2, just to see a party of Gendarmerie (an officer and 4 men) disappearing over the horizon into O10. This again caused a certain amount of soulsearching: could the whole thing have been an elaborate bluff and had the remainder of the regiment made off elsewhere? No, this could not have been the case, there had been no other possible contacts and indeed, on move 3, the enemy declared his presence in N10 as well. Now, here indeed was the crunch. Was he pressing southwards to Trarbach, in time to occupy it and to prevent the mustering of the jäger battalion? To the great relief of the Marshal General, move 4 still showed only the N10 reference, so Trarbach was safe! During the day Seydlitz, with the Ahlefeldt Kürassiere, moved to Stevenswert and took up a position a little to the east of the town, the idea being still to cut off the intruders, as soon as it was known in which direction they were heading. At the end of the day Kronstadt had reached the road junction in N10 but could see no enemy who were now obviously heading west and were very near the M10 square, in another subsquare of N10 in fact to that occupied by Kronstadt.

At dawn on 24th July the new jäger battalion mustered on the Burgplatz of Trarbach and, to the general satisfaction and relief of the city's burgers, on move 2 crossed the bridges leading from the city and set off on the road towards N10, to do its bit in chasing the importunate Lorraine raiders. East of Stevenswert, as we have said, stood Seydlitz's heavy cavalry, and promptly at the end of move 1 there appeared from the east the heavy masses of enemy cavalry: not one, in fact, but two full regiments of horse! In the lead came the Gendarmerie du Roi, who had been expected, and following them the red-clad Mêstre-de-Camp Général Dragoons, the two together outnumbering Ahlefeldt by two to one. Well, as a certain famous light cavalry leader said later, the wine was drawn and now must be drunk, so without

The confrontation at Stevenswert. Von Seydlitz with the Ahlefeldt Kürassiere (on the left) is about to try conclusions with the Lorraine cavalry raiders (Gendarmerie du Roi and Mestre de Camp Général Dragoons).

hesitation Seydlitz and his men charged the oncoming enemy who, nothing loath, countercharged. There followed a confused and whirling cavalry fight, on the Lorraine side the Gendarmerie taking the brunt of the battle, while the dragoons swung off round to the north, with the intention of attacking the VFS troops from flank or rear. Before this could be done, both Ahlefeldt and the Gendarmerie fell back (after the normal two moves of mêlée) and Seydlitz, who had been in the thick of the fight, saw that his casualties had been rather heavier than those of his opponents. Consequently, although his regiment was still 'fightable' (ie it had not been reduced to 50% or less), he decided to draw off to the south, away from the still complete regiment of dragoons, and await assistance. This he did, taking up a position near the wood (south side of M10), perforce allowing the Lorrainers to pick up their casualties and hasten on their way due west into L10. On move 2, Seydlitz was joined by Kronstadt, and the jäger also made their appearance later, reaching Stevenswert by the end of the day, by which time Seydlitz had reorganised and had led his entire brigade, albeit with one regiment seriously reduced, into L10. It was calculated that the enemy would be in the south-west corner of L10, heading west.

At this point, a rather grim spectre raised its ugly head: it bore the name Andau, this place being in I10 (*vide* the map). Referred to previously and somewhat mysteriously, it was the town where there was stationed a rather weak company of militia whose function, it can now be revealed, was to act as guard at a Prisoner-of-War camp wherein were some 103 Lorraine prisoners, the equivalent of nearly two infantry regiments, taken by the VFS earlier in the campaign. It was in the direction of Andau and its lightly guarded POW's that the enemy cavalry appeared to be moving. Balatre was out of course, and other than Andau, there was no crossing of the Schwarzwasser. Although over the river was Lorraine territory, VFS light cavalry patrols were operating there, although not in sufficient strength to provide much opposition for the Lorraine heavies. The situation appeared pretty fraught, and, as the fighting at Balatre appeared to have died down, a battalion of light infantry, the Jägerkorps zu Fuss, was directed from there towards Andau, although there was little chance of its being able to get there before the Lorraine raiders.

To continue the story, then, on 25th July, Seydlitz carried on with his pursuit, the enemy moving away in front of him, and by the last move of the day, move 4, the Lorraine horsemen had entered I10 and were nearing Andau, wherein there was considerable agitation. Seydlitz was still some distance behind, about halfway across J10, having left the Feldjägerkorps far to the rear. The Jägerkorps zu Fuss, coming from Balatre, had just passed the junction in J9.

The climax of the operation took place the following day when the Lorraine cavalry rode into Andau on move 1 without meeting any opposition, the militia having decamped during the night; the morale throw, plus their weakened state, had produced a perfectly wretched morale index. In the streets of the town were the delighted Lorraine ex-prisoners of war, now well and truly liberated. There was no question, in the mind of the Lorraine commander, but of joining the POW's to his force and carrying on across the bridge into the safety of Lorraine. Seydlitz and his men arrived later, to be followed at the end of the day by the jäger from Balatre.

Thus was the task completed, although there was a sort of sequel when the light troops across the Schwarzwasser made an attempt to impede the progress of the raiders moving west and north from Andau, but this effected nothing other than to cause a few casualties to each side.

The whole story, it seems to me, illustrates a most realistic operation and shows how exciting and suprising war game campaigning can be. Something indeed can be learned from it, if it is only the really apparent one that it is ever necessary to have a cavalry screen operating in every area. If, for instance, the Marshal General had had a cavalry post at Ruremonde, with its men operating all along the river line, the fog of war would never have been such an impenetrable blanket as it was. Of course it is true to say that the material benefit in the shape of the restoration of the prisoners, which event had a definite effect on the campaign for some time, was by way of being an unexpected bonus for the Grand Duke of Lorraine, who had no idea that a 'cage' had been set up at Andau, but 'c'est la guerre', as they say in Lorraine.

XXIV
Pioneers and their Duties

Field fortifications, which included any sort of device, trench or raised work whereby the progress of an enemy could be impeded or which would assist in his discomfiture, played a considerable part in eighteenth-century warfare, but it is important, before we consider the question in a war game context, to have a clear idea of just what the definition embraced. Many stratagems were used and the most readily available material employed to cause pain or grief to an enemy, some being so well known that they need little description. Felled trees provided an immediate solution to many a problem of defence. They could simply be cut down and left lying in positions where they could delay guns or transport or they could, time permitting, be arranged into an 'abatis' consisting of trees and branches sunk in the earth with their sharpened ends projecting towards the enemy. In the assault on Fort Ticonderoga in 1758 the Black Watch, even though using their claymores to hack down the obstacles, found it impossible to break through the dense 'abatis' the French had erected, and fell back with heavy losses. A more formal sort of thing was the 'chevaux de frises', a murderous-looking obstacle consisting of a beam of timber through which had been driven long iron spikes, set in such a manner that there was always a row of spikes facing the enemy. This could be used in a special area to close a gap in a continuous line of earthworks, but it could be dragged away by a resolute enemy. The diagram shows these field works.

The mention of earthworks brings us to that with which we are really concerned. In the field, there is really little difference between what a soldier of today and one of 1760 will do if told, in the idiom of the time, to dig himself in. The spade and pickaxe are similar and what they are used for does not differ materially from century to century: the man in question will go about digging a hole of the required size, at the same time piling the excavated soil in front of the excavation in the direction of the foe, increasing his protection and providing a firing parapet as well. Now the British *Manual of Field Engineering,* published in 1911 at the startling cost of 9d, is packed with information including the statement that to dig a 5 feet long trench, such as that illustrated, 3 feet in depth and width and about 4½ feet from the bottom to the top of the parapet, will take an untrained man 1½ hours in moderately easy ground.

'Abatis': sharpened tree trunks embedded in earthworks.

'Chevaux de Frises': sharp iron spikes embedded in a length of timber.

A simple trench with parapet.

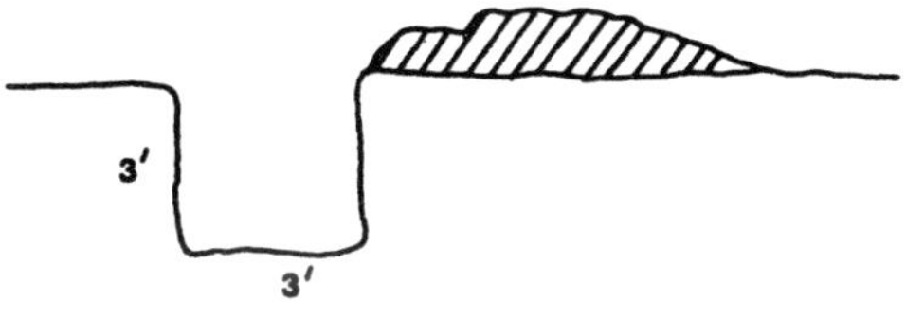

'Revetting': the shaded area is excavated soil.

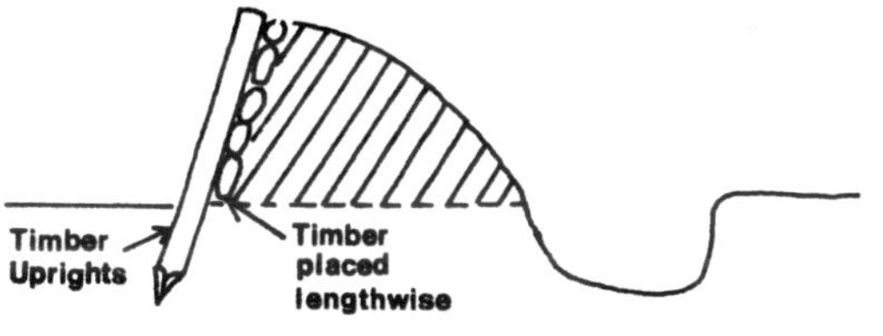

This is a very elementary form of earthwork and is highly unlikely to be met in eighteenth-century warfare; even so, we shall devote a few words to its construction before passing on to more important things. Throughout the eighteenth-century, such instant defences are exceedingly rare, because when battle was joined, there was usually neither the time nor the inclination to begin 'throwing dirt' as was done so frequently in the later stages of the American Civil War. To detach substantial portions of one's infantry to dig trenches in the proximity of enemy cavalry or light infantry was not considered the wisest of moves, and it is abundantly clear that it is not a good thing to have numbers of men working for dear life with their arms piled possibly some distance away and the enemy close by. However, should it be found necessary at short notice to construct such rudimentary defences, it takes place in this manner.

As we have already quoted, it takes one man 90 minutes to dig his five foot trench. Our scale is 1" = 10 yards = 30 feet, so it will take 6 men 90 minutes to dig a length of 10 yards or 1" on the table. If a large number of men can lend a hand and the working parties are doubled, possibly the time may be halved, thus making it 45 moves.

Even this is still far too long for any normal war game. It is really impracticable to contemplate digging trenches on the spot with action imminent. This must not cause undue dismay, however, because as we have pointed out it was historically very rare for such work to be carried out during a battle. In the most important conflicts of the century in which any sort of field works played a part it will be found that some time elapsed between their being made and the battle in which they figured. The redoubts at Malplaquet (1709) and Fontenoy (1745) are examples of such fortfications being completed before the arrival of the attacking troops, as was the case at Poltava (1709). The Battle for Bunker Hill (1775) is another notable case, of which considerably more anon. Here the fortifications were raised on Breed's Hill the night before the British made their attack. This all tends to demonstrate that eighteenth-century defences were of some elaboration and more often than not would be revetted. This means that the earth thrown up by the digging, which normally would not stand by itself at more than 45 degrees from the horizontal, was supported by sods, brushwood, stones, or best of all, by timber. In this case, strong timbers were driven into the ground and others placed lengthwise between them, with the earth thrown up, a very strong defensive system was created, one wherein apertures could be left for artillery (as in the Fontenoy redoubts), and this type of field fortification provides an exceedingly tough proposition for even the most aggressive troops. The complexity of such works give rise to another thought, though, concerning what sort of troops are capable of erecting them.

The untrained soldier is certainly able to toil and moil, but cannot draw a plan for how the defences can best be sited, this being the task of the trained engineer. This brings us to a convenient point where we can add another type of unit to our army.

As the business of erecting the more sophisticated type of field fortification is to be our concern, rather than the hastily prepared weapon-pit or foxhole, it seems that this comes within the province of specialist troops, engineers, or more properly pioneers, and it will simplify matters if we enact a quick rule: field fortifications can be constructed only by pioneers.

It may be proper at this stage to describe their organisation or at least that which I use in mid-eighteenth-century battles and campaigns. Pioneers are best employed in battalion strength and the unit's composition is Colonel, three officers, and 24 rank and file pioneers. They have no standard bearer, like light cavalrymen preserving their colours in their headquarters (or so they do in the Vereinigte Freie Städte), and they are armed, move and fight as infantry of the line. Morale points are normal, with the Colonel rating 3 and the officers 1 each, making the correct Morale Index of 6 for the unit. Now, one very good reason why only pioneer troops can construct redoubts and the like is that only they have the necessary tools to do so, picks, axes, spades and so on being carried in the wagon which is an integral part of the pioneer battalion. It is drawn by a pair of horses conducted by teamsters who, in the fashion of the time, are altogether civilian and menial, having no fighting value.

So, with the pioneer battalion plus impedimenta on the spot, we make the rules as to what they are able to do in their special rôle. We have noted and discarded the notion of digging fieldworks in battles where the 1 minute = 1 move is adhered to, thus leaving the procedure to be followed in reconstruction encounters and in campaigns. In the case of the former, where a move lasts not one minute but several, depending on the ground scale, the average seems to be about ten minutes per move (Mollwitz was a little less, seven minutes it will be remembered), so let us take ten minutes as being the ordinary move time. Transferring the fact that one man digs 5 feet of trench in 1½ hours to our time scale, we have 9 moves (each of 10 minutes). Now what we are thinking of is something very much more ambitious than a mere trench, most probably the revetted structure we have considered. This would naturally take a very much longer time to construct, even with several men working on a section instead of just one with a spade. It would most probably be at least twice as long, and without going too deeply into the mathematics of it, it has been found that if we rule that 4 men (these are actual figures on the table) throw up 1″ of breastwork in 20 moves, this is about right. This time includes that period devoted to the marking out of the lines to be followed by the earthworks, and for collecting and distributing the tools from the wagon. This means, in very general terms, that a battalion of pioneers, working hard, can construct 60 yards of fortification in just under 3½ hours. This may not seem a great deal, but we must not forget we are dealing with a fairly complex operation.

With this in mind we carry on with the campaign equivalent. In this format, we allow eight hours per day for military activity, marching, fighting and so on. This allows for the inevitable delay in getting the troops together, conducting the roll call and so on, so the 3½ hours referred to above is just under half a day's campaign time. Thus the pioneer battalion will complete its allocated length of fortification in half a day: it is best to take the nearest substantial fraction of the day. In other words, thinking back, we allocated four map moves to a day's operations, so the 60 yards will be thrown up in two map moves.

We are now left with the question: once up, how can they be demolished? The answer is easy: they can be thrown down at twice the speed at which they were erected, in 10 moves, in fact, or a quarter of a campaign day, should this be applicable.

One point must be observed: officers of the pioneer battalion are not included in the working parties but simply direct operations, although they fight when this becomes necessary.

Although it is something of a digression, it becomes necessary here, somewhat out of context, to detail the effect of artillery on the fortifications we have discussed. This will be roundshot only, shell having little effect on the construction. Again we use a cumulative system, as we did for the destruction of enemy guns or buildings, and the roundshot procedure is as before. The Three-Colour Stick is placed over the fortification being bombarded, black end at the gun muzzle, and the three-colour die is thrown. If the colour which comes up is that one on the earthwork, a numerical die is thrown for effect, and the deductions for distant and medium range (2 and 1 respectively) are made. When a total of 10 has been reached for one particular inch of the earthworks, that inch is considered to be levelled, ie destroyed. It will be seen that it is a protracted business to open a breach in such fortifications. A last point is that if the roundshot hits the breastwork, in no case does it continue farther.

Returning to our pioneers, there is one more highly important duty they carry out, this being the erection of pontoon bridges. Again this requires a considerable body of pioneers to carry out and the rule is that one officer and 12 pioneers are the minimum necessary. The pontoons are simple affairs, horse drawn of course, and to avoid complication we suppose that all rivers are of the same width, requiring the same number of pontoons to make the necessary bridge. What happens when the pontoon train arrives at the river bank is this:

Moves 1 and 2	1st pontoon launched
3 and 4	1st bridge section in place, from near bank to 1st pontoon
5 and 6	2nd pontoon launched
7 and 8	second bridge section in place, joining 1st and 2nd pontoons
9 and 10	3rd bridge section in place, linking 2nd pontoon to farther bank

A word concerning the equipment. It is home-made, pontoons being put together from balsa wood, the material from which the bridge sections are also made; the wheels are spare artillery wheels and the horses, whose harness is pretty crude, are cavalry horses with the unwanted rider removed with the aid of a knife. As with the engineer wagons, the pontoon train has teamsters whose presence is merely decorative.

The ten moves for bridge building are the ten minute moves, and in campaign terms, the operation is carried out in one map move.

On the subject of bridges (now referring to permanent, probably stone structures already in existence), there comes a time when these have to be destroyed, to hold up an enemy advance, for example. Again a job for the pioneers, and in this case we have a sort of sliding scale of numbers required, noting that there must always be one officer present. To prepare a bridge for demolition requires:

With one officer and 8 pioneers	8 moves
With one officer and 6 or 7 pioneers	9 moves
With one officer and 4 or 5 pioneers	10 moves

With less than four men the operation is impossible, as it is without an officer.

Once prepared, with explosive in position, the bridge may be blown at any time, provided a dice throw produces 5 or 6. This indicates that the bridge has gone up in smoke, but if the required throw is not obtained, the procedure has to be repeated once each move, until a 5 or 6 is thrown.

XXV
River Transport

The use of rivers and other waterways as avenues of transport was an important feature of eighteenth-century warfare, particularly in Europe and especially so in the Low Countries. Roads were very far from being modern motorways and guns, pontoon trains and siege equipment were far more conveniently carried by waterborne means than otherwise. The fact that this can be duplicated in war game campaigns is yet another factor tending to ensure realism by making players keep a sharp eye on any rivers or canals of strategic importance in their own or in occupied territory (witness the effect of the 'Andau operation' as narrated in Chapter XXIII). The control of waterways is patently of considerable importance; a regiment posted in a commanding position on a river bank or maybe at the junction of two canals, possibly with artillery support, could interdict the passage of enemy shipping and have a powerful effect on the conduct of a campaign.

As far as the war game is concerned, the vessels or barges used need not be tremendously elaborate. In fact they are of stout card, painted in some customary nautical hue and equipped with a three-man crew. This last is the personnel used in the Vereinigte Freie Städte and Lorraine. These crewmen are non-combatants, which is rather more credible than the alternative, which is to make them a species of marine. This is up to the wargamer, of course.

Stipulating a move for our barge, supposing it to be waterborne and under way, is not difficult. There will have to be at least two moves to allow for progress upstream and downstream, and of these the latter will be fairly rapid. The move in this case can be equated to that of heavy cavalry and will be 9″ (our rivers are not foaming torrents). Upstream, the thing becomes more of an effort and the move will be of 6″ only. These two moves apply to rivers, but in the still waters of a canal or a lake, where there are unlikely to be currents, we split the difference and are left with a canal move of 7½″.

With the barge alongside the wharf or jetty where loading and unloading take place, the time of such operations becomes important as does the number of personnel carried per barge. It seems that in the eighteenth century the ordinary troop-carrying barge took some 50 infantrymen, and this is approximately twice the number we load in one of our standard barges, or in round figures two of our barges take a regiment of 5 officers and 48 men. By this token then, two of our barges equal the number which in real life would be required to accommodate a battalion of infantry. This is only a passing thought, however, and we might also note that one of our battalions (those of 24 rank and file) or one regiment of cavalry would also fill one barge, which would alternatively carry a battery of our artillery, that is the two-gun variety we use in the Vereinigte Freie Städte.

River transport in action, with a troop-carrying barge loaded with half a regiment of line infantry (not forgetting the crew of three with oars).

The question of loading comes next, and here the infantry will naturally take the least time, being able to double on board and get into position very quickly; it would be generous to allow 20 minutes. So we allow two moves of the ten-minute type for the embarkation of one infantry regiment. Cavalry and artillery present problems, the loading of horses being an awkward business, and in both cases we have to allow an hour and a half for a regiment of cavalry or a battery of guns, that is 9 moves. Even this may be a trifle fast, but we assume that the operations proceed without undue snags.

If the enemy happen to be about and venture to assail a loaded barge from the river or canal bank, the effect of its musketry on the crowded barge will be exactly similar to the results of musketry on land, and casualties are calculated normally. For gunfire on barges we have to show a reference table of effect. As in all cases when roundshot is employed, we operate the Roundshot Measuring Stick plus the Three-Coloured Die, the former being laid across the barge and ordinary procedure followed. Here is the table of effect, given that the die comes up with the colour of the stick section covering the barge.

Close range	1	No effect
	2, 3	Damaged, reduced to half speed
	4, 5, 6	Sinks
Medium range	1, 2, 3	No effect
	4	Damaged, reduced to half speed
	5, 6	Sinks
Distant range	1, 2, 3, 4	No effect
	5	Damaged, reduced to half speed
	6	Sinks

When the barge is damaged, it proceeds at half speed to the nearest river port for repairs. This takes one campaign day, or four map moves, whichever applies.

In the unhappy event of the vessels being sunk, certainly a proportion of the passengers will go with it—infantry, cavalry or other personnel. Half the total, however, will save themselves, and get to the bank farther from the enemy. Guns, limbers and teams go down, however, and cannot be retrieved.

The effect of howitzer fire is assessed in the normal way, using the Shell Burst Indicator. For a hit on a particular barge, a 6 must be obtained and, should this be done, a second dice throw is made for immediate effect on the barge itself. Now the vessel is a pretty stout sort of thing and it will take a further throw of 6 to sink it. If the second 6 comes up, then the barge goes down, taking half the passengers with it. The other half are saved, and get out of the water on the bank away from the enemy. If the second 6 does not come up, then the normal dice throws are made for the personnel within the inner circle of the SBI, the 6 area. Here, the normal 4, 5 or 6 kills.

Disembarking troops and so on may take a little less time than the reverse process but not enough to make an appreciable difference, so to unload is 2 moves for infantry and 9 for cavalry and artillery.

XXVI
Campaign Casualties

In considering the niceties of conducting a campaign we come to the question of the casualties suffered in the engagements during it and to the discussion of what they represent. In the normal war game without strategic context the figures are taken off the table as they become casualties and that is an end to it. This means, in effect, the removal of all men who have been hit, however slightly, as well as those who have had it permanently. This is unreal, of course, when the consequences of the fighting have some long-term importance and where it is necessary to preserve as much of one's army as possible. By making allowance, for differing degrees of wound severity, the campaign is made that much more realistic, above all in respect of the battle's not being an end in itself but simply one of a lengthy series of actions. A general has a reason for holding out, if he has the opportunity by so doing of saving large numbers of only slightly wounded men, and also, in contrast, he is prevented from carrying out unreal operations if there was any likelihood of his placing himself thereby in a situation in which he might be unable to save even slightly wounded troops.

In the eighteenth century, medical science, especially in the field, was nothing if not rudimentary, and the proportion of men who died of wounds very high. This is the reason why the 'fatal' section of the following casualty table is higher than is normal for casualties immediately after a battle.

Briefly, at the end of a campaign battle, casualties on each side are divided thus:

a $\frac{1}{5}$ of the total (ie of all figures removed from the table) are dead.
b $\frac{1}{5}$ are only slightly wounded and can resume their place in the line the day following the battle.
c $\frac{1}{5}$ are wounded, and can resume in five days, ie the 6th day after wounding.
d $\frac{1}{5}$ are wounded, and resume 10 days after the battle.
e $\frac{1}{5}$ are wounded, and resume 15 days after the battle.

If the wound takes longer than 15 days to heal it is held that the sufferer comes into the first category in so far as he is so badly wounded as to be unable to take part in the remainder of the campaign.

In effect, this means that category *b* men are back in the line the day following the battle, and the more severely wounded must be dealt with medically, if this can be done. It is not, in fact, always possible for a defeated army to carry off all its casualties. In the case of an army which retires from the table in good order, the following rules apply:

> Wounded must be removed from the battlefield by helpers from their own regiment or unit.
> Category *b*, the walking wounded, require no assistance.
> Categories *c*, *d* and *e* each require one, two and three helpers per wounded man respectively.

An example: an infantry regiment of 48 rank and file suffers 20 casualties but retires in good order. Dividing the losses into the five categories thus:

> It has lost 4 dead
> 4 are slightly wounded and get away without help
> 4 wounded each require 1 helper, 4 in all
> 4 wounded each require 2 helpers, 8 in all
> 4 wounded each require 3 helpers, 12 in all

Thus it requires 24 men to care for the wounded, and as the regiment retired 28 strong, it can do so. That is, unless any officers have been hit, when others may be required. On the point of officers, they do not fall into the normal categories, but dice are thrown for each fallen officer individually. This results in the following:

Dice throw of	
1 or 2	the officer is dead
3	slightly wounded, resumes the following day
4	wounded, resumes in 5 days
5	wounded, resumes in 10 days
6	wounded, resumes in 15 days

Wounded officers require the same degree of assistance as do other ranks and no officer may act as a helper. Rank and file only are eligible for such duty.

All this applies to troops of good morale. A regiment in flight cannot take its wounded, each fit man participating in the 'sauve qui peut', although the walking wounded are allowed to get away.

The foregoing concerns simply the action taken on the battlefield and not the subsequent proceedings, these being regulated by the following precepts:

1. In one's own national territory it is assumed that country people of good will will take over the transport of the wounded, and proceed with them to hospital at infantry pace.
2. In enemy territory, however, the wounded have to be conveyed by their own fellows, but once off the battlefield this need not necessarily be done by men of the same regiment, but by units returning home through losses, or for

regrouping or for some other cause. The proportion of helpers to wounded at this stage must be three to two, ie 30 helpers are required for 20 wounded, irrespective of the degree of disability of the latter.

Incidentally, travelling time naturally counts towards the recovery period, and an agreed number of hospitals should have been established at the beginning of the campaign in one's national territory. They can be moved only after three days' preparation and then only at infantry speed.

Obviously, wounded men cannot go wandering about the countryside and the route to hospital must be as direct as possible. Indeed, if wounded men do not arrive at hospital within five days of their being wounded, their particular group begins to lose, until arrival at the hospital, one man in ten for each complete day in excess of the five. These losses will be taken in the first instance from the 'fifteen-day' men, then if necessary, from the 'ten-day' men and so on.

It has not been found necessary to have surgeons and other medical practitioners as part of one's actual army of figures, unless desired of course, but they would have to be male, the days of the nubile young nurse being a long way in the future.

XXVII
Campaign Recruiting and Replacements

An important feature of war game campaigning, even an essential one, is the replacement of battle casualties by recruits, and this can provide even more realistic logistics to cause the wargamer to scratch his head. Naturally, as a campaign progresses, recruits must be levied and trained to replace wastage and ordinarily these will be provided from one's national territory as a whole, with some emphasis on the urban areas, whether they be cities or towns. By employing a system whereby recruits in definite proportions come from such centres, a steady if sometimes only partial flow of replacements may be assured. This will give a higher degree of realism to the campaign operations, with particular reference to the value of occupied enemy territory, an important facet of eighteenth-century strategy. All that is required is a little preparation. Since we are campaigning we shall have maps of our own country and of the enemy's, and on these will be shown cities and towns. Should these be actual maps, the towns etc can be graded or on a fictitious map they can be indicated in particular ways to indicate their replacement potential.

The first thing which must be decided is how often recruits can be mustered and experience has shown that this is most suitably carried out every twentieth campaign day. This means that on this day a certain number of replacement troops become available to fill gaps in depleted units, and this mustering, fairly logically, will take place in one's capital city, where it would be natural to have one's headquarters and other military establishments. With this in mind we have to determine how many replacements will be forthcoming and this is done by totalling the losses of each of the belligerent sides. This is not done on a simple numerical basis, but by a system of points values for different types of troops, such as:

Infantryman	1
Light infantryman	3
Light cavalryman	4
Heavy cavalryman	6
A field gun	15
A gun team	10 and so on

When the points losses have been totalled, each side may levy on the twentieth day replacements of his own choice (*vide* the points system) to the value of points lost by the side losing least during the previous twenty days. For example, during one twenty-day period, Lorraine had lost 286 points worth of men and material, and Teutoburg-Althaufen 370 points. The replacements for both would therefore be 286 points, thus making sure that the emphasis was on the infliction of losses in the field, although it is important also to occupy territory and to deny the enemy the resources thereof. This is achieved in this wise.

When preparing your national map, start with one capital city, a number of lesser cities and a number of towns, all being centres of bureaucratic activity and military organisation. Let the capital represent 10% of the total resources, each city 6% and each town 3%. Villages are ignored. Organise the number of centres so that the total is 100%. The total reflects the condition when all centres are in a position to furnish the appropriate quota of recruits, and all localities are free from enemy presence, which would most certainly disrupt any possible recruiting. If, shall we say, town Zub is a 3% metropolis, and is in enemy hands, its civic functions are disrupted and no recruits can be had from it. From this point of view it can be written off. Enemy occupation would have to be something more prolonged than a mere flying raid, and it is decreed that:

> Should a city or town be occupied by enemy forces for 8 consecutive days in a twenty day replacement period, it will not contribute its total of recruits to the muster as it should.

An example: the city of Mudd, 6%, and the towns of Zub and Burp, 3% each, have been occupied by the enemy for the required time, and the Teutoburg-Althaufen recruits will have a total of 12% deducted from their number. In the case already cited, when Lorraine and Teutoburg-Althaufen receive 286 points each, the latter, with 12% of its recruit potential in enemy hands, will receive that much less, ie 286 less 34, or 252 points only.

All this must indicate that, although it is essential to seek out the enemy and inflict losses upon him, it is not without some consequence to occupy as much of his territory as might be practicable.

Following this, it might be noted that any inclination to pool one's troops and rush into enemy territory by unrealistically denuding one's own defences can be curbed by the formation of militia battalions (always good for creating some picturesque uniforms) which cannot be moved beyond the borders of one's homeland. These 'Grenze' or frontier battalions act as normal line infantry, consist of 24 men with a Colonel, 2 officers and a drummer, making a morale index total of 5, one less than that of a regular unit. Thus their morale, as befits militia, is slightly less reliable than that of regular line troops. They are nevertheless of great use in many circumstances.

XXVIII
The Battle for Bunker Hill

For our final battle, one chosen primarily to illustrate an infantry attack on field fortifications, which process was discussed in Chapter VII, we leave our customary scene of operations in the European theatre of war, and transport ourselves many thousands of miles to the west, indeed as far as what were called in our eighteenth-century parlance the American Colonies, although at this time the inhabitants of those lands were in the process of dissociating themselves with some vigour from the Mother Country. The year, in fact, is 1775, the scene is the city of Boston, Massachusetts, in which, as a result of the action some weeks before at Lexington and Concord, the British forces were penned, being now under what was not far removed from being a siege. A nearly complete blockade had been established on the landward side, although the waters of the Atlantic and more especially those around Boston (a city occupying at that time a peninsula) were well controlled by the ships of the British Navy.

Boston and the surrounding country is set out in its essentials in map 1 overleaf, and it is immediately very plain that to a force beleaguered in the town the Charlestown Peninsula is of paramount importance, and should guns be placed there on the hilly ground occupying most of the peninsula, they could very quickly make the town quite untenable. No effort was made by the British commander to occupy this important feature for some time, until in early June it was determined that troops should take possession of both the Charlestown Peninsula and Dorchester Heights. But General Gage, commanding in Boston, reckoned without his hosts for in the shape of 'The Committee of Safety', they had decided to move a force onto the Charlestown Peninsula and to hold Bunker Hill 'by a sufficient force posted there'.

So it was that during the night of 16th/17th June a thousand or so American Militiamen marched on to the Charlestown Peninsula, and when dawn broke the British in Boston saw the dark, earth-brown lines of a redoubt which had been thrown up under cover of darkness. In point of fact, it actually crowned not Bunker Hill but Breed's Hill, to the east of the former, but through the vagaries of history, the battle has always been called Bunker Hill and not by the name of the hill over which it was fought. It was to be a most bloody conflict.

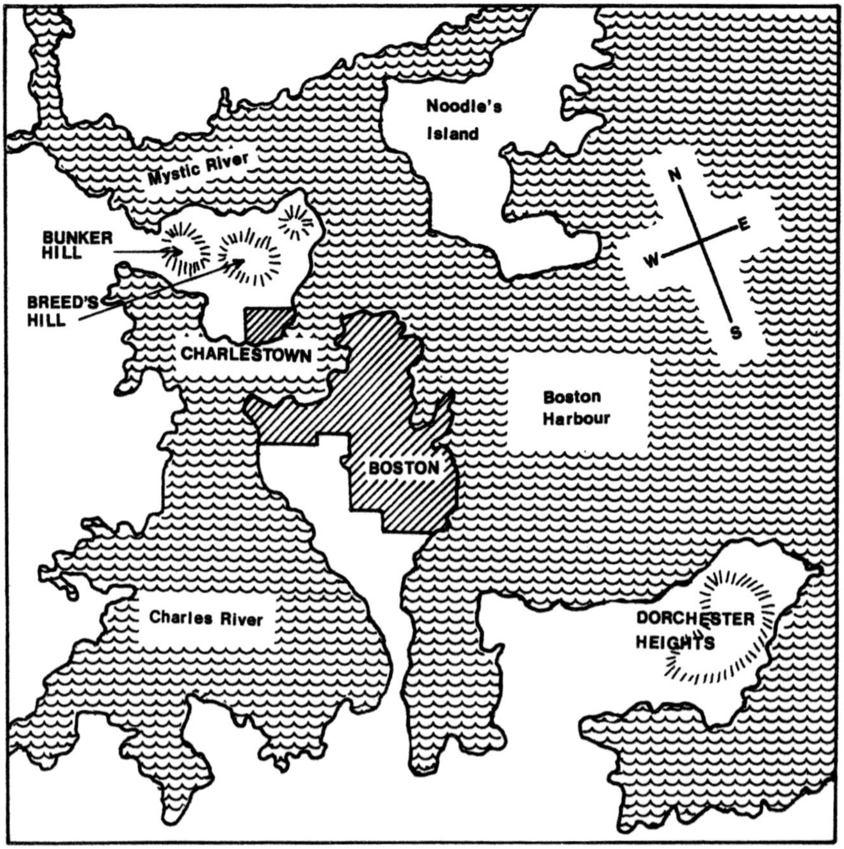

The Battle for Bunker Hill, map 1 : Boston and the surrounding country.

Faced with the unpleasant fact of the American presence on the Peninsula, the British went into action with a vengeance, and by the early afternoon some 2,200 infantry had been ferried over from Boston and had landed on the east side of the Peninsula without opposition. During this time the American position on the hill had been under a considerable bombardment, both from a battery in Boston and from the men-o'-war in the harbour, but this had not had any marked success, other than scaring a fairly large number of the untrained militia into flight. What happened next can be briefly told. Marching in beautifully arrayed lines, the redcoats twice assaulted the American defence line, but were flung back on each occasion with the most ghastly losses. Some 400 fresh infantry were brought over from Boston and a third attack was launched, this time successfully, although it was touch and go, and it was quite possibly because the defenders ran out of ammunition that the British were finally able to pour over the earthworks and wreak havoc among the Americans, few of whom had bayonets. Thus was fought the Battle for Bunker Hill (and a first rate account of it may be found in *The Battle for Bunker Hill* by Richard Ketchum, published by the Cresset Press in 1963).

Now to set out the details of how the historical event was converted into a war game, starting with the number of troops involved. These were in round figures 1,000 Americans and 2,200 British, and when the war game table was prepared and the troops placed in their initial position, this resulted in a total of 280 Americans and 530 British, in actual figures, that is. This is a considerably less favourable ratio to the regulars than the actual figure, but because of certain advantages enjoyed by the latter, it was considered to be just and proper.

Incidentally, as well as myself, also involved in refighting this battle were three professional military men, Lieutenants David Pinder, Prince of Wales's Own Regiment of Yorkshire, Charles Stewart Grant, Queen's Own Highlanders, and Michael Lindsay Stuart, Black Watch.

To obtain an accurate appraisal of the quality and capability of the Americans was a problem. They were pretty enthusiastic but quite untrained; many of them were fine shots but unused to the fury and din of battle, and in adversity extremely likely to break. To allow for this uncertainty of behaviour, it was decided that the American force be composed of militia units, such as were described in Chapter XXVII, with an initial morale index of 5 instead of the customary 6 for regulars. The defenders then numbered ten of these militia battalions.

It was easier to assess the British Army. Following the procedure of the time, the flank companies of all the British regiments (the grenadiers and light infantry) were removed from their parent battalions and organised as special élite units. In our battle, the light companies did not really function as such, but were simply used as storm troops. So to avoid confusion, such special units are simply described as grenadiers. They formed about $\frac{2}{5}$ of the British force. A most important point, which has already been briefly referred to, was that almost all the Americans were without bayonets. Thus, were it to come to a hand-to-hand struggle they were going to be at a severe disadvantage against the regulars, who were all so equipped. Obviously, the latter were entitled to some benefit, and it was enacted that for this battle the British infantry would receive a bonus of 1 point in respect of every dice throw made for hand-to-hand combat. It was momentarily debated whether or not the grenadiers should have yet another bonus point, but this was thought to be too high, and the idea was abandoned. They were, however, allowed to have the privilege their counterparts had had at Mollwitz, and fired in groups of four, instead of the normal sixes. As it happened, this turned out be irrelevant.

The general scheme for the war game was that the situation should be set out on the table at the time when the British were drawn up ready to make their first advance, and that the British generals should be left to decide just how they would go about the operation, ie they did not have to follow slavishly historical precedent. It is this situation which the reader will see in map 2, regarding which a few words of explanation might be advantageous. In the actual battle, Charlestown had been set on fire

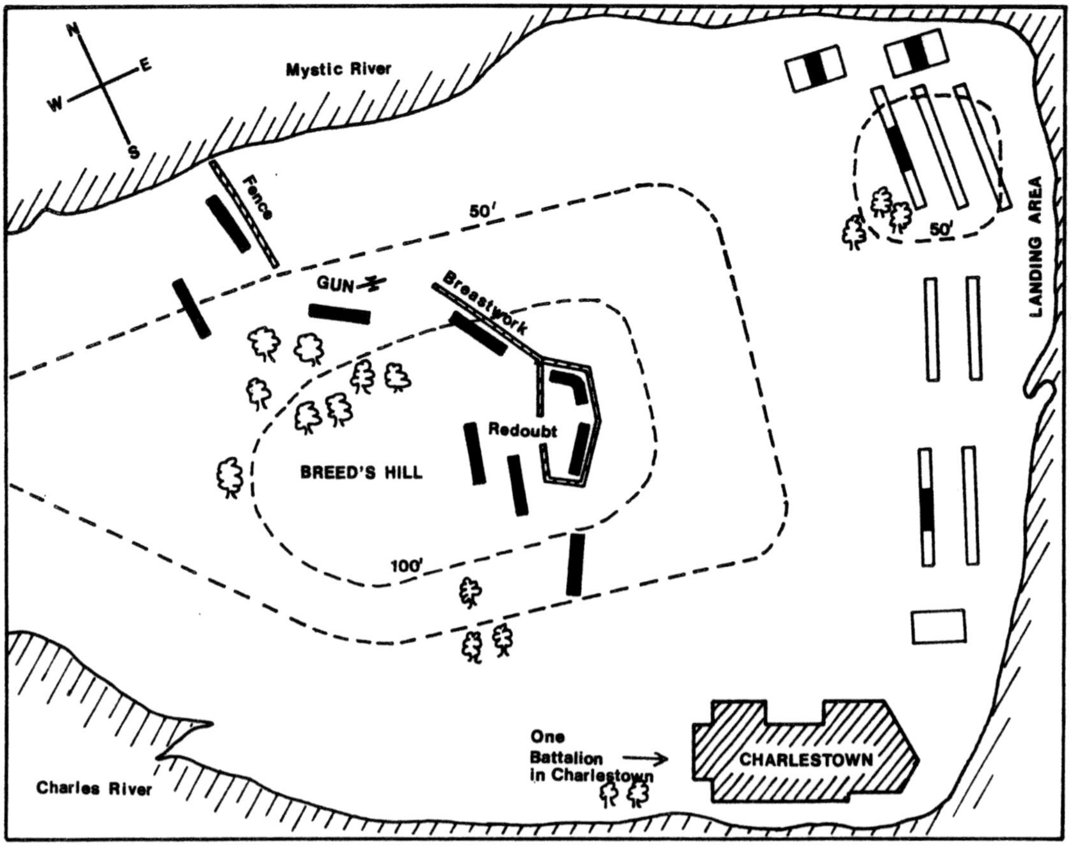

The Battle for Bunker Hill, map 2: the initial situation.

and was virtually destroyed, but in this case it was assumed to be unconsumed, and in fact was garrisoned by an American battalion. The fence on the north side of Breed's Hill was an extremely substantial sort of thing, reinforced by sods and brushwood, to a width of about ten feet according to one participant. Although several pieces of artillery had been brought into the redoubt, the gunners removed them and fled. Two guns were in action between the breastwork and the fence and have been replaced by one (this was the correct ratio) and this did a modicum of damage.

Some calculation concerning the distance between the 50′ and the 100′ contours (Breed's Hill is stated to be between 107 and 110 feet above sea level) and a reference to contemporary authorities quickly showed that the British would be able to reach the summit of the hill far more quickly and easily than was done in the actual battle. The slope, it seems, was criss-crossed with stone walls and fences and covered with high unmown grass concealing obstacles and pot-holes so, to allow for the necessary halting and dressing to maintain the lines, the British movement had to be cut down. It was therefore decreed that between the contours the infantry move uphill was cut

The Battle for Bunker Hill. The British infantry are about to assault the American position, with the left flanking columns moving round to the south side of the hill.

by half, to 3″ in fact. Once on the upper contour, which was somewhat smoother, the normal capability was restored.

Thus, with orders issued to both armies, those to the British being simply to advance with the bayonet and to dislodge the Americans from their earthworks (they did not indeed fire at any time during the assault on Breed's Hill), the game began.

At once it was apparent that the British commander had decided to avoid the easy advance along the north shore towards the fence (it had been there in 1775 that the light infantry had been shattered by musketry) and that the entire force was veering towards its left, with the regiment on the extreme left flank deploying into line to face Charlestown, from which effective American fire was already coming. As soon as the British regiment was in line, its heavy fire began to take effect and American casualties began to mount.

Meanwhile three grenadier and one line regiment had deployed into line and were setting their faces to the ascent, while behind them the move to the left continued, this being covered by the regiment in the firefight with the American battalion in the town.

On move 5 the field gun came into action but was not tremendously effective, and on the southern side of the hill one of the battalion from the rear of the redoubt moved down to join its fellow, the two making a line to face the anticipated thrust from that direction. At the same time one of the battalions from behind the fence began to move southwards over the hill. The Americans had seen that there was to be little action on the north shore.

The next two moves saw considerable development. As they advanced up the hill the four regiments had converged to such an extent that one of the grenadier units had been forced to drop back behind the others, so the advancing line now consisted of three regiments. The 'left hook' was making progress and at the end of move 7 the situation was as shown in map 3. Here we see that two of the left wing American battalions are on their way across the hill and that the defenders of Charlestown have been eliminated (the battalion was reduced to half strength by very effective British fire). The advancing line was now running into very heavy fire from the redoubt and at the end of the move the left flank regiment, the line one, had lost an officer and 11 men (the morale throw was a good one, however). The right hand regiment suffered a total of 6 losses on the move, two being from a roundshot from the gun.

During the ensuing two moves the advance went on, at the cost of rapidly mounting casualties; the flanking two regiments lost an officer and 26 men in the two moves. On the extreme left the British suffered a reverse, a regiment there having to halt after a bad morale throw. The two battalions from the American left were now crossing the summit of the hill to the support of their right, but by this time the field gun's field of fire was masked by the American defences.

However, the advance flowed steadily upwards, each move seeing the British swept by increasingly effective musketry. At the end of move 10, the left hand regiment of the advancing line had been reduced to half its strength, and was falling back. The

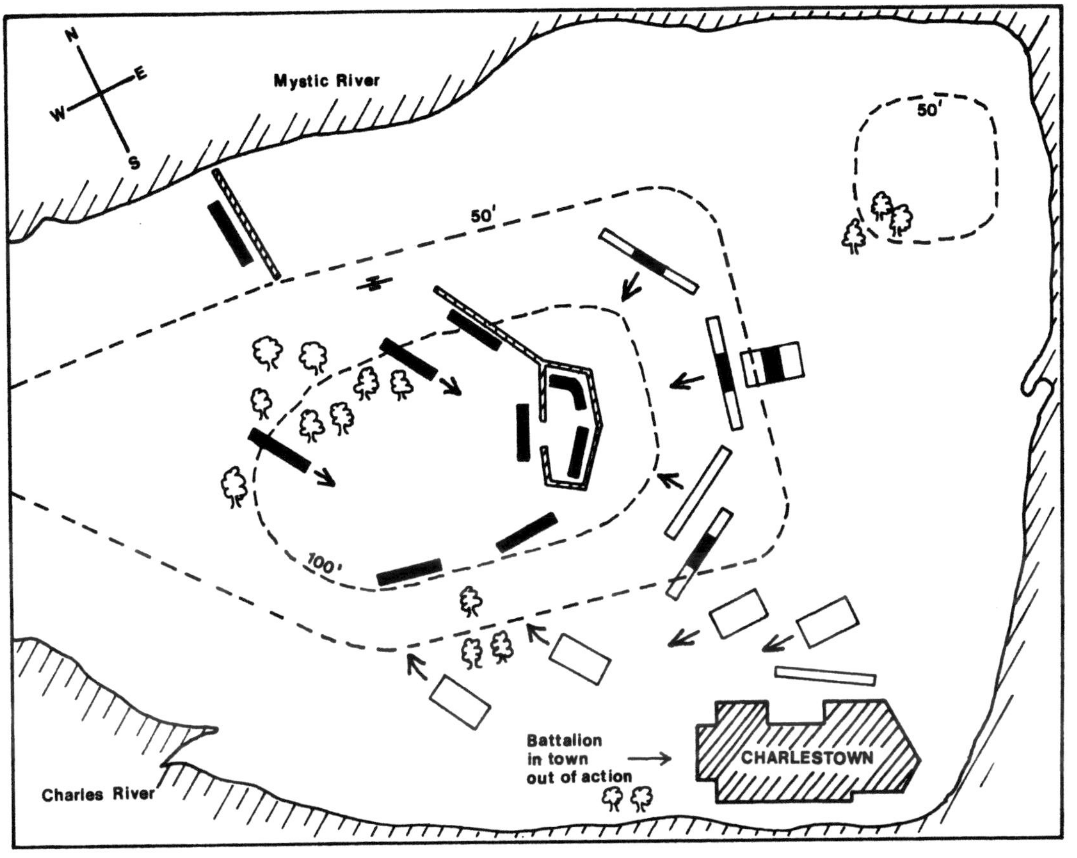

The Battle for Bunker Hill, map 3: the 'left hook' making ground, while the British lines advance directly up the hill.

centre regiment had had a bad morale throw and had halted, but on the British extreme left the one which had halted on the previous move recovered, and continued its advance. The two militia battalions covering the southern approach were now firing with effect on the British storming columns. At this point no less than 98 British infantrymen had fallen, and as there had been no firing from their side, no American had suffered (I exclude the battalion destroyed in Charlestown).

On move 11 the first contacts were made, in the centre the British attempting to force their way over the breastworks and on the left a British regiment coming up the slope with a rush to meet one of the American units (see map 4, on p. 181). Two British regiments had recoiled with 50% losses and were moving together to regroup while the grenadiers at *A* had a bad morale throw and halted. The threat to the American right wing was obvious, and while the fighting across the breastworks was only just in favour of the attackers, in the other combat the American battalion lost an officer and 8 men, no casualties being suffered by their assailants.

The fighting over the breastworks was very severe, drawing two more reserve battalions into the redoubt from which the first assaulting unit had to fall back. Although it had succeeded in getting several men across the fortifications, the resulting 'head-count' times dice throw was insufficient to maintain them there. It was at once replaced by the follow-up grenadier unit which stormed across the earthworks in great style and drove the Americans back towards the only exit. On the American right the British were pressing forward, although one of the regiments had halted through bad morale, but the second wave came up fast and soon the entire American right wing was crumbling (the lack of bayonets, i e the additional 1 point to the British regulars, was a great handicap to the militiamen). At the end of move 15 the situation was as shown in map 5. The entire American garrison was in retreat, the British pressing upon their rear, only the battalions at the fence and between the extension to the redoubt, neither of whom had seen fighting, being other than down to half strength or under. At this stage, the American commanders decided to concede, and it was indeed an unequivocal British victory. 157 Americans were casualties.

It was an expensive one, however, 162 actual figures being lost out of the original British strength of 530, not indeed as high a proportion as in the actual battle, but nevertheless very severe. The British, of course, did have the benefit of hindsight and did not commit the error of plunging into the defile on the north side. The question as to whether the Americans should have had increased firepower remains; at least a largish proportion of them were reputed to be marksmen, but then again, they did get the benefit of the defences they had erected and were not fired upon at all. No use was made of the British naval bombardment, not that it did a great deal of good anyway. For myself, I think (not being too overbold, I hope) that had the British not held the Americans in such contempt, in the actual battle they would have taken rather more time to organise an attack which would have cost much less than the one they did launch.

As a war game, it was interesting more as an experiment than anything else; it lacked the manoeuvre and fluidity of many other battles I have taken part in, but then it did show that a two to one superiority was necessary to overcome field defences, and this really was the object of the exercise.

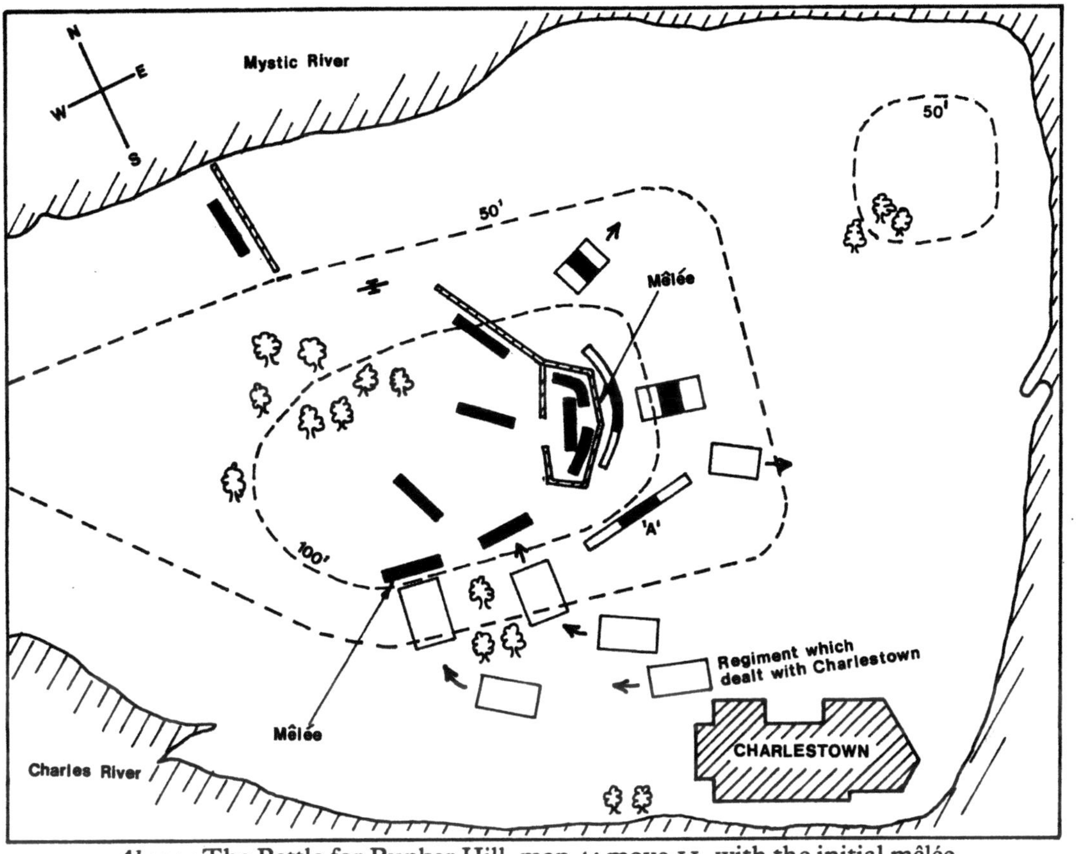

Above: The Battle for Bunker Hill, map 4: move 11, with the initial mêlée.
Below: The Battle for Bunker Hill, map 5: the situation at the end of the with the British units regrouping at points *A* and *B*.

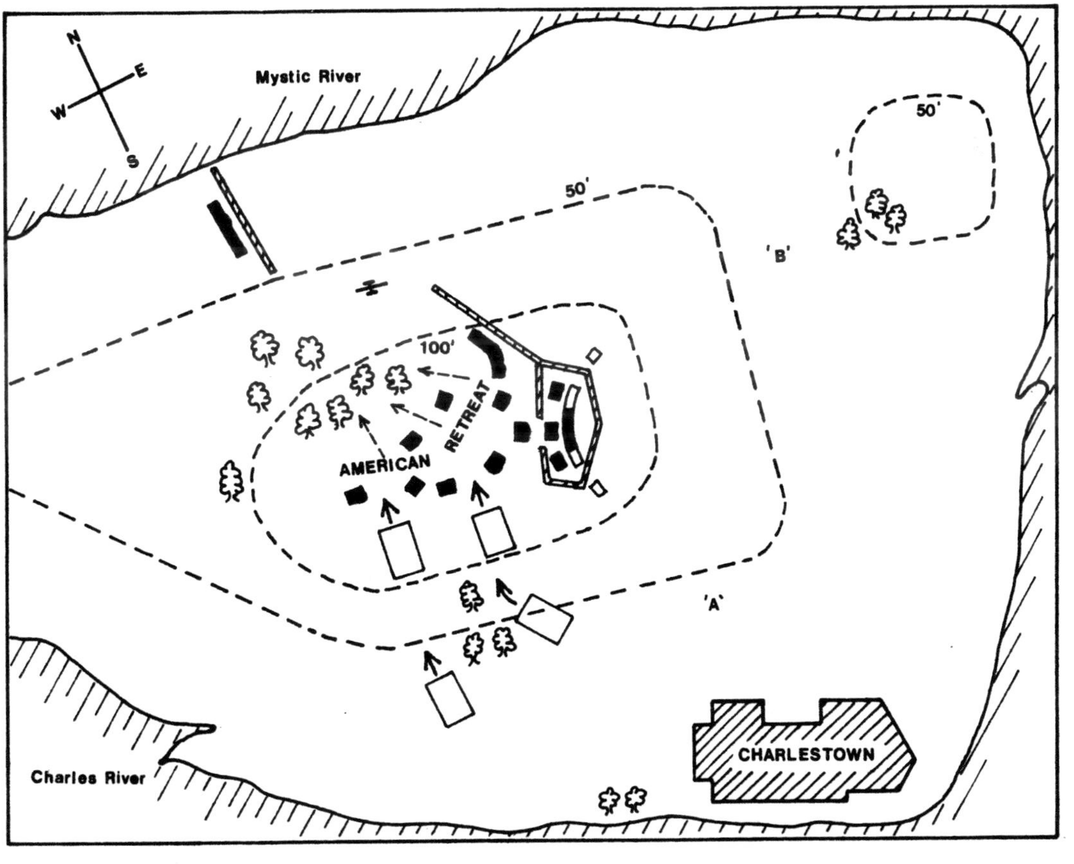

XXIX
Marlburian Warfare

In all its important factors, warfare of the middle eighteenth century was similar to that of the great days of Marlborough, the first decade of the century, the time of his great victories. Weaponry and tactics for both heavy cavalry and line infantry were the same as they were to remain for the sixty years following the great Duke, and for us to enact the battles of that earlier period, we have little to do save to omit certain types of troops and add but one unfamiliar one.

Quite simply, we leave out both light infantry and light cavalry, neither of which species made their appearance until much later. This leaves us with line infantry and heavy cavalry, but the latter should, to be accurate, be divided itself into horse (the true heavy type) and dragoons. The latter, as is well known, were introduced towards the middle of the seventeenth century, their rôle being ideally to fight as well on foot as on horse. It seems, though, that they were never an unqualified success in this dual role, and by the middle of the eighteenth century were in no way different from the regiments of horse. Even by the age of Marlborough this dragooning role was rarely seen, but there are examples from time to time of dragoons dismounting and fighting as infantry. One which comes to mind is in the assault on the Schellenberg not long before Blenheim when the Royal Scots Greys, then the Royal North British Dragoons, were dismounted to make an infantry-type attack on the enemy trenches.

What we have to do then is to make a simple rule for the dismounting of our dragoons. In essence, the process of dismounting or of mounting must take one move, and when dismounted the dragoons obey normal infantry rules. An important point concerns horse holders. For every four horses left without their riders there must be one horse holder, that is, you have one mounted dragoon left with three horses. The problem is how to go about the dismounting process with one's miniature figures, some of whom are not detachable from their steeds. This will entail the provision of a foot figure for every dragoon, and some means of showing when a dragoon regiment has dismounted for foot action, say by placing some sort of coloured counter with the regiment. In the case of figures which can be detached from their mounts, they are simply removed and the substitute figures used. The posture of a detachable horseman is such that he cannot with dignity be used by himself, even though he may have a long sabre scabbard which has the advantage of acting as a third point of support along with his feet.

The second additional type of soldier which might be called upon for service is the grenadier, not just the élite soldier but the true grenadier, throwing his heavy bomb. I feel that by the time of Marlborough the use of the device giving these men their title had almost completely fallen into disuse, but in the event of their still being used in this sort of action we must cater for it.

The proportion of grenadiers (those actually employed as bomb-throwers) in a war game regiment of Marlburian style would not be more than about a tenth or an eighth, I feel, and they would operate as follows. The grenades were pretty heavy and cumbersome affairs and the throw would be a good one to reach 30 yards so, to be generous, we give the grenadier a 3″ range for his bomb. Its burst area would not be enormous and with its poor degree of fragmentation a burst circle of ten yards diameter (1″ on the table) would be about right. So with a small wire circle of this size, we throw for whatever might be in the device, and 4, 5 or 6 on the dice throw would kill whatever is enclosed therein, mounted or foot.

The grenadiers could well be used against defended houses, of course, in which case they would rush up to doors or windows and pop their missiles inside. Should they succeed in so doing, we enact that dice throws be made for every figure in the house, and in this case it takes a 5 or a 6 to kill.

Apart from the above it would be logical to give grenadiers the powers already suggested; they were, after all, the biggest and most powerful men in the regiment and must be considered as quite a crack force, one to be reckoned with in all circumstances.

XXX
War Game Figures and Equipment

What follows are brief references to the principal manufacturers of war game soldiers and ancillary equipment. It does not pretend to be exhaustive and indeed new firms keep appearing and putting new figures on the market, but today, happily, a great many hobby and model shops are stocking quantities of war game figures which enables the player to select his troops in the best possible way: by going along and examining them. We all have our own favourites, there is no doubt, so any comment I may make relates solely to my personal preference and is not designed to denigrate in any way figures which simply do not appeal to my own particular taste. The fact that I mention them I take to be sufficient indication that they are all of considerable merit. Nor is there any point in mentioning prices, these varying with every passing month. At the time of writing, 20–25mm figures can be said to be between 5p and 10p each, although bulk buying will bring the price down considerably. Now for the figures:

1 *Hinton Hunt Figures,* Rowsley, River Road, Taplow, Maidenhead, Berks.
Produces a wide range of 20mm figures, ranging from the Norman Conquest to the Crimean War. Excellent figures, the English Civil War troops being particularly fine, as indeed are the Napoleonics.

2 *Rose Miniatures,* 45 Sundorne Road, London SE7.
Best known for his 54mm pieces, Russell Gammage, the proprietor and designer, has a good line of war game figures for the Napoleonic and American Civil War periods. Of a very high standard in design and finish, these figures deserve to be much better known than they are.

3 *Les Higgins Miniatures,* 78 Northampton Road, Wellingborough, Northants.
Has two lines, 20mm and 30mm, and so far specialises in the English Civil War and Marlburian periods. They are splendid types, and in the 20mm size there is certainly nothing better on the market at the moment. The cavalry of the latter period especially are absolutely exquisite little figures.

4 '*Willie' Figures,* 60 Lower Sloane Street, London SW1.
Renowned for really high quality 30mm figures (they are really a shade larger).

Has types of practically all periods, with particular emphasis on the Napoleonic Wars and the middle eighteenth century. If figures of character are required these are unsurpassed, each one having its own identity, often whimsical, sometimes a downright caricature—very attractive figures, indeed.

5 *Norman Newton Figures,* 188 Piccadilly, London SW1.
Anything produced by designer Charles Stadden needs little recommendation. The figures are 30mm and in wide variety, with the ubiquitous Napoleonics pretty numerous. The eighteenth century is well represented, though, and all are well worth having as showpieces if, like the 'Willie' types of this size, they are somewhat too expensive for the average impecunious wargamer to buy in bulk.

6 *Douglas Miniatures,* 41 Trinity Road, St Johns, Narborough, Leicester.
20mm figures of Marlborough, Seven Years War, Napoleonic and Crimean War periods. The Crimean list is an extensive one and the Seven Years War series, although not numerous at the moment, has a number of attractive little figures.

7 *'Garrison' Figures* (Greenwood and Ball), Martinhoe, East End Way, Pinner, Middlesex.
Producing the finest range of ancient figures, predominantly Greek, Roman and Persian, the firm is now bringing out Napoleonic war game figures in 25mm. The cavalry is particularly fine, in vigorous attitudes, and finish and detail of casting is superlatively good.

8 *Miniature Figurines,* 5 Northam Road, Southampton.
Puts out a truly immense variety of 25mm figures, possibly the widest range of any manufacturer, from the ancients up to the Franco-Prussian War. Has a splendid selection of eighteenth century troops, including figures for the 1745 Jacobite Rising and the American War of Independence.

9 *Airfix Ltd.,* Haldane Place, Garratt Lane, London SW18.
It would be improper not to mention the products of this firm, whose inexpensive plastic war game figures (20mm to 25mm—they do vary) have started the career of many a junior and not a few senior wargamers. They are quite the cheapest on the market (about 15p for boxes of 20 to 30 figures) and the war-gaming world owes Airfix a not inconsiderable debt.

A word now about other equipment.

In the realm of artillery, *Hinchliffe Models,* Meltham, Huddersfield, takes the leading position without a doubt. Producing cannon in 20mm, 30mm and 54mm scale, these pieces are of the highest possible workmanship and will do the greatest credit to any army. Field guns of various calibres and howitzers as well for the eighteenth and nineteenth centuries are in remarkable detail for such tiny pieces. In the 20mm size prices are round about 30p and they are worth every penny.

Very useful war game terrain is produced by *Bellona Ltd,* Hawthorne Hill, Bracknell, Berks. The river sections, straight, curved, and undulating, are particularly useful for the war game table, as well as wall sections, bridges and so on. The firm also has a line of large terrain sections: trench systems, fortifications and beach defences are only three examples. Made of plastic they can be cut to shape if necessary and painted easily and quickly, to give a most striking and realistic effect. Well worth fighting over, without a doubt.

Bibliography

Ralph Willet Adye: *The Bombardier and Pocket Gunner*. London 1804.

C. T. Atkinson: *History of Germany 1715-1815*. Methuen 1908.

Howard L. Blackmore: *British Military Firearms 1650-1850*. Jenkins 1961.

Leonard Cooper: *British Regular Cavalry 1644-1914*. Chapman and Hall 1965.

Lt.-Col. G. T. Denison: *History of Cavalry*. Macmillan 1877.

Christopher Duffy: *The Wild Goose and the Eagle*. Chatto & Windus 1964.

Cyril Falls: *Armageddon 1918*. Weidenfeld 1964.
Great Military Battles. Weidenfeld 1964.

Major-General J. F. C. Fuller: *British Light Infantry in the Eighteenth Century*. Hutchinson 1925.

German General Staff: *Der Erste Schlesische Krieg*. Berlin 1893.

R. Glover: *Peninsular Preparation*. Cambridge University Press 1963.

Charles James: *New and Enlarged Military Dictionary*. London 1810.

Lee Kennett: *The French Armies in the Seven Years War*. Duke University Press 1967.

Richard Ketchum: *The Battle for Bunker Hill*. Cresset Press 1963.

W. R. Livermore: *The American Kriegsspiel*. Boston 1882.

E. M. Lloyd: *A Review of the History of Infantry*. Longmans 1908.

H. Lloyd: *History of the Late War in Germany*. London 1766.

James Lunt: *Scarlet Lancer*. Hart-Davis 1964.

Manual of Field Engineering. HMSO 1911.

Cavalié Mercer: *Journal of the Waterloo Campaign*. Peter Davies 1969.

John Muller: *A Treatise of Artillery*. London 1768.

John Naylor: *Waterloo*. Batsford 1960.

New Regulations for the Prussian Infantry. Berlin 1757.

Lieutenant Charles d'Ollone: *Historique de 10me Regiment de Dragons*. Paris 1893.

Sir Reginald Savory: *His Britannic Majesty's Army in Germany during the Seven Years War*. Oxford University Press 1966.

R. E. Scouller: *The Armies of Queen Anne*. Oxford University Press 1966.

F. H. B. Skrine: *Fontenoy and Great Britain's Share in the War of the Austrian Succession*. Blackwood 1906.

H. G. Wells: *Little Wars*. London 1913.
Jon Menchip White: *Marshal of France: the Life and Times of Maurice, Comte de Saxe*. Hamish Hamilton 1962.
Rex Whitworth: *Field Marshal Lord Ligonier*. Oxford University Press 1958.
Henry Spenser Wilkinson: *Essays on the War Game*. Manchester 1887.
Brigadier Peter Young: *The British Army 1642-1970*. Kimber 1967.

Index

RULES FOR THE WAR GAME

When "The War Game" was first published it did not include a synopsis of the rules.
This reprint provides the opportunity to do so.

PLAY SEQUENCE

The sequence of play for each move is:

Declare charges
Normal Moves (simultaneous)
Artillery fire
Musketry fire
Melee
Compulsory moves

MOVEMENT

Line Infantry		
In line	6"	
In line and firing	4"	
In column	7 ½"	
Charging	9"	
Light Infantry		
At all times	7 ½"	
Heavy Cavalry		
Normal	9"	
Battle move	12"	(for each period of rest)
Charge	18"	
Light Cavalry		
Normal	12"	
Charge	18"	
Artillery		
Team	6"	
Manhandle	1"	
Wagons		
All types	6"	
Barges		
Up River	6"	
Down River	9"	
Canal	7 ½ "	

MOVEMENT AND TERRAIN

HILL

Contours:
Uphill moves for all troop types are halved
On the level all moves are normal.
Downhill gives no distance advantage but note the impetus when charging.
Scenic Terrain;
All movement is halved.

WOOD

Line infantry	-	half move.
Light infantry	-	normal.
Heavy cavalry	-	no movement.
Light cavalry	-	no movement.
Artillery/Wagons	-	no movement.

SWAMP/MARSH

Infantry only, in open order at half move distance.

RIVERS/STREAMS

If fordable, infantry and cavalry take 2 moves while artillery and wagons take 4 moves.

RANGES

MUSKETRY

Line	18"
Light	18"

ARTILLERY

Ball	60"
Canister	24"
Howitzer	20" to 50"

ESTABLISHMENTS

Line Infantry	5 and 48
Light Infantry	3 and 24
Garrison Infantry	4 and 24
Heavy Cavalry	3 and 24
Light Cavalry	3 and 24
Engineers	4 and 24
Artillery Battery	3 and 10 (2 guns)
Barges	3

MUSKETRY

BASIC MUSKETRY

Players throw dice to determine who fires first in a mutual exchange. When the decision is a draw the firing is simultaneous. The firer throws one dice for each group of 6 firers and deductions are made for range and cover as follows:

RANGE	NORMAL VOLLEY		FIRST VOLLEY	
	Open	Cover	Open	Cover
0 to 6"	2	3	1	2
6 to12"	3	4	2	3
1 to18"	4	5	3	4

Each target group is numbered 1 to 6 and dice are throw (one for each casualty caused) to determine which men are hit. In this way a figure may be hit more than once. If firing has not been simultaneous, the side to fire second does so replying with those figures left after removing the casualties inflicted on him.

LIGHT INFANTRY MUSKETRY

Light infantry fire as individuals using a single dice for each figure firing.

Firing at organised bodies of troops (in to the brown).
Range 0 to 9" - 5 or 6 kills.
Range 9 to 18"- 6 kills.

Firing at specially selected individuals (picking off officers etc).
Range 0 to 9" - 6 kills.
Range 9 to 18"- Cannot be done except for mounted officers when 6 kills.

Firing at line infantry in cover (in houses, behind walls or earthworks):
Range 0 to 9" - 6 kills (no picking off).
Range 9 to 18"- nil.

Light infantry firing at light infantry:

In the open	0 to 9"	-	5 or 6 kills.
	9 to 18"	-	6 kills.
In cover	0 to 9"	-	6 kills.
	9 to 18"	-	nil.

THE CHARGE

INFANTRY

Infantry may only charge if they are in column, however they may move a normal move to contact. In the latter case they get none of the advantages of the charge. Rules for this are covered separately.

In column, the head of the column, that is the front rank, are moved directly forward to made contact with the enemy. The two men from each flank of the second rank are moved forward and outwards to meet the enemy to either side of the original column while the centre men close up behind the centre of the column. Similarly, one man from each flank of the third and forth rank is moved outwards and forwards, the centre men closing up to their front and behind the remaining column up to the full extent of the 9" move.

FIRING AT A CHARGING UNIT

An advancing unit is fired on each move until the move in which the charge comes to contact. On this occasion both sides throw a single dice. If the defender wins he fires at close rang: if the attacker wins he comes to contact without receiving a volley.

CAVALRY

Cavalry may only use the charge to contact the enemy.
Heavy cavalry must complete the whole 18" move in a straight line. There will be no wheeling.
Light cavalry may wheel through 45 deg. only in the first 6" of the charge move.
There will be no change of formation during the charge.
There will be no change of formation on striking the enemy in the first move to contact.

MELEE

Melee occurs when two sides are in base contact either as a result of one or both sides charging or coming in contact within a normal move.
The melee is resolved by throwing the dice for each individual combat in the following manner:-

1 inf vs 1 inf:	straight throw, highest wins.
2 inf vs 1 inf:	add 50% of 1 die for the 2 inf.
1 cav vs 1 cav:	straight throw.
1 cav vs 2 inf:	cavalry doubles throw.
1 cav vs 2 inf:	straight throw.
1 cav vs 3 inf:	infantry add 50% to throw of one die.
1 cav vs 2 cav:	latter adds 50% to throw of one die.

It is not possible for the same troop types to fight more than 2 to1.
In all cases the higher throw (or score) wins.
[Subsequent to the publication of *The WarGame* 'highest wins' was replaced by a difference of more than one between the combatants]

ADVANTAGES IN MELEE

Add 1 to each throw if:
- Charging
- Attacking down hill
- Heavy cavalry against Light
- Infantry behind a wall
- Attacking exhausted troops who have had only one move of rest (see Exhaustion).

Add 2 to each throw if:
- Attacking exhausted troops who have had no rest.
- Defending in a house against as attacker outside.

The first move of melee is quite formal, whether infantry vs. infantry, infantry vs. cavalry or cavalry vs. cavalry, there is little scope for independent movement. Musketry and artillery casualties inflicted by those defending unit which are contacted count towards the melee.

THE SECOND MOVE OF MELEE

In the second move, however, the combat is free flowing. If both sides are to stand and continue the melee for a second move then each throws a single die to determine who moves first. The winner may move 4 figures of infantry or 2 of cavalry to contact the enemy figures. Once contacted, a figure is pinned down and may not be moved. The other side then does the same, moving 4 figures of infantry and so on until all that can move to contact within the normal move distance have done so. The aim of each side will be to get as many advantageous combats as possible (that is 2 to 1). This mechanical system represents what is in reality a simultaneous flowing together of the two sides.

The second move of melee is conducted as the first except that the charging impetus of +1 is lost.

DURATION OF MELEE

A melee will last no more than 2 moves unless it is taking place in a built up area in which case it can continue for a further move. This is because fewer troops will actually be engaged at one time because of the defiles.

DECIDING THE OUTCOME OF A MELEE

The outcome of a melee may be decided by one of the following ways:-

First move:

If one side looses twice the casualties of the other side including those casualties inflicted by artillery and musketry, then it must withdraw on the next move.

If any casualties have been inflicted then the side in question must test for morale - if the result is bad, the unit must withdraw in the next move.

Second move:

If one side looses twice the casualties of the other in the melee then it must withdraw on the next move.

If either side has a bad morale then that side must withdraw on the next move.

If neither of the above factors apply, then the result is a draw. In this case both sides will retire unless one is a defender who has written orders to hold ground.

ACTIONS AFTER A MELEE

Units which have had two moves of melee and have drawn the combat will fall back two normal moves and will then rest a further two moves before being allowed to take part in further offensive action. They may defend themselves if attacked.

If a unit is attacked by fresh troops during their four moves of exhaustion (two of retreat and two of rest) the attackers add 2 to each individual combat throw if the move is immediately following the fighting moves of the exhausted side and 1 to each throw if the exhausted side has had a clear move without combat. If fighting is continued for another move, the additions are increased to 3 and 2 respectively.

HEAVY CAVALRY VS. INFANTRY

If heavy cavalry charge infantry who are formed in less than 4 ranks deep, they may actually ride down the men and burst through.

Each cavalry figure moving up to contact throws one die.
3 ranks deep : throw of 5 or 6, breaks through.
2 ranks deep : throw of 4,5 or 6, breaks through.

In the event of a break through, the front figure is removed as a casualty. The second and third rank figures are moved back and to the side a total of 3". The horsemen continue through to the extent of the charge move to contact another enemy if possible. They may veer up to 30 degrees to do this.

MORALE

The morale of a unit is based on three factors. These are:-

Command and Control.
Losses in Action.
The Imponderable.

Command and Control is based on the number of officers and supernumeraries present. Each is worth a certain number of points:-

Line infantry.

Mounted Colonel		2
Four other officers/NCO's		1 each
	TOTAL	6

Light infantry.

Mounted Colonel		3
Two other officers		
the first at 2		
the second at 1		
	TOTAL	6

Cavalry.

Colonel		3
Two other officers		
the first at		2
the second at		1
	TOTAL	6

Losses in Action concern morale as follows:-

One sixth of original rank & file strength lost:- 1 point
One quarter of original rank & files strength lost:- 2 points
One half of original rank & file strength lost:- see 50% rule.

The imponderable is determined by the throw of one ordinary die.

Morale is calculated by the following:-

Command Points - Points for Losses + Throw of 1 die.

If the result is 6 or better the morale is good, the unit continues with its task.

If the result is less than its task.6 the morale is bad! The unit must fall back or behave as follows:-

If it is actually at grips, in a melee, with the enemy it breaks off the struggle and makes a complete move the rear.

If it is advancing, or stationary and firing, it remains halted on the following move and cannot fire.

Once a unit has incurred a bad morale it must be tested on each successive move until it rallies or flees the field, but on each of the ensuing moves the requirement to rally increases by 1: i.e. 7, 8, 9 and then 10 after which it is considered dispersed.

THE FIFTY PERCENT RULES

When any unit is reduced to 50% or less of its rank and file it must break off from whatever it is doing and move directly to the rear in the next move. It will play no further part in the action.

The exceptions are:-

1. If it takes place in the first move of melee it may complete the second move of the melee.
2. If occupying houses the unit may remain in the houses.

GENERALS RALLY

A general may rally a retiring unit (unless it is at 50% or less) by moving to the unit and attaching himself to it. When he reaches the unit a single die is thrown to see how many moves it will take before the unit is fit for action. Once this happens, the General may not leave the unit during the battle.

THE SAVE THROW FOR OFFICER

Because the number of officers in each unit's organisation do not fully represent the total officers and NCO's in an actual unit and because they were so important to a unit's morale in action, a saving throw is used. When an officer is lost in combat or from enemy fire the player may throw a single die to save himself: if he gets a 5 or 6 he is saved and continues in the battle; any throw of less and he is dead and is removed.

ARTILLERY

ROUNDSHOT

A measuring stick is used made up from ¼ inch wide half round 60" or 5 feet long. The first 18" are clear after which it is divided into three sections of 8" coloured black, white and yellow, three sections of 4" of similar colour and again with 2" sections. The stick is positioned on the line of fire from the gun to target. A single dice is thrown a 1 or 2 being black, a 3 or 4 white and 5 or 6 being yellow. Alternatively a dice can be appropriately painted, two sides in each colour and used for the purpose. Those under the stick, in the appropriate colour, are in the line of fire and are diced for

Near group	3,4,5, or 6 kills
Mid group	4,5, or 6 kills
Distant group	5, or 6 kills

[The following rules for roundshot where brought in shortly after the book *The War Game* was published and replace the above rules.]

Round shot range is 60 inches. A measuring stick is used made from ½" square rod and calibrated in inches. On the stick is a 4" long sliding scale sleeve made of card. The stick is positioned on the line of fire from the gun to target and the sleeve moved until it is over the desired target. Two differently coloured dice are thrown; one is designated plus and the other minus. If the plus is higher the sleeve is moved away from the gun the same number of inches as the difference between the two dice, and if the throw is minus the sleeve is moved towards the gun the difference between the two dice. There is no movement of the sleeve if the throws are equal. The heads of figures covered by the sleeve are then diced for as follows to determine if they are casualties:-

Range 0 - 24"	3,4,5 and 6 kills
Range 24 - 36"	4,5 and 6 kills
Range 36 - 48	5 and 6 kills
Range 48 - 60"	6 kills

Each figure is thrown for individually

COUNTER BATTERY FIRE

Counter battery fire uses the system above except that when working out the effect on the gun it is done as follows:-

> If the gun is under the appropriate colour sector or sleeve a single die is thrown and the result from 1 to 6 is noted. When the accumulated total reaches 10 the gun is reduced to firing on alternative moves. When 20 is reached the gun is destroyed.

Because of the reduction in velocity with distance however a reduction of 2 is made to each throw if the range is 48" or more. and 1 from 36" to 48".

CANISTER

The canister device is explained and illustrated in Chapter X.

The device is placed with its apex at the muzzle of the gun.
Figures within the device are diced for as follows: -

Near	4,5 and 6 kills
Middle	5 and 6 kills
Far	6 kills

HOWITZER

Howitzer range is 20" to 50". The centre of impact is worked out using the Shell Burst Indicator (SBI) which is shown in Chapter IX. The SBI has 5 selectors numbered 2 to 6. The centre sector is numbered 6 and the outer sectors clockwise from 5 to 2.

The firing procedure is to place the SBI on the chosen target with the centre section over the point of aim and with the 5 section furthest from the gun. A die is thrown to show area of impact (1 is a misfire). Dice are then thrown for the effect of each figure within the sector in which the shell impacted. A 1,2 or 3 has no effect while a 4,5 or 6 kills.

It can be seen from the above that with the device a 5 is an overshoot, a 3 an undershoot and 2 and 4 are errors to the left and right. Nevertheless, casualties still occur if troops are in the particular sector.

The counter-battery fire the procedure and accumulation of hits is as for round shot.
At less than 20” howitzers may fire canister as for normal artillery.

ROUNDSHOT ON HOUSES

When a house is hit by round shot a single die is thrown with the following results:-

Range	Dice Throw 1 or 2	3	4	5	6
0 - 36"	no penetration	penetrates kills 1 stops	penetrates kills 1 stops	penetrates kills 2 goes on	penetrates kills 3 goes on
36 - 48"	no penetration	no penetration	penetrates kills 1 stops	penetrates kills 2 stops	penetrates kills 2 goes on
48 - 60"	no penetration	no penetration	no penetration	penetrates kills 1 stops	penetrates kills 1 stops

Houses are destroyed by an accumulation of hits on the target until a total of 20 points are achieved using the above table in the same manner as with counter battery fire. At this point the body of the house is removed to leave a ruined shell.

With howitzer fire the same accumulated score system is used but the effect and casualty systems are different. The SBI is placed on the house if that is the target and a die is thrown to see if a hit has been achieved. If a hit on the house occurs then a second die is thrown to determine the effect:

Throw of 1,2 or 3	-	No casualties
4	-	1 killed
5	-	2 killed
6	-	3 killed

In addition to determining the number of men lost, the hits are added as for roundshot to determine the effect on the house. (This includes 1,2 and 3 which count towards damage although killing no men). When the total reaches 10 the house is set on fire. All the troops in the house must leave retiring at least 3" away from the fire. The house will burn for 15 moves during which time no troops may move within 3" of the house.

When a house is in 2 sections there is a strong chance that the second section will catch fire. In each move that the first section burns a die is thrown to see if the second section catches: 3,4,5 or 6 means that the second section catches fire: 1 or 2 it does not.

Model flames are placed on the building for the duration of the fire. At the end of the 15 moves the flames are removed as is the building to reveal the ruins.

GUNNERS

If a dismounted officer becomes a casualty the mounted colonel of the battery may take his place. Gunners and drivers are armed with side arms and may fight in melee – they have no muskets. A normal gun crew consists of an officer and four gunners. A gun may be operated by three gunners or by one officer and one gunner.

[Note: subsequently the rules were modified to allow two gunners to fire a gun on alternate moves.]

SUPPLEMENTARY RULES FOR GRENADIERS

Musketry: Grenadiers fire in groups of 4 instead of the usual line infantry groups of 6. A volley from a full grenadier regiment consists then of 12 groups as opposed to the 8 from the ordinary line infantry.

Melee: In hand to hand fighting the throw of a grenadier is always increased by 1, substantially increasing his fighting capability.

Morale: No reduction to the Morale Index for rank and file casualties is made until the losses have reached 25% (i.e. 12 men have fallen), when 1 is deducted from the throw for morale.